CONSTRUCTION MATERIALS AN

D1759540

PROJECT MANAGEMENT

Construction Materials and Engineering

Additional books in this series can be found on Nova's website under the Series tab.

Additional E-books in this series can be found on Nova's website under the E-books tab.

Management Science – Theory and Applications

Additional books in this series can be found on Nova's website under the Series tab.

Additional E-books in this series can be found on Nova's website under the E-books tab.

CONSTRUCTION MATERIALS AND ENGINEERING

PROJECT MANAGEMENT

ROBERT J. COLLINS
EDITOR

Nova Science Publishers, Inc.
New York

Copyright © 2011 by Nova Science Publishers, Inc.

All rights reserved. No part of this book may be reproduced, stored in a retrieval system or transmitted in any form or by any means: electronic, electrostatic, magnetic, tape, mechanical photocopying, recording or otherwise without the written permission of the Publisher.

For permission to use material from this book please contact us:
Telephone 631-231-7269; Fax 631-231-8175
Web Site: http://www.novapublishers.com

NOTICE TO THE READER

The Publisher has taken reasonable care in the preparation of this book, but makes no expressed or implied warranty of any kind and assumes no responsibility for any errors or omissions. No liability is assumed for incidental or consequential damages in connection with or arising out of information contained in this book. The Publisher shall not be liable for any special, consequential, or exemplary damages resulting, in whole or in part, from the readers' use of, or reliance upon, this material. Any parts of this book based on government reports are so indicated and copyright is claimed for those parts to the extent applicable to compilations of such works.

Independent verification should be sought for any data, advice or recommendations contained in this book. In addition, no responsibility is assumed by the publisher for any injury and/or damage to persons or property arising from any methods, products, instructions, ideas or otherwise contained in this publication.

This publication is designed to provide accurate and authoritative information with regard to the subject matter covered herein. It is sold with the clear understanding that the Publisher is not engaged in rendering legal or any other professional services. If legal or any other expert assistance is required, the services of a competent person should be sought. FROM A DECLARATION OF PARTICIPANTS JOINTLY ADOPTED BY A COMMITTEE OF THE AMERICAN BAR ASSOCIATION AND A COMMITTEE OF PUBLISHERS.

Additional color graphics may be available in the e-book version of this book.

Library of Congress Cataloging-in-Publication Data
Project management / Robert J. Collins [editor].
p. cm.
Includes index.
ISBN 978-1-61761-460-6 (hardcover)
1. Building--Superintendence. 2. Construction industry--Management. I. Collins, Robert J., 1950-
TH438.P756 2010
690.068'4--dc22
2010031166

Published by Nova Science Publishers, Inc. † New York

CONTENTS

PREFACE

Project management is the discipline of planning, organizing, and managing resources to bring about the successful completion of specific project goals and objectives. This book presents current research in the study of project management, including sustainable project management in building and infrastructure projects; the project management consultant; the application of systems engineering and systems thinking to project management; the impact of project duration on IT project success; as well as the traditional and virtual models as instruments of value in construction projects.

Chapter 1- This chapter focuses on the topic of sustainable project management. Project managers are pivotal figures in assessing, addressing and enforcing sustainable project practices through the different project phases. The chapter reports on recent research by the authors aimed at addressing the broad research question: how is sustainability applied through project management practices in the US construction industry? To address this question data has been collected from interviews with staff working in US-based consultancy firms engaged in architecture/engineering and landscape/urban planning and covering building and infrastructure projects. Specifically the chapter focuses on a number of specific aspects of sustainable project management: firstly, the impact of project management practices on key stakeholders and their communities, from the perspective of project managers, is assessed to see if the projects deliver against sustainability-related goals; secondly, how project managers define sustainability is explored to see if definitions are consistent with conceptual developments in the field, particularly in respect of the environmental, economic and social elements of the triple bottom line (TBL); thirdly, the extent to which companies integrate sustainability into their project management systems is investigated to see if companies are undertaking specific actions to promote sustainability-related practices in their projects; fourthly, the methods used to apply sustainability principles at the project level is explored to assess the extent to which sustainability is operationalised on a day-to-day basis; finally, a sustainable project management evaluation model, adapted from the corporate sustainability management reference model developed by the Centre for Sustainable Innovation (www.sustainableinnovation.org), that takes an holistic view of the subject based on the TBL, is used to assess the validity and usefulness of such an evaluation model to project practitioners.

Chapter 2- The world's current energy situation requires the use of a complex set of resources in order to satisfy the wide range of energy demand. Nuclear power should be seen not only as a possibility among other energy options, but also as a significant contribution to respond to the need for allowing a limited use of fossil fuels. In general, electrical energy projects are characterized by a highly dynamic and frequently unpredictable context. Plant modularity provides a high level of flexibility in the development of this kind of project. This means that, if flexibility is appropriately exploited, it is possible to change the course of the project in a favorable direction. In particular, focusing on project execution, building modularity into investments allows us to view investments as a sequence of expansion options. In this perspective, consistent with the real options framework, uncertainty can actually increase the value of the project as long as flexibility is preserved and investment not irreversibly committed. Furthermore, during plant construction, there are usually only cash outflows; in contrast, during construction of a modular plant cash outflows may be accompanied by cash inflows deriving from modules that have been completed and become operational. The chapter aims to estimate the value deriving for a project related to the realization of a nuclear power plant from the modularity exploited in terms of sequential options. A Monte Carlo simulation model has been developed in order to integrate discounted cash flow method and real options approach. Moreover, this model has general relevance: it can be used in order to evaluate complex modular power plant projects and then isolate the contribution of project flexibility, independently from the energy source. We demonstrate the utility of the proposed model through the application to a real nuclear power plant project: we consider a III+ generation reactor, whose modularity allows for a high level of project flexibility and is associated with a number of options to expand equal to the number of units/modules that make up the plant. The example demonstrates the effectiveness of the proposed approach and provides illustrative numerical results.

Chapter 3- Following some basic steps, the project manager can move from organizational project management into the field of project management consulting. This requires the development of a solid business plan for the proposed consulting business. The first step is self-assessment of consulting competencies. This includes an evaluation of personal competencies using the Compleat Consultant Assessment, developing a matrix of consulting skills and a SWOT analysis of personal strengths and weaknesses, followed by action items for improvement. An examination of preferred consulting approach and the reasoning behind selecting the process consulting approach, along with a discussion of personal assumptions and beliefs should follow. The next step deals with the development and operationalization of the mission and values for the proposed consulting business. This discussion leads to an analysis of consulting methods and techniques, consulting focus, and the development of a personal philosophy of consulting and underlying reasons for the consulting focus chosen. Next is the development of a marketing strategy which should focus on several marketing activities (not sales), and include the specific market niche, value proposition, and branding. As an important next step in marketing includes strategies regarding establishing value-based fees and proposed attraction and retention of talent must be developed. Finally, the implementation plan should include discussions on sustaining revenue, developing a clientele or stable group of clients, and potential challenges to the implementation plan and action item(s) to overcome weaknesses.

Chapter 4- Common to periods of economic downturn, many companies seek to reduce budgets, cut costs and minimize the risk of project failure. In line with these initiatives, we have seen many firms over the last few years shorten project timelines, in an effort to heighten control over project outcomes, providing more accountability and sustainability in an uncertain business environment. While much has been written regarding measures of project success and the incidence of project success or failure throughout the years, the corporate landscape has now significantly changed, giving rise to new assessments and determinants of project success or failure.

This study is composed of 2 phases, whereby IT recruiters were asked to identify a set of criteria best indicative of successful project managers, Composed into the Hiring Criteria Index, these criteria, along with questions regarding measurements of project success, project duration and perceptions of short term or long term project success were sent by questionnaire to 3,258 IT managers and executives nationwide. Respondents were asked to identify, on a 10 point Likert scale, what percentage of projects were considered successful across 5 measures of success: Cost, On Schedule, Quality1 (Met Tech Specs), Quality2 (Met Client-Defined Business Requirements) and Client/User Satisfaction. Results indicated that respondents achieved greater than 70 % of project success, as measured across all five factors. However, when assessing the relationship between these measures of success and project duration, respondents indicated that they experienced more success for short term projects (i.e. projects a year or less in duration), as measured by all indicators, except Client/User Satisfaction. It appeared that the ability to satisfy the customer was unaffected by length of project cycle. Of those measurements of success that appeared to be associated with shorter project durations, On Schedule and Quality2 – Met Client-Defined Business Requirements, were indicated to have the strongest relationship to successful short term projects.

Chapter 5- Building project management requires real time information systems and in present scenario required information systems can be achieved by effective use of Information Communication Technologies [ICT] at the industry level. This chapter reports a benchmarking framework developed to rate the construction organizations for their ICT adoption for building project management, administration of its first phase comprising rating of organizations and through Data Envelopment Analysis measurement of their efficiency in implementing strategic adoption of ICT for building project management. Data analysis leads to the development of a model for defining a 'Best Practice Organization' for ICT adoption for building project management.

Chapter 6- The management of technology and engineering projects within an organizational context continues to fall short on a number of levels, especially when considering that projects and programs undertaken across different industries do not always achieve the required project outputs satisfactorily. Moreover, there is also an apparent disconnect between technical activities and project management processes as well as difficulties caused by inadequate project planning. In order to address these issues, engineering systems thinking has been found to contribute to a number of favourable project management features. Consequently, this chapter will identify approaches for improving the project management process through exploring the application of systems engineering and systems thinking to the management of projects. This will be undertaken through an extensive literature review of supporting material and conceptual analysis of how systems engineering and systems thinking can be applied to project planning. Through building on this analysis and from work in the literature, a new model for project management has been developed that is based on four systems-based levers, which are: multidisciplinary and holistic; requirements-driven; project interdependencies; and systems techniques. The utility and flexibility of this innovative management framework has been explored through an initial application to a case study involving a technology project on the development of composite materials for aerospace applications. This case study revealed that there are a range of systems methodologies that can be deployed in order to improve the project planning process and ultimately contribute to project success.

Chapter 7- This chapter documents the institutional arrangements in China's construction industry. It concentrates on the three major differences between China and the UK system, namely, the mandatory tender evaluation by an Independent Specialist Committee (ISC), the mandatory construction supervision system, as well as the mandatory use of bills of quantities procurement method for government funded projects. It is hoped that this will provide some insights for international construction professionals seeking to work in China. The effects of the former two arrangements on the efficiency of property developers, and the quality and safety performance of construction projects will be evaluated. The study indicates that the ISC tender evaluation system has actually reduced the efficiency of property developers in terms of capital-output ratio. However, the mandatory construction supervising system has improved both the safety during construction and the quality of finished projects. The reasons why the old Quota procurement system is still widely used is also discussed.

Chapter 8- Physical face-to-face interaction is often used in traditional construction product delivery. However, in recent times a progressively important concept (the virtual model) has emerged in construction project delivery. Via the virtual model, construction actors maintain less physical presence and rely on information and communication technology (ICT) tools to operate irrespective of time and space constraints to deliver common value delivery goals. This paper explores the perceived utility in the use of the 2 models (traditional and virtual) in value delivery in construction projects.

The study uses qualitative methods to examine the topic. Twenty-nine semi-structured interviews were done. Cross-verified data were analyzed and consolidated into themes. The results were then examined by 8 experts to illuminate the findings.

The following four segmented views emerged. First, the virtual model is seen as better than the traditional concept in value delivery in projects. Second, the 2 concepts are perceived to be complementary in value delivery in projects. Third, value delivery via the 2 media are seen to be the same. Fourth, the traditional concept is perceived to provide better value than the virtual concept in construction project delivery. The complementary use of the strengths of both concepts in a synergistic manner is, however, recommended to attain improved value delivery in construction projects.

Chapter 9- This research aims to investigate the adoption of good practices in the construction industry based on practices applied in other sectors that could help to gain competitive advantage. Typical practices such as Concurrent

Engineering and Supply Chain Management are already established and have been applied by other researchers, however their deployment in the field of construction has not been widely explored.

The research methodology adopted is based on Action Research, in which researchers are involved in the change process. This method has been chosen because it is realistic and practical oriented.

Research carried out in the last three years has focused on the implementation of these practices with a view to improve performance of a case firm in the construction industry sector .The outcome is a total cost reduction achieved through production and assembly productivity increases as well as significant improvement in on-time deliveries to customers. The conclusion is that the benefits of the implementation of these principles in the construction sector are completely demonstrated.

In: Project Management
Editor: Robert J. Collins, pp. 1-72

ISBN: 978-1-61761-460-6
© 2011 Nova Science Publishers, Inc.

Chapter 1

SUSTAINABLE PROJECT MANAGEMENT ASSESSMENT IN BUILDING AND INFRASTRUCTURE PROJECTS

David Bryde * ***and Frances Maravelea*** **

[1]Built Environment and Sustainable Technologies (BEST) Research Centre
School of the Built Environment Faculty of Technology and
Environment Liverpool John Moores University Room 208c,
Peter Jost Building Byrom Street, Liverpool,L3 3AF.UK
[2]Liverpool John Moores University Room 208c, Peter Jost
Building Byrom Street, Liverpool,L3 3AF UK/ 52 South
Main Street Essex, CT 06426 USA

This chapter focuses on the topic of sustainable project management. Project managers are pivotal figures in assessing, addressing and enforcing sustainable project practices through the different project phases. The chapter reports on recent research by the authors aimed at addressing the broad research question: how is sustainability applied through project management practices in the US construction industry? To address this question data has been collected from interviews with staff working in US-based consultancy firms engaged in architecture/engineering and landscape/urban planning and covering building and infrastructure projects. Specifically the chapter focuses on a number of specific aspects of sustainable project management: firstly, the impact of project management practices on key stakeholders and their communities, from the perspective of project managers, is assessed to see if the projects deliver against sustainability-related goals; secondly, how project managers define sustainability is explored to see if definitions are consistent with conceptual developments in the field, particularly in respect of the environmental, economic and social elements of the triple bottom line (TBL); thirdly, the extent to which companies integrate sustainability into their project management systems is investigated to see if companies are

* Corresponding author: Email: d.j.bryde@ljmu.ac.uk Tel: +44 (151) 232 3353
** Email: fmaravelea@gmail.com Tel: +1 (312) 952 4960

undertaking specific actions to promote sustainability-related practices in their projects; fourthly, the methods used to apply sustainability principles at the project level is explored to assess the extent to which sustainability is operationalised on a day-to-day basis; finally, a sustainable project management evaluation model, adapted from the corporate sustainability management reference model developed by the Centre for Sustainable Innovation (www.sustainableinnovation.org), that takes an holistic view of the subject based on the TBL, is used to assess the validity and usefulness of such an evaluation model to project practitioners.

1. Introduction

In today's society businesses are encouraged as a matter of good practice to incorporate sustainability as part of their corporate culture (Boswell, 2005). In the construction industry the design and construction of buildings can make significant contribution to the mission of sustainable development (Shen et al., 2002). Based on the current US economy, President Barack Obama's federal stimulus package is expected to allocate more than $25 billion for energy-efficiency and renewable-energy initiatives, including many hefty tax breaks for green buildings. Clients´ interest therefore has started to increase in eco-friendly projects, especially those that may help them save money in a down-turn market (Brite, 2009). Construction activity is commonly considered to have adverse impacts on the environment, which is the basis of sustainable development for human beings. The application of sustainable practices has economic, environmental and social benefits, creating a win-win situation for both shareholders and stakeholders (Boswell, 2005). In this respect project management plays a vital role in applying sustainable practices to construction projects. Since the management of construction projects continues to be a challenging occupation, as the environment in which projects are constructed increases in complexity, project managers seek to adapt methods that help them overcome those challenges. Such complexity arises from the increasing technological, social and economical forces that impact on the process of constructing the world's buildings and infrastructure. Those forces have also led to emerging stakeholders who can now claim socially acceptable interest in projects to which clients are required to acknowledged and respond (Walker et al., 2003).

The research reported in this chapter focuses on the area of sustainability in the management of projects. The decision to research this topic was motivated by the conviction that sustainability is one of the salient issues managers face and will have to face more and more over the coming years. This is supported by recent global surveys which report the criticality of sustainability-related issues to corporate organisations in the real estate sector (Jones Lang LaSalle, 2009). Specifically, the research seeks to investigate how sustainability is applied through project management practices in the construction industry. The nature of the research particularly lends itself to the collection of qualitative data and exploratory research approach therefore the chosen research method was interviews with senior project managers who work in consultancy firms, servicing the construction sector in the US. The research utilizes an existing reference model which is customized in order generate a new sustainability project management assessment model pertinent to the construction industry.

In the next section a brief overview of the construction industry, with specific reference to sustainability is provided, the research question and objectives are stated and the structure of the chapter outlined.

1.1. Background of Sustainability and the Construction Industry

In the US and elsewhere many companies have been taking their social role seriously for a long period of time, often under the banner of "corporate sustainability". In the US, however, there are no universally accepted standards for defining a corporate approach to sustainability. Indeed many companies are struggling with what sustainability actually means for their company and how to apply sustainability-related principles in practice (Kielstra, 2008). The literature on sustainability for instance offers managers virtually no guidance about the mechanics of the sustainable decision-making process, or about their degree of public accountability (e.g. Aguilera et al., 2007, Xing et al., 2009). At the same time greater pressure is being put on companies to adhere to more sustainable practices. The Economist (2008) reported that company after company has been shaken into adopting a sustainability policy, with it being now regarded as unthinkable for any big global corporation to be without one. Climate change has added further impetus to the sustainability agenda. Investors are taking an ever greater interest, and the message is moving across supply chains and spreading around the world. Yet at present few companies would be able to articulate their exact policies, as sustainability decisions often rely more on instinct than on evidence. But a sustainability assessment industry of sorts is developing, such as the Global Reporting Initiative (GRI, 2006), and many big firms have started to publish their own sustainability reports, full of targets and commitments (Economist, 2008).

In respect of the construction industry, the Charted Institute of Building (CIOB) in U.K. for example, reports that the concern for sustainability has grown out of the wider recognition that rising populations and economic development are threatening a progressive degradation of the earth's resources (CIOB, 2009). Because buildings have a fundamental impact on the environment - consume large quantities of resources, involve large numbers of workers, and represent a large proportion of economic activity - decisions made during all stages of the design and construction management process are vital for maximising sustainability. Sustainable buildings aim for an overall net positive environmental burden by considering a building's total economic and environmental impact and performance, from raw material extraction and product manufacture to building design, construction, operations and maintenance, and building reuse or disposal. Although sustainable building practices have, so far, been primarily voluntary it is anticipated they will become more prominent, and be reflected more strongly in procurement and project delivery systems (Augenbroe and Pearce, 1998). Because of their role, project managers are pivotal figures in assessing, addressing and enforcing sustainable project practices in all project stages (PMI, 2004). As such project managers are increasingly seeking to implement – on their own initiative and at the request of clients – project management practices and processes designed more precisely to deliver sustainable buildings (Graham et al., 2003). Also the increase in legislation pertaining to sustainable performance (such as the US Energy Policy Act of 1992) has prompted the incorporation of sustainable project management practices into the project delivery process

(FCGB, 2003). The end result of the project management process being a building that performs to a prescribed level against sustainable-related criteria (McCartney, 2007).

Construction sustainability performance therefore is crucial to the attainment of sustainable development and the literature indicates that in the past various techniques and management skills had been developed to help improve such performance in construction projects. However, these techniques are often ineffective due to the fragmentation and poor coordination among various construction participants. There is a lack of consistency and a failure to take an holistic perspective that hinders participants from implementing sustainable construction practices at various stages of project realisation. A recognition of this problem led to an interest in "sustainability management" which is a generic term for environmental and social management, and corporate governance. It refers to the processes or structures that an organisation uses to meet its sustainability goals and objectives while transforming inputs into a product or service (UNEP, 2006). "Sustainable project management" is an off-shoot of sustainability management and, as a somewhat new discipline that is also attracting increasing attention, which requires project managers to control and facilitate the project phases carefully in order to achieve sustainable results.

1.2. Research Question

The construction industry has been perceived to be under-performing in each of the key sustainability theme groups: environmental, social and economic (CIRIA, 2001) – the three groups representing the three pillars of sustainability or the "triple bottom line" (TBL) (Elkington, 1997). Various organizations are dedicated to implementing sustainable principles into the construction industry and generating best practices in sustainable construction, such as the creation and application of new knowledge within new practices, as well as sustainable construction assessment indicators and methods (Egan, 1998). However, historically, most of these sustainability practices have not been documented or structured in a way that allows construction companies to share and reuse these best practices and lessons learned. There is a need to build formal and structured methods for a seamless exchange of information between the construction and sustainability domains (CIRIA, 2001). Addressing this need informs the following research question: "How is the issue of sustainability applied through project management practices in the construction industry?" To answer this question the research focused on US-based consultancy firms of small (1-10 people), medium (11-50) and large (51-100) sizes, with the firms engaged in the disciplines of Architecture/Engineering and Landscape Architecture/Urban Planning, and covering building and infrastructure projects. With the focus being on investigating the awareness of the practitioners on sustainability issues and how they applied sustainability in their practices.

1.3. Research Objectives

To support the research question and gather the appropriate information needed to assess sustainability project management for building and infrastructure projects, the six following objectives were derived:

- To assess how, from the project mangers′ perspective, their policies impact the stakeholders and their communities. The stakeholders and the community as a whole always benefit or suffer by the way companies carry their agendas. Here the impact of those project management practices is considered.
- To evaluate how project managers define sustainability. Since there are no specific guidelines that project managers can follow, an understanding on how the TBL is interpreted in the construction industry and for construction projects is important.
- To investigate if firms integrate sustainability into their core management systems. By having an integrated sustainability policy companies can better succeed in promoting sustainable practices for all their projects, regardless of size or location, and they all can benefit from the outcome.
- To evaluate how sustainability is applied to construction projects. Here the tools and techniques will be investigated in order to assess the methods used to successfully apply sustainability principles to construction projects.
- To explore to what extend are the practitioners aware of the TBL assessment model elements presented to them. Since this model aims to encompass a more holistic view on sustainability, it is pertinent to see if the practitioners view each of the three elements as important, and if they currently using them in their project management assessments.
- To assess the validity of a sustainable project management assessment model that has been used for this research and its applicability to the construction industry. Since this model has not been used in any previous research that pertains specifically to the construction industry, its validity and appropriateness, based on the research results, will be examined.

1.4. Chapter Structure

The remainder of the chapter is structured as follows: the next section provides a literature review which examines the existing theories of corporate sustainability with specific reference to stakeholder theory, the link between strategy sustainability management, sustainability in construction projects and certification systems applicable in today's construction projects and measuring and reporting on sustainability-related performance criteria. This review supports the development of the research question and objectives stated in the previous section. Then, based on the Corporate Sustainability Management Reference Model, the Sustainable Project Management Assessment model is developed. This is followed by a section documenting the research method, which includes a discussion of the methodological approach, research strategy, the primary data collection method, and how the issues of reliability, validity and generalisability have been addressed. The following section presents the key interview findings, which reflect the current situation in relation to sustainable project management of the US consultancies in the construction industry. The key findings are then discussed and elaborated upon, with their relevance to the literature analyzed. The next section discusses some emergent issues that provide additional and supplementary insight into the subject area. The concluding section of the chapter summarizes the research and makes recommendations for future research in this area.

2. Literature Review

2.1. Corporate Sustainability and Stakeholder Theory

At the organisational level, the notion of sustainable development finds its equivalent in the term corporate sustainability. According to Wilson (2003), corporate sustainability can be viewed as an evolving management concept that poses an alternative to the traditional models of short-time wealth maximization. Since a completely sustainable company does not, or cannot, exist, corporate sustainability is conceptualized as a process of permanent improvement. Therefore, it is defined as a relative concept that describes the planned and strategic management processes of working towards a balance of economic, social, and environmental goals and values (Paech and Pfriem, 2004).

Many scholars had identified the fact that it is hard to translate the theory of corporate sustainability into practice, and one of the reasons why lays in the nature of the concept itself. Critics argue that "sustainability" is an arbitrary and fuzzy concept, whilst supporters see it as a chance for firms and stakeholders to engage in a constructive dialogue (WBCSD, 2002). Although for the large part of the 1990's and 2000's corporate sustainability has been viewed through an environmental-focused lens, recent years have seen the other pillars of the TBL: social and financial, gaining prominence.

As interest in the study of corporate social performance has grown, scholars have empirically examined why companies engage in activities that benefit society. Their research reveals that business managers are motivated by ethical as well as instrumental considerations, and by internal values as well as by external pressures (Bronn and Vidaver, 2009). These motivations frequently overlap, and it is often difficult to determine whether corporate social initiatives are genuinely guided by moral values or whether they are driven by more strategic concerns such as protecting profitability or preserving organizational legitimacy within the context of changing institutional norms (Graafland and van de Ven, 2006). Environmental (and in recent years increasingly social) management systems are implemented as means to manage and control organisation's environmental and social performance. However, the real impact of such systems is often low, as research by the Institute for Economy and the Environment (IEE) has found (Dyllick and Hamschmidt, 2000, cited in Bieker et al., 2002). The IEE research found that environmental and social sustainability remains largely separated from the traditional core business strategies and management systems, which are geared towards financial performance indicators. Accordingly, management tools are needed that help firms to integrate financial, environmental and social management systems (Bieker et al., 2002).

One problem is that, like the terms "green", "eco-efficient", "ethical", or "socially responsible", the term "sustainable" has proven to be remarkably difficult to distil into one generally accepted definition (Bieker et al., 2002). "Sustainable" has become a buzzword, which everybody interprets in a different way. Things become even more complicated once the term is associated with firms. Some business people simply equal corporate sustainability to successfully surviving in the market place. It is not made easy by the fact that definitions of sustainability are abundant. As early as the 1970's Massachusetts Institute of Technology used the term "sustainability" to describe "an economy [...] in equilibrium with basic ecological support systems [...]" (Stivers, 1976: 187, cited in Bieker et al., 2002). However, it took until the late 1980s in the wake of the Brundtland Commission's report the term "sustainable development" founds its predominant definition as "[meeting] the needs of the present without compromising the ability of future generations to meet their own needs" (Brundtland, 1987).

The term corporate sustainability encompasses concepts that directly or indirectly refer to the role of business in society (Loew et al., 2004; Wilson, 2003). Among these concepts are the approaches of corporate social responsibility (CSR), corporate citizenship and other related concepts, such as corporate social performance, social accountability/triple bottom line (TBL), people-planet-profit (PPP), corporate governance and a stakeholder approach. So in many organisations corporate sustainability is increasingly becoming a corporate value and an integrative part of the business strategy. It challenges many of the principles underpinning the role, structure, and functioning of corporate governance. Thus, mainly among large-sized companies, tools such as triple-bottom-line accounting, sustainability balanced scorecard, life-cycle assessment, eco-efficiency, and environmental information and management systems have been implemented in an attempt to make business processes more sustainable (economically viable, socially responsible, and environmentally sound) and, as a consequence, to extend long-term profit maximization (Signitzer and Prexl, 2008). With all these tools predicated upon the TBL as the preeminent model for firms to interpret sustainability (see figure 2.1).

Although on the face of it a simple concept, each sustainability dimension of the TBL represents an immense challenge in terms of delivering against related performance criteria, and even more so when companies are expected to address the three dimensions simultaneously. One suggestion is that partial integration may be the answer i.e. "...some of the most interesting challenges, however, are found not within but between the areas covered by the economic, social, and environmental bottom lines. [...] new concepts and requirements (are) emerging at the interfaces between each of these great agendas in the shear zones" (Elkington, 1997: 70). Concentrating on the shear zones between two dimensions opens the possibility for companies to think about the links between two dimensions separately (Elkington, 1997: 78, 91). Bieker et al., (2002) links each two dimensions separately and derives three different sustainability cases: the Business Case, the Human Case, and the Green Case as described in figure 2.2.

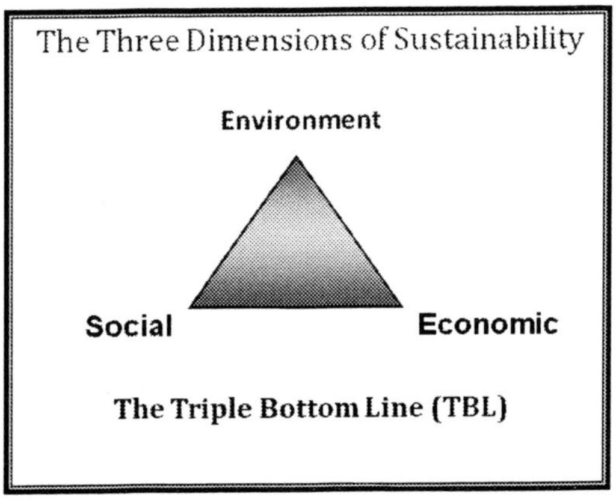

Figure 2.1. The Triple Bottom Line (TBL).

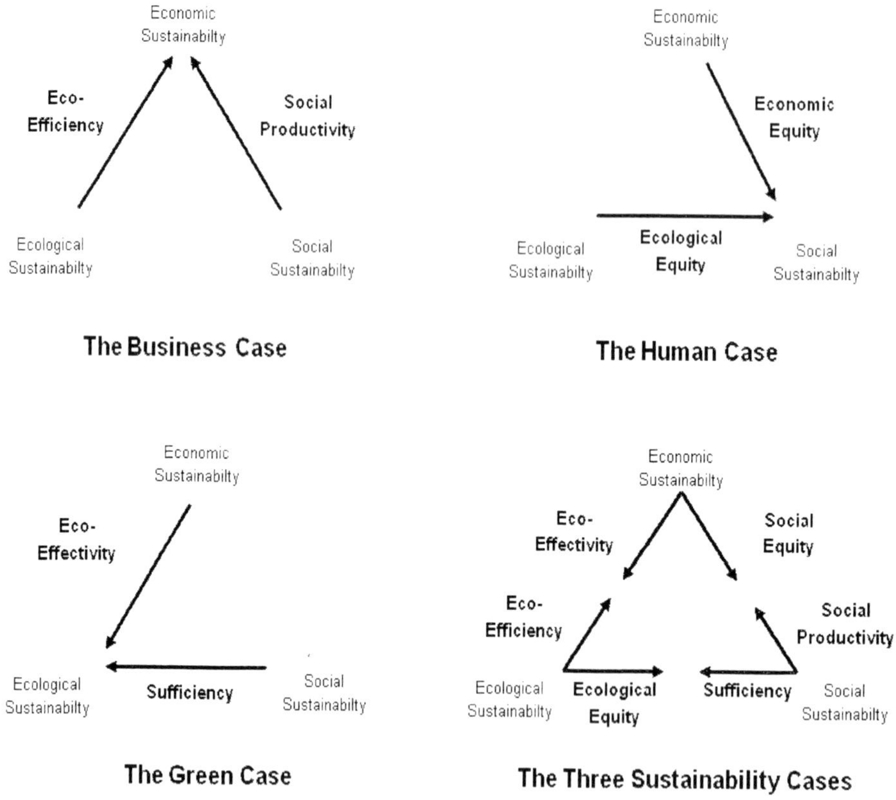

Source: Adaptation of Hockerts (1996; 1999b)

Figure 2.2. The Three Sustainability Cases (Bieker et al., 2002).

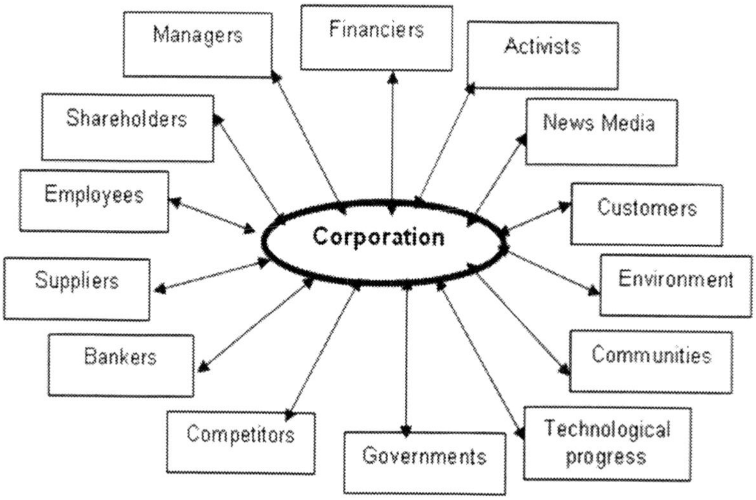

Figure 2.3. A map of global stakeholder groups of a multinational corporation, (Hampel, 1998; Metcalfe, 1998).

The Business Case of sustainability allows a firm to pursue shareholder strategies through environmental or social sustainability. Strategies would aim for "eco-efficiency" and "social productivity". The Human Case of sustainability would favour strategies of "economic and environmental equity" and the Green Case would aim for "eco-effectivity" and "sufficiency" strategies. All three cases are integrated to provide an holistic view of sustainability - as shown in Item 4 in figure 2.2.

Donaldson and Preston (1995), suggested that the research on stakeholder theory has proceeded along three often confused lines. First, there is instrumental stakeholder theory, which assumes that if managers want to maximise the objective function of their firms, then they must take stakeholder interests into account. Second is the descriptive research about how managers, firms, and stakeholders in fact interact. Third is a normative sense of stakeholder theory that prescribes what managers ought to do. According to Freeman (1984) successful transactions with stakeholders are built on understanding the legitimacy of the stakeholders and having processes to routinely surface their concerns. In its final report The Hampel Committee (1998: paragraph 15) (cited in Elias and Cavana, 2003), stated that:

> "Corporate governance must contribute both to business prosperity and accountability, and that the purpose of those responsible for corporate governance is to safeguard the interests of shareholders and to protect and promote the interests of other stakeholders, such as managers, employees, customers, suppliers, governments and the communities where the company operates."

Metcalfe (1998: 12) argues that in a corporate context, stakeholder theory states that:

> "…a stakeholder is entitled to consideration in some ways similar to a shareholder, and stakeholders may thus include employees, customers, shareholders, suppliers, the state, and the local communities…" Both the Hampel Report's and Metcalfe's lists of stakeholder groups can be shown in figure 2:3.

Looking at it from a stakeholder perspective a Board of Directors of a global corporation should not have profits for shareholders as its only responsibility. Each stakeholder group in figure 2.3 has a role and contributes to the success of the corporation and without their contribution in some shape or form there would be no profit for shareholders. Jansen (2001: 1) proposes the goal of value when discussing stakeholder theory, stating that: "…a firm cannot maximise value if it ignores the interests of its stakeholders." Jansen points out that "...the big challenge facing corporate boards and managements is determining the trade-off between the firm's objectives and the interests of its stakeholder groups." The solution to global stakeholders' interests requires management to take into account global business and make ethical decisions beyond shareholder profit objectives. It is not enough to say that the business of multinational corporations is to create shareholder value without considering how such value creation will affect both local and global communities.

In the three sustainability cases, described in figure 2.2, the stakeholder view of strategy is very much linked to an instrumental theory of the corporation, integrating both the resource-based view (i.e. the Green Case in respect of the use of natural resources) as well as the market-based view (i.e. the Business Case in respect of being efficient and productive), and adding a socio-political view (i.e. the Human Case in respect of the notion of equity). These views define the specific stakeholders of a corporation (Donaldson and Preston, 1995). To maximize shareholder value over an uncertain timeframe, managers are encouraged to pay attention to key stakeholder relationships and recognise that their firms have a stake in the behaviour of their stakeholders. Therefore, prudent management of firms' operating environments, including relationships with their stakeholders, and good stakeholder management has clear instrumental value for firms (Berman et al., 1999).

2.2. The Link between Strategy and Sustainability Management

Although many researchers contend that strategic reasons have replaced altruistic motives for corporate social engagement (e.g. Kotler and Lee, 2005), others have found that personal moral values and the desire to make a positive contribution to society's future continue to be powerful drivers of the corporate social agenda. Some studies have documented instances in which doing the right thing appears to be a stronger motive for social-related sustainability initiatives than the practical benefits these activities can generate for the firm (e.g. Bertoin, 1992; Hahn and Scheermesser, 2006). Others have found that moral motives share the stage with strategic perspectives. To illustrate the latter point, a recent study of Dutch managers showed that while respondents believed social initiatives could improve profitability, enhance reputation, and strengthen employee commitment to the firm, they also expressed an equally strong desire to make the world a better place (Graafland and van de Ven, 2006).

The key role of companies in achieving sustainability has been stressed and discussed both on the strategic (e.g. Hart, 1995; Hart, 1997; Roome, 1998; Dyllick and Hockerts, 2002; cited in Figge et al., 2002) and on the instrumental level (e.g. Schaltegger and Burritt, 2000; Bennett and James, 1999; cited in Figge et al., 2002). In the capitalist market-based system economic scarcities are reflected by market prices. Environmental and social scarcities, however, are only partially reflected in economic transactions, although they have become increasingly important in business. Management reacts to perceived scarcities with the use of management instruments and the degree to which environmental and social issues are increasingly recognised in market transactions is reflected in the growing importance of environmental or social management systems. These systems, however, are rarely integrated with the general management system of a firm. As a consequence, environmental and social management is often not oriented towards the economic success of the firm and the economic contribution of environmental and social management remains unclear (Figge et al., 2002). Studies concerning the relation between the environmental and social performance of the firm with its economic performance are mainly based on empirical tests which refer to the correlation but not to the causality between environmental and social measures and the economic success of firms (e.g. Griffin and Mahon, 1997). If firms are to achieve simultaneous improvements of the economic, environmental and social performance of their business and their projects, this lack of integration can be a major obstacle.

Sustainability has to be addressed at the strategic level in organisations and accordingly it requires the correct tools for proper implementation. On the strategic level Kearney (2007: 4) defines sustainable development as the following:

> "For the business enterprise, sustainable development means adopting business strategies and activities that meet the needs of the enterprise and its stakeholders today while protecting, sustaining and enhancing the human and natural resources that will be needed in the future."

In order for each sustainability strategy to be implemented successfully, a set of objectives has to be set and followed. According to Drucker (1954) an organization without clear objectives is like a ship without a rudder. The procedure of setting objectives and monitoring progress towards them should permeate the entire organization from top to bottom. Managing by objectives (MBO) relies on the defining of objectives for each employee and then comparing and directing their performance against the objectives that have been set. MBO aims to increase the performance of the organization by matching organizational goals with the objectives of subordinates throughout the organization. In the 1990's, Drucker put the significance of this organization management method into perspective, by saying that in order for it to be successful, organizations must have a clear understanding of their objectives. The use of MBO needs to be carefully aligned with the culture of the organization. Engagement of employees in the objective setting process is seen as a strategic advantage. Likewise, having clear sustainability objectives will aid to set and achieve the organisation's sustainability goals.

Once objectives have been set organisations need to establish performance management systems (PMS) to ensure that operational targets and measure align with strategy. Kaplan and Norton (1992) developed the Balanced Scorecard (BSC) as a strategic management tool that serves to identify and hence measure the major strategically relevant issues of a business. It describes and depicts the casual contribution of those issues that contribute to a successful achievement of a firm's strategy. Given the pre-eminence of the BSC in the PMS literature it is unsurprising that a number of authors have focused on the development of a scorecard to define and assess sustainability in project environments (e.g. Bieker et al., 2002; Figge et al., 2002).

Other researchers who recognised the lack of a comprehensive to properly assess sustainability on the business level created their own models based on empirical studies and research. Some of the models been used in the past are the Project Sustainability Management (PSM) model – developed by the International Federation of Consulting Engineers (FIDIC) in 2006, which introduces guidelines of how project owners and engineers can incorporate the principles of sustainable development into individual projects. The Civil Engineering Environmental Quality Assessment and Award Scheme (CEEQUAL) provide assessment of the environmental quality of civil engineering projects, which publicly recognises the achievement of high environmental performance. Awards are made to projects in which clients, designers and constructors go beyond the legal and environmental minima to achieve distinctive environmental standards in their work. Also, the Center for Sustainable Innovation (CSI) developed a generic corporate sustainability management reference model that helps to integrate the three pillars of sustainability into a single and overarching management tool, which is not limited to one industry, but rather can be customized to serve different industry sectors. In order for a sustainability assessment model to be successful, all aspects relevant for achieving a permanent competitive advantage need to be included. The creation and presentation of competitive advantage helps to secure the long term success of the firm (Figge et al., 2002). Optimised sustainability management then can perhaps be best represented graphically as shown in figure 2.4 below. All three TBL pillars of sustainability intersect, giving strategic focus and bringing maximum benefits to the organisation (Kearney, 2007).

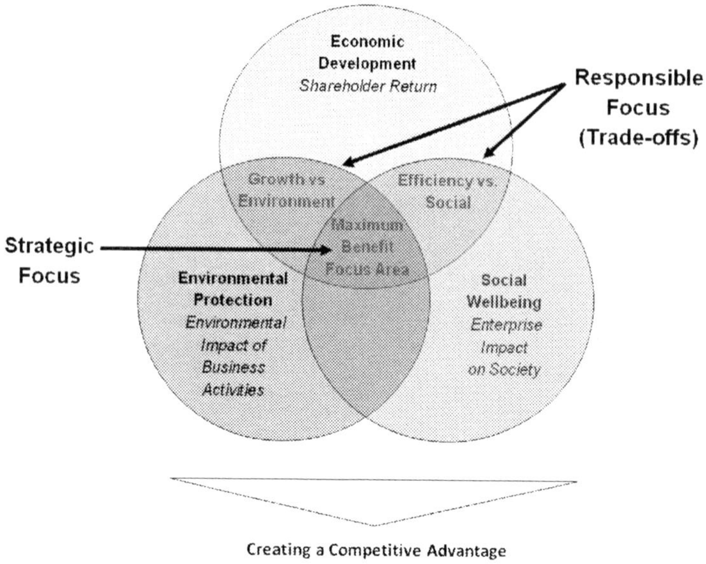

Figure 2.4. Strategic Focus and Trade-offs of Sustainable Management (Kearney, 2007).

2.3. Sustainability in Construction Projects

On the project level, implementing sustainability starts at the strategic/concept planning and project programming stage, where the technical and economic feasibility of alternatives will be compared in order to select the best possible solutions. Sustainability decisions made at the beginning of a project life-cycle have a far greater influence than those made at later stages, since design and construction decisions will influence the continuing operating costs and, in many cases, revenues over the building's lifetime (Boswell and Walker, 2004).

The concept of sustainable construction is relatively new and aims at integrating the objectives of sustainable development into the construction activities. The concept is generally well-understood in relation to the environmental performances of construction products and assets, though as discussed earlier in the chapter, it should more largely refer to a balanced economical, ecological and social approach to sustainability that reflects all three TBL elements.

An early definition of sustainable construction was presented by Charles Kibert at the First International Conference on Sustainable Construction held in Tampa, Florida, US, in 1994. He stated (cited in Kibert, 1994) that sustainable construction is the creation and responsible management of a healthy built environment based on resource efficient and ecological principles. One view of sustainable construction is as a process, which starts from the planning, and designing phase and proceeds even after the construction teams leave the project (Hill et al., 1996; Hill and Bowen, 1997). Sustainable construction has been understood by many nations to be a reflection on the way the building industry responds to achieve sustainable development. Hill et al. (1994), further qualify sustainable construction as a special case of sustainable development which targets the specific group of construction industry. This group being tasked to develop, plan design, build, alter or maintain the built environment including the building materials manufacturers and suppliers with due reference to sustainability-related principles.

The concept basis of sustainability and the list of definitions expanded as more disciplines entered the terminological debate: economists called for a sustainable "economies", agriculturalists for sustainable "harvest" and sociologists for sustainable "societies". What was lacking though was a consensus on a definition of the term sustainability and the 991 update of the World Conservation Union stated that the term "sustainable development" was open to criticism as ambiguous and liable to a range of interpretations, many of which were contradictory. Such a charge still has resonance. Hill et al. (1994) suggest that this is because the term had been used interchangeably with "sustainable growth" – and this in itself is a contradiction in terms because nothing physical can grow indefinitely. `Caring for the Earth´ defined sustainable development as development which improves the quality of human life while living within the carrying capacity of supporting ecosystems (IUCN/UNEP, 1991).

Griffith (1997) draws attention to the environmental effects of construction activities resulting in a number of comfort disturbances to individuals living and working in the areas surrounding construction projects. This is manifested through noise of construction operations and equipment, dust from construction process and traffic, hazardous contamination, for example toxic waste and other visual disturbances such as signs and advertising boards, as environmental problems associated with construction sites. In addressing the complex problem of construction and the environment, efforts towards sustainable design are fundamentally an attempt to put into place practice that restores the balance between the natural and built environment. It is a search for an ecological model that views both realms as fundamentally interconnected. It should be recognised that mankind is locked into a highly dynamic relationship with the natural world and that the two are acutely interdependent (Schaefer, 1994). Any one definition of sustainability cannot however, adequately cover the various facets of sustainable construction. The construction industry does not exist in a vacuum and its actions impact on, and are impacted upon, by economic, social, environmental, technical and policy issues.

2.4. Certification Systems for Sustainability

Although, as mentioned above, sustainability is not a term that everyone can agree upon, it has not prevented different countries from having developed systems that practitioners can use to achieve certain sustainability levels in their construction projects. In the US the Leadership in Energy and Environmental Design (LEED) Green Building Rating System™ encourages and accelerates global adoption of sustainable green building and development practices through the creation and implementation of universally understood and accepted tools and performance criteria. LEED is a third-party certification program and the nationally accepted benchmark for the design, construction and operation of high performance green buildings, and gives building owners and operators the tools they need to have an immediate and measurable impact on their buildings' performance (USGBC, 2009). In the U.K., BREEAM (Building Research Establishment Environmental Assessment Method) also takes account of planning management and aspects such as health and comfort, but the main emphasis is placed on ecology.

The German DGNB rating system, which is also one of the newest, from the German Sustainability Building Council, is arguably the one that most reflects the holistic perspective of the TBL. The sustainability seal is awarded on the basis of a system divided into five categories and comprising of forty nine criteria. These are related to ecological and economic quality, as well as to socio-cultural and functional aspects, technical efficiency and process quality. With this approach, the DGNB differs from other evaluative systems that have established themselves internationally. As LEED certification is oriented towards the environment, it makes far lower overall requirements than that of the DGNB and it lacks the broad range of components that the DGNB certification has (Jäger and Hunziker, 2009). One other major differentiation the DGNB certification has, in comparison to LEED and BREEAM, which is particularly pertinent to the topic of sustainable project management, is the emphasis it gives to process quality, as illustrated in Figure 2.5.

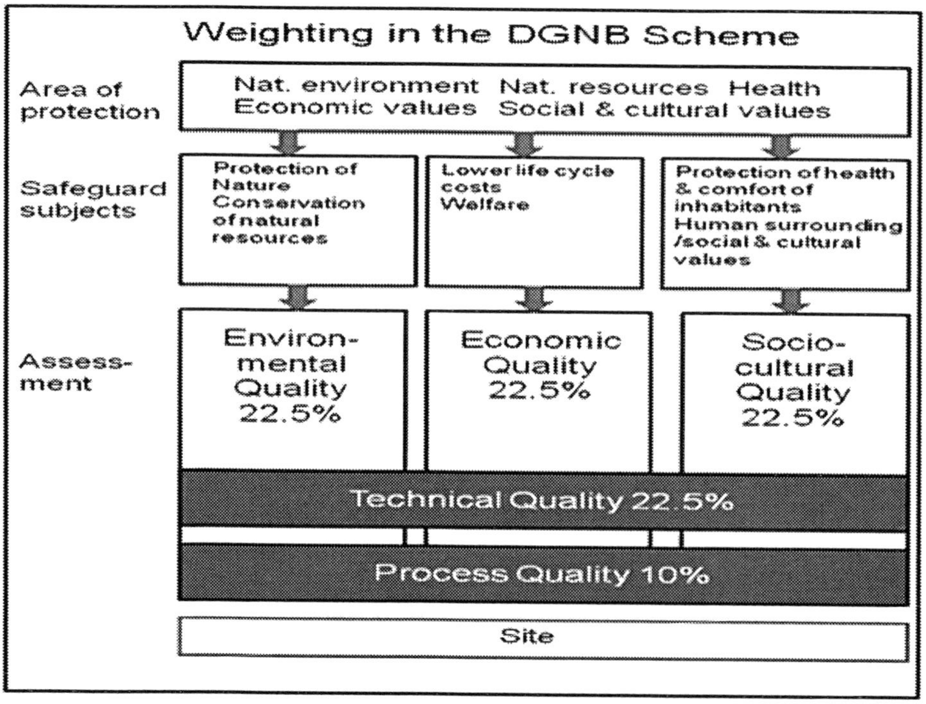

CERTIFICATION DGNB - EXTRACT			
	CRITERIA	INDICATORS	ENGINEERING SERVICES
Process	Quality of design	Holistic design	Interdisciplinary design team, Energy concept
	Quality of construction	Waste, noise	Logistic on the construction site

Figure 2.5. DGNB Sustainability Measurements (Fraunhofer-Institut für Bauphysik, 2008; Bilfinger and Berger, 2008).

The criterion of process quality encompasses the quality of design and the quality of construction. The design is viewed in an holistic manner from all disciples, integrating interdisciplinary design teams and abiding to energy concepts; while the quality of construction focuses on the waste and noise that is being created and the logistics involved on the construction site. Using the DGNB as a framework, project managers, regardless of location and country of origin are able to take an approach to sustainability that goes beyond a rating system - which evaluates based on a set of criteria and points - in order to achieve maximum results (Brite, 2009).

2.5. Advantages of Measuring and Reporting Sustainability Performance

As a result of official responses to both the Brundtland Commission (WCED, 1987) and the United Nations Conference on Environment and Development in 1992 (the "Earth Summit"), many national governments have adopted sustainable development as a goal. This has resulted in a plethora of proposals to monitor progress towards corporate sustainability (Atkinson, 2000). Since environmental and social policy is becoming increasingly important to the government, the media, pressure groups, investors, consumers and clients, measuring and reporting on the evolving sustainable business practices can give firms a competitive advantage over companies not yet addressing the issue. Furthermore, measurement is fundamental to progress, as it is important to recognise and learn from changes that have been implemented (CIOB, 2004).

Utilizing sustainable project management models that enable the measuring and reporting of performance against the TBL ensures that construction projects are managed to include sustainable environmental practices in their design, construction and operational phases. If the model also takes into account the social and economic aspects of the TBL, it potentially provides management with a tool to measure, drive and even reward outstanding behaviour on a project (Griffiths, 2005). Some of the benefits that an holistic sustainable project management assessment model or framework provide are:

- Championing a commitment to balance and sustainability at a project management level.
- Incorporating sustainability criteria into design and assessing options against the relevant criteria.
- Incorporating sustainability criteria into the construction phase of the project.
- Establishing simple sustainability performance measures and putting monitoring and measurement systems in place.
- Raising awareness within the project team and establishing a culture of care and ownership related to the natural environment and to people.
- Linking project sustainability objectives to individual and team performance through Key Performance Indicators and a focus on continuous improvement.
- Reporting project performance against the TBL and using this to communicate to stakeholders.
- Working alongside stakeholders to ensure the project meets the needs of the communities involved in, and affected, by the project.

- Ensuring that the chosen project delivery model works to achieve sustainable outcomes (Griffiths, 2005: 13).

Based on a generic sustainable project management assessment framework best practices can be established, which are best supported by committed management and a sustainability manager/champion on the project. This manager/champion can work with others to develop a customised model for the project and support the designers and construction teams to identify opportunities and risks, to take appropriate action and to monitor progress. The framework also guides on-going performance management across the dimensions of sustainability, helps to establish project and stakeholder reporting and provides inspiration and motivation (Griffiths, 2005).

2.6. Concluding Remarks

Within the construction industry, companies have long been aware of the need to consider the environmental impacts of a building. Managing community relations have also been seen as an integral part of construction, since buildings typically have a high impact on society at the local, national and even international level. However, the recent demand from various stakeholders, such as shareholders, government, consumer groups and the public for products and services to be 'socially responsible' extends the scope of sustainability to an extent that it can no longer be assumed that traditional construction management process and procedures will suffice. Furthermore, many clients are beginning to demand that the sector takes a proactive role in furthering the sustainability agenda and it is likely that in some cases this will become a determining factor between securing a contract for work or not. But incorporating sustainable construction practices into an organization does not mean compromising business standards or values. It means taking a fresh approach to one's objectives and strategic position in order to reduce the social and environmental impacts of an organisation's business activities, meet the needs of the stakeholders, whilst at the same time maintaining a successful financial bottom line.

In the construction industry, the reputation of businesses and the quality of their work is constantly under scrutiny from environmental pressure groups, the media and the public, as well as from clients and investors. Having a competitive edge is crucial to the survival of any construction firm and the concept of sustainable practices provides an opportunity for individuals and companies to demonstrate industry leadership. It is therefore crucial for construction professionals to realise that sustainability does not provide a new set of business objectives to be met; rather, identifying sustainability targets for the business provides a fresh approach to fulfil existing targets and will illustrate to the stakeholders that components of the TBL have always been and will continue to be an integral part of operations. Project managers play therefore a key role, being in a leadership position, to develop and manage processes that enable all project participants to work towards achieving sustainability-related objectives and to carry all related tasks in a measurable and reportable manner.

3. Development of Sustainable Project Management Assessment Model

Comprehensive and coordinated planning is the cornerstone to sustainability. But planning cannot be done properly, unless it occurs in a methodical way, and by a set model or framework which encompasses and addresses all the proper assessment steps needed, to achieve desirable results. This section documents the development of a sustainable project management assessment model pertinent to the construction industry, in order to evaluate the sustainability activities of the project participants.

3.1. Sustainability Transformation of the Iron Triangle to the Global Context

With today's business expectations and requirements, diversion from the classical "iron triangle" scenario of meeting time, cost and quality-related success criteria is deemed necessary. Aiming for a sustainable built environment requires more than that. It requires a paradigm shift in the way we approach time, cost and quality constraints, which forces us to take a much broader look at the iron triangle components than have been used so far in traditional project management. This broader perspective can be made operational through the introduction of suitable sustainability indicators (Augenbroe and Pearce, 1998). Figure 3.1 shows the evolution of the sustainable construction concept over the passage of time (Bourdeau, 1999). The traditional building process was to focus on time, cost and quality (the Iron Triangle) during construction. Next issues such as resource depletion, emissions and conservation of bio-diversity were layered onto the triangle and a bigger picture encompassing these issues emerged, as supported by Agenda 21 on sustainable construction (CIB, 1999). Finally, a broader concept evolved to suite the global context and to cover environmental, economic and social sustainability-related issues as well.

Therefore project management practices can no longer solely evaluate their success in respect of the traditional Iron triangle-related criteria only. Rather they should encompass the economic constraints, the environmental quality, and the social equity and cultural heritage of communities, people and natural resources, as it translates to quality of living. Hence, for any sustainable project management assessment model to be comprehensive it should reflect the new paradigm of sustainable construction. With this in mind the assessment model will be derived accordingly.

3.2. Generic Reference Model and New Evaluation Model

In developing a sustainable project management assessment model that meets the requirements of the construction sector a useful starting point is a generic model that can act as a reference point. One such model that fits this purpose is the Corporate Sustainability Management Reference Model (CSMRM) developed by the CSI (see figure 3.2).

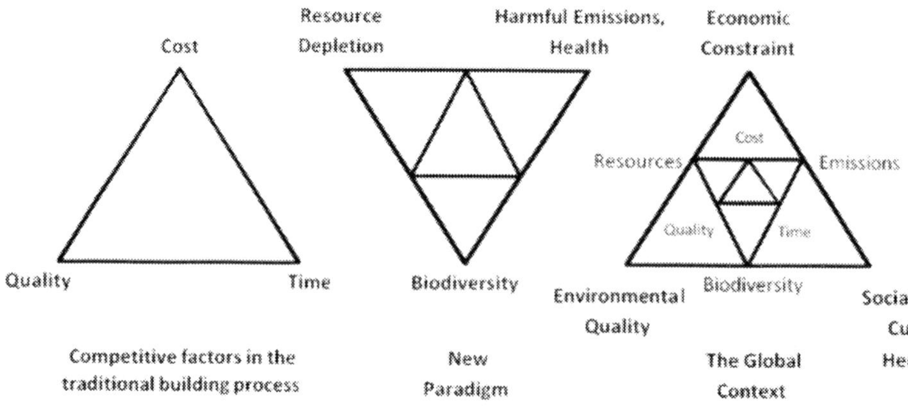

Figure 3.1. Concept of Sustainable Construction (Bourdeau, 1999).

The CSMRM takes a multi-faceted approach to corporate sustainability management that reflects the holistic TBL perspective discussed early in the chapter. The authors contacted Dr. Mark W. McElroy, who is the Board Chair of CSI, to ascertain whether the model had been used in prior research. Dr. McElroy indicated that elements of the model had been used in several research projects, which included the food industry, accounting and environmental (water treatment) assessments, yet it had not yet been used to assess sustainability-related practices in the construction industry. But as Dr. McElroy confirmed, conceptually the model is committed to the core sustainability theory, encompassing the TBL policies, and therefore adapting it to the project management of construction projects gave the potential to make an original contribution to knowledge in relation to the assessment of sustainability.

As shown in figure 3.2 the CSMRM has an outer layer of four broad practice areas that are informed by the inner layers that reflect the theory of sustainability and the policy of meeting the TBL. The practice areas are as follows:

Stakeholder Relations: This area focuses on the need for stakeholder relations that incorporate transparency, inclusiveness, dialogues, trainings, appropriate disposition of corporate governance towards all stakeholders, and good media relations to promote awareness and a culture of care. Appropriate marketing to reach all those groups is also deemed important in this section.

Program Strategy and Operations: has elements that deal mainly with internal issues. These include: the goals and objectives of the organization, the identification of gaps between practices and performances, strategically designed policies to identify necessary funding programs, finding the right people to run those programs, building a suitable infrastructure. Managing by goals and objectives provides clear guidelines and active participation of corporate governance within the organization.

Research and Development: deals with research towards more sustainable materials and practices, training the staff, the stakeholders and other relevant parties through conferences, informal meetings and other means, and promoting innovation through experimentation, prototyping tools and alternative solutions.

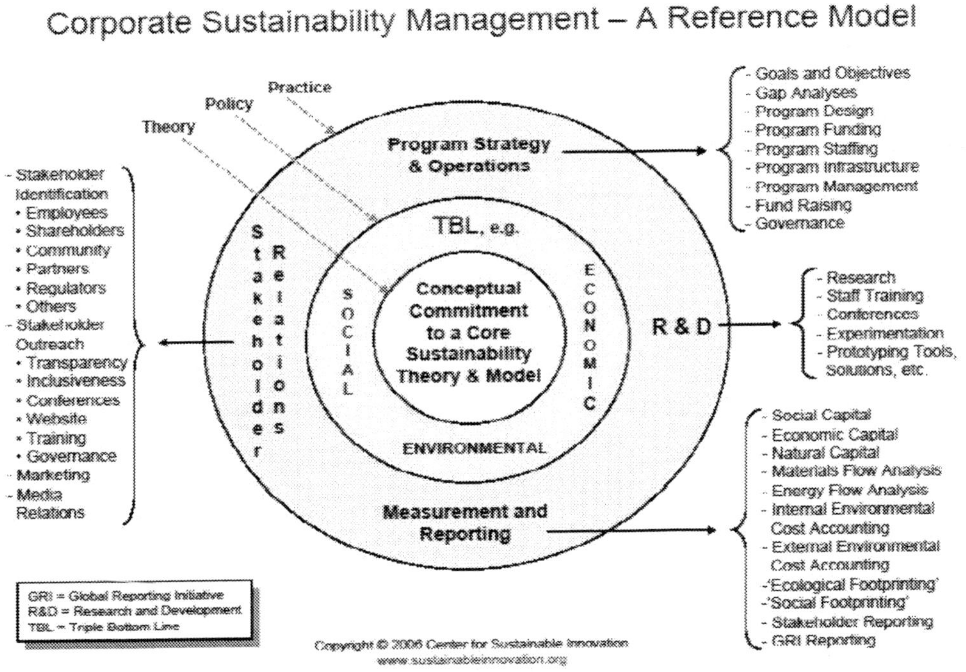

Figure 3.2. Corporate Sustainability Management Reference Model (CSI, 2006).

Measuring and Reporting: is the final area and focuses on the importance of measuring and reporting progress in practices related to social, environmental and economic capital, materials flow analysis, energy flow analysis, internal environmental cost accounting, impacts of practices on the ecological and social footprint, stakeholder reporting and GRI reporting.

All of the above elements within the four practice groups validate the concept of sustainable construction which reflects the progression from the iron triangle to the global context (see Figure 3.1. earlier). Therefore it is useful to assess sustainability practices that project managers utilize in the construction industry in these four broad areas (though it is recognised that the elements in each of the practice categories are indicative and can be added to or subtracted from to make the model industry specific).

3.3. Sustainable Project Management Assessment Model

Thus, the Sustainable Project Management Assessment (SPMA) model, adapted from CSMRM that will be used as a framework for this research is shown in Table 3.1. The model does not intend to measure sustainability and it does not give parameters or weight factors, but rather it aims to assess how sustainability principals are applied through project management practices in construction projects.

As with the CSMRM, the SPMA is based on the same four practice categories as described above. The elements within each category are derived based on the indicators that were identified through review of the extant literature, the authors' knowledge of the industry and discussions with other practitioners.

Table 3.1. Sustainable Project Management Assessment Model for the Construction Industry.

Sustainability management in the construction industry
Evaluation model
Tbl: social - environmental - economic
Stakeholder relations & impacts
Communicating sustainability goals to all stakeholders
Managing relationships between stakeholders
Stakeholder participation in decision making
Sustainability impacts on stakeholders and communities
Program strategy & operations
Understanding sustainability goals
Planning the implementation of sustainability goals to each project phase
Leadership and advocacy to keep sustainability goals on track
Strategic planning in different project phases
Motivating project teams to effectively implement strategies
Develop specific strategies for clients, design and construction team
Use of sustainable design strategies
On-going operations strategy and planning
Education, research & development
Empowering project team & stakeholders by educating, explaining and translating sustainability issues
Awareness and use of sustainability tools and materials
Training & education programs for clients, sub-contractors and consultants
Education and awareness of international sustainability standards
Research to alternative methods and innovation
Assessment, measurement & reporting
Economic & financial studies
Environmental consideration factors
Environmental measures and monitoring
Social & community reporting
Building product & life cycle assessment
Develop framework for measuring, tracking and evaluating goal setting performance methodology
Financial incentive analysis including available subsidies, tax credits, and potential rebates
Feasibility study to determine incremental cost & scheduling implications for potential leed or green globes prerequisites and credits

In the ***Stakeholders Relations and Impacts*** section, the focus is on how sustainability goals are communicated to all stakeholders and relations managed between the organizations and the stakeholder groups. For example, are stakeholders participating in decision making processes in regards to sustainability issues? And how do sustainable practices impact stakeholders and communities at large? The ***Program Strategy and Operations*** section enables evaluation of the organization from within. First it is important to understand how project managers define sustainability and to establish how they strategically plan their goals and objectives and incorporate them into the project phases. Also what tools and techniques are used to assess sustainability? Other relations between the organization and the client are also examined here. The ***Education, Research and Development*** section focuses on evaluating how organizations interact with their staff, clients, sub-contractors and other stakeholders in providing educational and training programs on sustainability issues. Also the project manager's awareness about sustainability systems, on national and international levels is considered and the methods they incorporate in their practices to educate others and promote research and innovation assessed. Finally, how do they incorporate all these aspects as part of their corporate strategies? Lastly, the ***Assessment, Measuring and Reporting*** assesses if the practitioners consider economic, environmental and social aspects when designing sustainable projects. How do they look at costs (in short and long term assessments)? Do they use any model/framework for measuring, tracking and evaluating their processes and outcomes? What kind of reporting methods do they use?

4. Research Method

This section outlines the research method adopted. Based on the research question and objectives, the research philosophy, approach and strategy are defined. The method and instrument used to gather data are indicated and the participants, from whom information was solicited, are described. At the end the method for analyzing the data is described and issues of the reliability, validity and generalisability of the research are covered.

4.1. Methodological Approach

While quantitative methods are based on a natural science, positivist model of testing theory, qualitative methods are based on interpretivism and are more focused around generating theories and accounts. Positivists treat the social world as something that is 'out there', external to the social scientist and waiting to be researched. Interpretivists, on the other hand believe that the social world is constructed by social agency and therefore any intervention by a researcher will affect social reality. Herein lies the supposed conflict between quantitative and qualitative approaches - quantitative approaches traditionally seek to minimise intervention in order to produce valid and reliable statistics, whereas qualitative approaches traditionally treat intervention as something that is necessary (Neuman, 2006). Research in the area of sustainability and corporate sustainability, undertaken from a managerial perspective in the construction industry, can be categorized as interpretivism. The aim in not to adhere to measurements from a quantitative perspective, but rather to find out how sustainability concepts and standards are defined by the practitioners in the industry and how are these standards applied to construction projects by the project managers in order for them to achieve sustainable results. Therefore the qualitative research perspective is deemed more appropriate in this case. The area of "sustainability" is still a relatively young discipline and there is a lack of general agreement on definition, and a lack of maturity in measurement. So studying its application through project management practices can be categorized as a real, certain and precise phenomenon, and collecting data that is factual, truthful and unambiguous is possible. Furthermore, the research approach can be categorized as inductive. Inductive reasoning applies to situations where specific observations or measurements are made towards developing broader conclusions, generalizations and theories (Saunders et al., 2003: 87-88). Opposed to inductive reasoning is deductive reasoning, where one starts thinking about generalizations, and then proceeds toward the specifics of how to prove or implement the generalizations (Saunders et al., 2003: 86-87), mostly applicable in disciplines where agreed facts and established theories are available (Remenyi et al., 2000: 75).

4.2. Research Strategy

The aim of this research is to expand our understanding on how sustainability is applied through project management practices to construction projects. In particular, the research seeks to examine how practitioners work in their field, and see if a distinction is made between the available theory and the real-world practices, with the intend to analyze similarities and gaps between the theories and the empirical evidence.

Many researchers use case studies as a way of doing research in social science and socially related events, and involve the intensive study of a single group, incident, or community (Shepard and Greene, 2003). Rather than using samples and following a rigid protocol to examine limited number of variables, case study methods involve an in-depth, longitudinal examination of a single instance or event: a case (Flyvbjerg, 2006). Since the intent of this research is to identify how project managers apply sustainability standards to their projects through project management practices, it will not focus on one or two cases but rather a cross-section of organisations. The research strategy therefore will involve an in-depth exploratory investigation of 10 US consultancy firms, located in the states of Illinois and Michigan.

Heterogeneous sampling has been used to collect data from different types of consultancies. These consultancies include architects, landscape architects/planners, and infrastructure engineers. This will enable the data collection processes to be gathered from diverse disciplines within the industry's consultancies. Therefore the unit of analysis will be at the industrial level: on the construction sector; on the organizational level: on architects, landscape architects/planners, and infrastructure engineers; and on the individual level: on senior project managers. As senior projects managers are the decisions makers and have direct access to the client, they are the appropriate unit of analysis for this study. It is through these project managers that decisions are made regarding sustainability issues, and they are the coordinators on how those policies should be applied in their projects and practices. Their direct client access gives them the power to influence client decisions. Thus the focus of this study will be on the individual level, with senior project managers and the data collected indicates how sustainability is applied by those project managers, through their practices, to construction projects. In all the organizations he/she is referred to as the "senior project manager" or just "project manager", which is abbreviated as PM.

4.3. Data Collection

The qualitative interview further allows for social argument to construct "depth, nuance, complexity and roundness in data" (Mason, 2002: 65). In this research it is important to obtain insight on how the participants apply project management methods to assess sustainability in their projects. These insights are generated by certain individual assumptions and beliefs that form the structure of sustainability management levels, therefore in-depth telephone interviews seem most appropriate. Due to the fact that project managers need to express their positions on the applications of sustainability, the interviewer must have some flexibility to further investigate pertaining issues in this area; therefore the semi-structured interview is deemed appropriate. The interview questions are provided in Appendix A. It comprises of six parts and are constructed as following: the first section gives the general information of the organizations; the second section deals with the stakeholders and community and how those are influenced and impacted by sustainability practices and sustainable projects; the third section deals with definitions of sustainable practices since it is important to assess how practitioners define sustainability in order to better evaluate how they apply it; the fourth section aims to investigate if sustainability is part of the core management of the organization, the fifth section assesses how sustainability is applied to construction projects, and the last section deals with the project life cycle and the application of sustainability on the different project stages.

All the potential interviewees were initially contacted either through a phone call or by email and were asked for participation consent in this research project. The interview questions were piloted with a small number of practitioners in the industry, and were modified accordingly based on the feedback received. Also through those same practitioners, a set of indicators were identified in order to validate the evaluation model and make it applicable to this research. All participants were contacted in the same manner and were informed of the purpose and desired outcome of the interviews and the intent of this research. The participants were asked permission for the interview to be recorded. Thus both hand transcribed and recorded information was obtained during the interview process. Finally the information was analyzed as indicated in the following section. All participants received by email a participant's information sheet, indicating in more detail the purpose of the interview, and assuring confidentiality and anonymity of all interview results.

4.4. Data Analysis

The data were analyzed using a template analysis. This means that firstly categories are drawn out, determined by the trends which can be identified from the collected data. Then the data were unitized according to the important categories identified. Finally, the units were placed into their respective categories (Saunders et al., 2003). The analysis aimed to generate what is central in the data, with the researcher's task being to find a central core category which is both at a high level of abstraction and grounded in the data that had been collected and analysed. This was done in three stages: finding conceptual categories of data; finding relationships between these categories; and conceptualizing and accounting for these relationships through establishing core categories. It is achieved by carrying out three kinds of coding: open coding to find the categories; axial coding to interconnect them; and selective coding to establish the core category or categories (Strauss and Corbin, 1998; cited in Robson, 2002: 492-493). This is referred to as a method of constant comparison, and intends throughout the analysis to build theory through the interaction with the data, making comparisons and asking questions (Pidgeon and Henwood, 1996: 92-4; cited in Robson, 2002: 493).

Based on the research strategy described above, the potential strengths and weaknesses of the chosen method were reviewed in terms of reliability, validity and generalisability, which are detailed in the next section.

4.5. Reliability, Validity and Generalisability

Both the validity and reliability of the secondary data should unarguably depict a valid and reliable picture (Bryman and Bell, 2003) of the sustainability and project management practices. However, this data does not provide an holistic picture of the subject matter, and therefore the planned collection of primary data in this research. The research approach entails the intensive study of a small number of cases, so its claims to validity are obviously limited. Also conducting the semi-structured interviews via telephone limits the sample even more due to time constraints. The way the researcher interacts with his subject has a further impediment on the results. Hence, because of the use of semi-structured interviews, and the inductive fashion of this exploratory research strategy, it is likely to be difficult for another researcher to duplicate the exact same results. A measure is considered reliable if it would give us the same result over and over again (Bryman, 2004). It is also apparent that due to the nature of the purposive sample claims of generalisability can only be made with extreme caution.

5. Findings

This section reports the findings from the semi-structured interviews. Table 5.1 below lists the interviewees and their organisations. The results are presented in relation to each of the four practice categories of the Sustainable Project Management Assessment Model (SPMA) presented in section 3.3 earlier in the chapter. A summarized table of the key findings, which are presented below can be found in Appendix B. Detailed interview responses can be found in Appendix C.

5.1. Stakeholder Relations and Impacts

In terms of stakeholder relations the majority of interviewees stated that the public is involved in decisions, particularly (and unsurprisingly) on public projects. In such environments the public are able to exert some influence. As articulated by project manager A (see table 5.1): *"The public makes their desires known to the boards and commissions either through public meetings or by writing their commissioner."* In the private sector there is no such uniformity of involvement, with projects having to be of a larger scale for communities to get involved (as stated by project managers A, C, D, H and K). There was also a common view that sustainable projects impact on wider stakeholders. A typical response was that of project manager J:

> "They benefit from improved operating costs, and a healthier indoor environment. They also contribute to renewable and recycled markets."

Eight out of the ten respondents believed that stakeholders do see some differences between a "green" project and a "conventional" one (project managers A, B, C, D, F, H, J and K). But as project manager J indicated in most projects the differences might be subtle, with lower operating costs for green projects being possibly the single most important difference. The general consensus amongst the project managers was that stakeholders prefer green projects to traditional ones because they believe they are better for the environment. However from the owner's point of view, as project manager E pointed out: "*Many see green projects as desirable but more costly*." Therefore the additional costs make many owners, especially in the private sector, steer away from sustainable buildings (project managers E, F and H). Also public policies and the media were seen to play an important role in influencing how stakeholders see and perceive sustainable projects in general (project manager F).

Commercial developers were perceived to promote sustainability to differentiate them from the competition. So sustainability becomes more of a marketing tool rather than a deeply held conviction to contribute to sustainable development (project managers D and H). As graphically described by project manager H:

> "I think many commercial developers see being green as a way to 'one-up' their projects from the competition, but now it has become almost too many doing that that the effect is lost. Hopefully someday Green will just be the way to go and will be the "conventional" project."

Some project managers perceive stakeholders as recognising the benefits from green projects based on their being educated and knowledgeable about the topic sustainability (project managers B, F and G). The long term benefits tended to be viewed as more environmental and social, but they also included economic criteria related to a longer payback period (project managers A, J and K).

The general consensus amongst project managers was that communities are not always aware of the positive impacts of sustainable projects. Better education and marketing, as well as publicized material from private and especially governmental agencies were seen to be needed to educate the public (project managers A, B, F, H and J). Project manager A described their situation:

> "I deal with the [ ] Forest Preserve. So, we with our project impact very directly on communities and the recreational public. With our projects we can educate the public on Green issues. Our projects tend to have sustainable design components. The Forest Preserve needs to publicize this better."

Table 5.1. Interviewees and their organizations.

participant code	company size*	project longevity (in yrs)	year of project commence	role in project	LEED accredited	types of projects described	type of project sector	average budget in USD	nature of business	type of org	length in current position
A	medium	2	2007-present	Project Manager	no	infrastruct, transport.	private/public	15-20m	Engineering	consultancy	3yrs
B	small	1 to 2	2007-present	Project Manager	yes	buildings	private/public	500k	Architecture, interiors, site	consultancy	2yrs
C	large	3	2007-present	Project Manager	no	buildings	private/public	20-50m	Architecture, engineering	consultancy	1.5yrs
D	small	1 to 2	2007-present	Project Manager	no	buildings	private/public	5-10m	Architecture, Interior design	consultancy	4yrs
E	medium	6mo-1yr	2007-present	Project Manager	no	buildings	private/public	10-15m	Architecture, Interior design	consultancy	4yrs
F	large	1 to 4	2007-present	Project Manager	yes	landscape, infrastruct	private/public	20-60m	Architecture, Land. Arch., Urban Planning	consultancy	1yr
G	large	2yrs	2004-2006	Project Manager	yes	landscape, infrastruct	private/public	5b	Architecture, Land. Arch., Engineering	consultancy	3yrs
H	large		2004-2006	Project Manager	yes	buildings	private/public	10-15m	Architecture, engineering	consultancy	4.5yrs
J	medium	2 to 3	2007-present	Project Manager	yes	buildings, landscape	private/public	10m	Architecture, engineering	consultancy	10yrs
K	small	6mo-2yr	2007-present	Project Manager	no	landscape, infrastruct	private/public	2-10m	Architecture, Land. Arch., Engineering	consultancy	3yrs

* small (1-10 employees) medium (11-50 employees) large (51-100 employees)

The advantages that communities are viewed as getting through the use of sustainable practices are: economic stimulus by using local resources and services, less waste in materials, less demand for energy, healthier environments with less pollution and healthier employees. When the benefits become more tangible or apparent, either through education or some other form of exposure, project managers believe communities have a greater sense of pride, global understanding of interrelatedness, and advocate promotion of sustainable practices to other communities (project managers A, B, C, E and F).

5.2. Program Strategy and Operations

In terms of definitions of sustainable development only project managers B and E gave definitions close to the Brundtland Commissions report (1987). As stated by project manager B: *"Sustainability means living and thriving today without depleting systems for future life."* Interviewee F defined it by the three pillars of the TBL, while the remaining project managers defined it in terms of sustainable materials and systems that have the least impact on the environment (project managers A, C, D, G, H and K). In terms of how participants perceived the TBL economic, social and environmental aspects of sustainability, most viewed the environmental and economical aspects as more tangible, while the social aspect seemed more abstract and harder to quantify (project managers A, B, C, E, K, H, J). This was seen to influence the focus in terms of selling the concept, as articulated by project manager J:

> "Economic aspects are generally the easiest to sell to the client, if sufficient funding is available up front. Environmental aspects make sense to people but are difficult to quantify. Social aspects are the most abstract and most difficult to quantify."

Most project managers defined the LEED rating system as primarily addressing environmental aspects, some economic ones, with a trickled down effect which impacts social aspects (project managers C, E, F, H, J and K). However, two project managers disagreed and indicated that in their assessment and for their purposes, LEED does cover all three dimension of sustainability (project managers A and G). Six of the project managers indicated that they worked to a set of standards to implement sustainability in their projects, typically using LEED (project managers B and C) or a quality management system (project manager K). However, sustainability was considered by most on a project-by-project basis or upon client's request. As explained by project manager H: *"It depends on the project type, the client's interests and knowledge of sustainability, along with the funds available."* Only project managers B, F and J said that they considered sustainability, to varying degrees, on all their projects. Central management was seen to have little involvement in providing a sustainability framework, with only project managers B, G and J stating such an involvement. Project manager J describes how such involvement worked: *"...a checklist has been developed that identifies relatively easy objectives and then notes other objectives that are likely, based on project type."* The response of project manager A suggests a lack of involvement is often a function of the size of the organisation:

> "We are a small civil engineering firm. We each manage our own projects and develop a rapport with the client. There is no central management." (Project Manager A.)

Most participants stated that corporate governance encouraged and promoted sustainable management practices (all except project managers D, E and K). A distinction was made between encouragement and support, as articulated by project manager H: *"Encourage – yes, support –no. It tends to fall upon the project manager, and the client and their goals."* Only project manager F′s organisation had a department for corporate social responsibility, though again the absence was in part a function of organisation size (project manager B) and project manager C's organisation had a *"designated person"*. Project managers H and J stated that they had sister/partner companies that did sustainability consulting with whom they both worked closely. Project manager F described those responsible for sustainability who staff could consult:

> "Within the firm there are numerous people who are identified as sustainable "leaders". Additionally, there is an internal "sustainability community" amongst many other design focus circles which confers typically on a monthly basis to exchange ideas."

Most project managers indicated that they do seek assistance from external consultants on sustainability, despite the fact that five out of the ten project managers were LEED accredited. A typical process was described by project manager C, who stated they *"…regularly meet with sales representatives and manufacturers to talk about their products, meet with other consultants as needed per project (such as a consultant who offers sustainability food service management to our clients)."* The majority of project managers felt they were involved in making decisions early in the project life cycle (all except H) and all carried the project through completion. They were all positive about their ability to influence the client and their team members. Most positive was project manager C, who stated: *"Absolutely. I consider myself the major influencing factor"*. Whilst project manager H was typical of those who were more circumspect:

> "Usually only later in the design phase which can be too late to influence major decisions, but I will take opportunities to influence decisions I can."

Likewise they generally affirmed that they coordinated the activities of the various project actors and provided the link between the disparate stakeholders, though project manager H described this as a shared role:

> "This is usually shared with the partner-in-charge (PIC). While I will be more in touch with the engineers and team and contractors, the PIC will be as much involved with the owner."

5.3. Education, Research and Development

To some degree or other all project managers (expect project manager E) were involved or aware of actions being taken to educate their team members and consultants on sustainability issues. Such an environment was graphically described by project manager F:

> "My firm is active in developing, innovating and implementing tools to create a vibrant sustainable practice and is very good in communicating these initiatives to all staff and consultants."

Project manager H recognised that education was a two-way process, stating that "…consultants, especially Mechanical, Electrical and Plant (MEP), are also educating us on issues as much of what they do is at the core of energy efficient operations."; whilst project manager J viewed project charters as a means to define project goals and educate staff in respect of sustainability-related goals at the start of the project. Project manager A's organisation selected sub-consultants that would have the same or higher LEED awareness than themselves.

In their dealings with clients there were mixed responses in terms of whether they sought to educate their clients on its benefits or merely saw it as an instrument to achieve business-related goals. The tension was typified by the comments of project manager C and project manager H:

> "Personally, many of us feel it's our duty to educate the client, but as a whole I don't think the company pushes as hard as it should. We definitely use it as a marketing tool to get clients (project manager C)". "I think the office would like to think it does, but other than a marketing statement I don't feel the office walks the talk (project manager H)."

Most of the project managers agreed that there is limited awareness of sustainability tools and materials provided by local Bodies. The exception was those who mentioned information on LEED (project managers B, E and J), local codes (project manager C) and more recently Green Globes, which is an alternative certification system for sustainability (project managers B and F).

5.4. Assessment, Measuring and Reporting

All project managers state that LEED standards are not the only ones used to measure sustainability in their projects. Many understood the limitations of the LEED system and used other local and national sustainability codes depending on the location of the project i.e. landscape architecture projects have access to a thorough set of guidelines specific to site development (project manager F). As articulated by project manager F:

> "My organization maintains a "sustainability checklist" as part of its Quality Management System which is a dynamic tool, lasting the duration of the project and meant to be revisited at opportune points of project development. This tool references LEED standards, but assumes that LEED is only the baseline of sustainability."

Interviewee J stated that they use a quality control checklist as part of their internal processes, though other project managers stated that they use no checklist to quality control the correct implementation of sustainability principles (project managers A, D, E and H).

In terms of the three elements of the TBL all project managers said that in some shape or form they address the environmental aspect of sustainability, typically as they relate to the life-cycle costs of the project. In terms of the social element the results were more mixed. Some stated low or minimal consideration (project managers A, D and E). Some felt that good design naturally incorporated social considerations (project managers C, G and K). Therefore even if most of the standards they used to assess sustainability did not measure the social aspects directly, they perceived their practices to take account of their social responsibility. Four project managers (B, C, H and J) detailed specific concerns for meeting social-related sustainability criteria. As articulated by project manager B: *"...we look at all aspects of products and services that we use. Are the companies socially responsible and how do they take care of their workers and communities?"*

The project managers all took a whole life cycle perspective when considering assessment, measuring and reporting, which often required involvement of different parties at different stages. As described by project manager A:

> "All the stages are considered. Often I have to educate the contractor and sub-contractor on why we are doing something. The low bidders tend to want to get done quickly and get out. We must insist on all the project elements being constructed because they tend to work in conjunction with each other."

This perspective, though, did not result in agreement that the primary focus was on total life cycle costs, with many project managers agreeing that the emphasis of the clients on the impact on up-front costs prevailed (project managers A, B, D, E, G and J). The conflict was graphically described by project manager H: *"...there is often a battle between up-front and life cycle. When changes start to affect the up-front costs it can be a battle to maintain the decisions based on the life of the project. The owners have good intentions but have to stay within their funding."*

The assessment, measuring and reporting was in most cases supporting the use of practices to enforce sustainability (all project managers except D and E). Multi-methods were adopted, involving: design/design research (project managers F and G), evaluation studies/specifications (project managers J and K), maintenance and testing programs (project managers B and C), material selection (project managers C, J and K) and value engineering (project manager H).

Reporting on sustainability was done differently by each organization. On public projects there were governmental publications that gave an update of the construction progress and monthly or quarterly meetings were held to inform the stakeholders (project managers A, C, F, G, H and J). On private projects the reporting was primarily internal or amongst the immediately involved parties, and it was done through memos, verbally in meetings and through the distribution of meeting minutes (project manager B, D, E and K). A number of project managers (C, E, G, H and J) described the sporadic use of checklist, for example if the project is seeking LEED certification or it is a specific request of the client. What was absent was any sense of there being a framework to achieve maximum results for their projects through their practices against all elements of the TBL. Project manager K described it in graphic detail:

> "There are no real reporting standards. We have meetings and internal memos, but we are not encouraged by the company to take such measures. If we can get corporate governance involved into providing a sustainability management framework, incorporating the TBL

principles, our jobs [as project managers] will become much easier, our projects can be evaluated more precisely and all of our staff will be more coordinated."

6. Discussion

In this section the key findings are discussed. The section is also divided into the same four categories of the SPMA Model as per the Findings section above.

6.1. Managing Stakeholder Relations and Impacts

In respect of how the policies of project managers impact on the stakeholders the findings indicate that managers seem to do the bare minimum to engage with the wider stakeholders, such as the communities in which their projects are undertaken. In public projects, and because of the public's involvement, the engagement is greater and project managers have an obligation to involve their stakeholders. In private projects, with no such obligation, that engagement is less evident. The instrumental stakeholder's theory indicates that it is in their interest for managers to take note of their stakeholders (Berman et al., 1999) and Jansen, (2001: 1) stated that "a firm cannot maximise value if it ignores the interests of its stakeholders." Freeman (1984) indicates that management should follow processes that give an opportunity to stakeholders to raise their concerns. Other literature suggests that sustainability is about working with community partners to increase their awareness. Therefore, moving the construction industry toward sustainability will involve collaboration on the part of all stakeholders to find common solutions to problems (Augenbroe and Pearce, 1998). Furthermore, talking to communities, pressure groups and the local press could prevent complaints and bad press relating to projects by generating reciprocal understanding and creating harmonious relations which can ultimately contribute to successfully meeting goals and objectives (CIOB, 2004).

The absence of any strong corporate governance in almost all of the participant organizations was perhaps the single strongest reason for failure to manage relationships with and between stakeholders. The Hampel Committee (1998: paragraph 15) states that *"corporate governance must contribute both to business prosperity and accountability..., and that the purpose of those responsible for corporate governance is to safeguard the interests of shareholders and to protect and promote the interests of other stakeholders..."* Clients, who are one of the key stakeholders, were described by most project managers in the survey as being concerned with costs over sustainability, which took precedence over the benefits of 'green' buildings. This is consistent with the prior literature, which indicates that additional cost is a common reason for projects diverting away from seeking sustainability-related objectives, especially when upfront costs are perceived as more important than whole life-cycle costs. In this respect recent local and Federal US government incentives i.e. stimulus packages providing incentives in the form of subsidies, tax credits and rebates to reduce costs (as described by Brite, 2009) have the potential for projects to meet sustainability-related targets whilst also maintaining harmonious relationships with clients by not adversely affecting up-front costs.

According to the project managers one of the reasons many stakeholders prefer ′green′ buildings over conventional buildings is because they believe they are better for the environment. However, there was also a view that whilst stakeholders and communities prefer sustainable projects they cannot necessary recognize sustainable projects from conventional ones. There is an obvious gap here that can be bridged by the closer engagement of organizations with the local communities, and by project organisations being more transparent. Part of this process will be seeking feedback and listening to stakeholders′ comments, which will create a constructive dialogue among all parties and increase awareness. Hence stakeholders and communities will see a difference from the beginning of each project and understand and recognize the differences between sustainable and conventional ones. In addition, project managers can ensure that any operatives and site staff understand the importance of sustainability and how to be socially responsible during construction; hence improving community relations and minimising complaints (CIOB, 2004).

The stakeholders′ perception on sustainability advantages and/or disadvantages, as far as the project managers could assess, seemed to be formed not so much from the influence of project management professionals, but rather on information received from the media and other public sources. This might explain why stakeholders could not identify sustainable projects, since their exposure to such issues from the professional organizations is minimal. Consequently, they form their opinions through other entities and by the degree of exposure they have to the subject. However, some of the advantages which the communities can see, which translate to immediate benefits, are the use of local labour, materials and resources on sustainable projects. As stressed in the literature, it is important that project organizations initiate external and internal stakeholder dialogue by talking to suppliers about where and how materials are sourced; talking with employees about what sustainability means to the organization; and encouraging all project participants to devise and implement new approaches which will deliver against sustainability-related objectives. Such constructive dialogues and involvement of the different parties might help to find ways for the business to also address social-related sustainability responsibilities that had not been thought of previously (CIOB, 2004). In buildings, recognised long term benefits that are observed include occupants feeling healthier and energy costs were lower. These are indeed benefits of ′green′ buildings, but some stakeholders and communities may need help in better understanding sustainability standards, through engagement in workshops on building design or best environmental practices.

6.2. Managing Program Strategy and Operations

In today's society businesses are encouraged as a matter of good practice to incorporate sustainability as part of their corporate culture (Boswell, 2005). This begs the question, what is meant by the term sustainability? Most of the definitions given by the project managers pertained to the usage of materials and systems as they impact on the environment. Only one project manager defined sustainability in a way that was consistent with the three components of the TBL. This is consistent with the literature, which indicates that the term "sustainable" has proven to be remarkably difficult to pinpoint to one generally accepted definition (Bieker et al., 2002). There was also little awareness of the sustainability definition given in 1994 at the First International Conference on Sustainable Construction in Tampa, Florida, US which defined sustainable construction as *"... the creation and responsible management of a healthy built environment based on resource efficient and ecological principles"* (Kibert, 1994). The emphasis here is on the management practices for the success of sustainable construction. Therefore sustainability is achieved through an orchestrated activity of the team of actors involved in the process of programming, designing, construction, use and recycling of the facility (Augenbroe and Pearce, 1998). This process has to be coordinated by the project manager to be deemed successful, so project management plays a vital role in applying sustainable practices to deliver sustainable projects (Walker et al., 2003). These findings seem to give a partial answer to the research question: How is sustainability applied through project management practices? In part it is through the level of understanding each project manager has regarding: 1) how to define sustainability i.e. in terms of the TBL and 2) their perceived role in coordinating the processes by which sustainability-targets are met.

Whilst the survey showed some awareness of the TBL concept amongst project managers this awareness had not translated to a use of components to apply and measure sustainability in their projects in respect of each of the three elements. Environmental and economic aspects of the TBL were most likely to be measured. Social aspects were not addressed individually, but rather were viewed as being an outcome of good design practices. This is consistent with literature which indicates that many companies are already being very socially responsible, but simply have not labelled their actions as such (CIOB, 2004). Construction sustainability performance in relation to all three elements of the TBL is necessary for the maximum attainment of sustainable development. In the past various techniques and management skills had been developed to help improve sustainable performance in construction projects. However, in the survey these techniques are not effectively implemented due to the fragmentation of the industry and the poor coordination among the various construction participants. As recognised previously (UNEP, 2006) there is a lack of consistency and existence of methods that take an holistic perspective to help participants implement sustainable construction practices at various stages of project realisation. As the project managers surveyed pointed out, each TBL component contributes to the overall impact of the project and even though the focus is more on environmental issues the total success of the project cannot be measured by that one component alone.

As the management of construction projects continues to be a challenging activity, as the environment in which projects are constructed increases in complexity, project managers seek to adapt methods to help them overcome those challenges (Walker et al., 2003). Most of the project managers surveyed viewed the LEED rating system as an incomplete way to apply sustainability, which confirms prior research that claims the LEED standard is oriented towards the environment and makes far lower overall requirements on the other two sustainability components (Jäger and Hunziker, 2009). That said, two project managers did state that LEED encompasses all the necessary components to achieve sustainability in projects, which shows some confusion as perceptions of what all the sustainability components are and how well LEED meets them. Contrast LEED with the German certification system DGNB, which, unlike LEED, explicitly includes all three TBL components of sustainability (Jäger and Hunziker, 2009). The project managers that did use additional sustainability standards, besides the LEED components, were taking them from local and national codes rather than from other established international sustainability systems. It was clear that there was limited exposure to and adoption of non-US national standards, such as BREEAM (UK) and DGNB (Germany).

Regardless of the fact that half of the project managers had obtained LEED accreditation, all of those surveyed stated the need for either external or internal consultation on sustainability-related issues. This enforces the fact that even the educational part of the LEED accreditation system does not provide adequate support for an accredited member to address all the sustainability components. Some of the project managers indicated that there was someone responsible for sustainability issues within their organization and two replied that they had sister companies which dealt with sustainability issues, with whom they consulted on a regular basis. These findings align with the recommendation of appointing sustainability managers, which is a similar role to the LEED accredited managers, that could be incorporated into job descriptions, or of creating sustainability committees, which would make, review and implement procedures and assess progress (Griffiths, 2005; CIOB, 2004).

Most of the project managers′ responses were consistent with indicative literature in respect of strategically planning the project phases to incorporate sustainability-related goals, when it is required. Integrating sustainability-related concerns into projects starts at the strategic and concept planning and project programming stage, where the technical and economic feasibility of alternatives will be compared in order to select the best possible project. Sustainability-related decisions made at the beginning of a project life-cycle have a far greater influence than those made at later stages, since design and construction decisions will influence the continuing operating costs and, in many cases, the revenues over the building's lifetime (Boswell, 2005). One project manager stated that sustainability has been used as a company marketing tool, while another stated that developers also considered it a selling-point for their buildings. For some, though not all, sustainability is an important area which will sets the organization apart, giving a competitive advantage over less sustainability-oriented organizations.

The majority of project managers surveyed had a tracking system in order to keep sustainability goals in check. But these tracking systems were comprised of the TBL components that were discussed above, which included the LEED rating system and in some cases additional local sustainability standards. Such tracking systems were typically used on certain projects, with only three project managers indicating that meeting sustainability targets was part of their standard practices, and in their case they used such a tracking system for all of their projects. It is important for organizations to develop useful tools that appeal to different actors, which can easily be embedded into existing practices. But rather than adapting the practice to the tool, the new generation of design tools needs to reflect the diversity in skills and objectives of its user base (Augenbroe and Pearce, 1998), which was the case for the three project managers with such tracking systems.

In most organizations corporate governance did not provide support for, or enforce, sustainable practices. This lack of engagement with and guidance to project managers, coupled with no standardized sustainability framework available to all project members, confirms the informal approach to sustainability taken in the strategic planning of businesses (CIOB, 2004). It also shows the lack of sustainability integration into their core management systems for most of those firms. The one organization in which central management was directly involved by providing a generic framework, and whose objectives could be customized for each project, had the most precise and defined formal processes. It is clear then that there are many strategic approaches to adopting sustainability as a way of business in project environments. The real value of corporate sustainability is that the concept can enable a business to approach existing objectives with a fresh perspective and encourage others to view the business from a new, often more favourable angle. Companies can use mission, vision and value statements oriented towards sustainability goals. From this they can set realistic sustainability-related targets and outcomes to be achieved, which projects can contribute to delivering. By explicitly stating how the planned actions will be beneficial to the company, to society and to the environment; and how they will meet the company's existing objectives, they can ensure employee awareness and present sustainable development as a new direction for the company to move forward and compete in today's markets, as suggested in the literature (CIOB, 2004).

Unsurprisingly, project managers see themselves as the pivotal figures in coordinating the project processes, in carrying the project through all the phases, being the link between all project actors and ultimately being able to influence on the client through their direct access. This is consistent with the literature (Boswell, 2005). Thus they are responsible for implementing sustainability policies in their projects. Some project managers attributed their success in this area to setting clear objectives throughout the project phases in order to implement sustainable practices effectively. Setting clear objectives has long been viewed as an important of successfully implementing strategy. As far back as the 1950's Peter Drucker described how the procedure of setting objectives and monitoring progress towards them should permeate the entire organization from top to bottom, in a process of "management by objectives" MBO (Drucker, 1954). MBO is a useful approach which helps to assess the achievement of sustainability objectives in an organization if it involves continuous tracking of the processes and ongoing feedback towards reaching those objectives. The concept of sustainable construction is a relatively new one, with its aim of integrating the objectives of sustainable development into the construction activities. Whilst it is generally becoming well understood in relation to the environmental performance of construction products and assets (environmental sustainability), objectives need to reflect a more holistic and balanced economical, ecological and social TBL approach. Although project sustainability's influence on market developments can be classed as indirect, it has an important role through the decisions of market actors integrating or not the objectives of sustainable development into their decision process (COM, 2007). Therefore its role can be enhanced if decisions are based on meeting objectives related to all three elements of the TBL.

6.3. Managing Education, Research and Development

Many organizations in the construction industry are dedicated to implementing sustainable principles into their processes, thus generating best sustainable construction practices, such as the creation and application of new knowledge within those practices (Egan, 1998). Therefore educating clients, as well as other key stakeholders, is crucial in achieving sustainable development. Education and training can also be expanded to include implementing new technologies and building practices (Augenbroe and Pearce, 1998). The project managers surveyed indicated that they did educate their clients and sub-consultants, along with the rest of the team members, to ensure maximum results. However education on sustainability issues did not extend to the community members, an important group as discussed earlier in the chapter, or to the end users. So these groups rely on acquiring knowledge through the media and publications - which is limiting since they do not all have the same exposure to such sources of knowledge - instead of purposeful trainings or workshops.

Although most organizations undertook education and training activities to selected stakeholders, this was only on projects that required sustainability conformance. Education beforehand and on a continuous basis, through sustainability brochures and publications geared towards future clients and the public is very important but was conspicuously lacking. Organizations that wish to practice sustainability need to come up with approaches and methods to show future clients the possible ways they can benefit from sustainable projects, both now and in the future. One area of activity amongst some project managers was the development of maintenance and testing programs, which ensured that the systems and materials they use were working as intended and were being maintained properly to guarantee long building life as well as the health of the occupants. Building showcases and monitoring and diagnosing systems in practice is another way to educate stakeholders, through innovation. Also developing a timely national database to cultivate and promote proven technologies, which could be extended to a life-cycle information system for constructed facilities, is another possible tool for compiling and disseminating knowledge to stakeholders. Prior literature highlights the benefits of the exchange of knowledge with other developed countries (Augenbroe and Pearce, 1998) and this could be achieved by adopting national and international sustainability metrics in exported technologies. The project managers did not indicate that there has been an effort to educate members of the construction community, or a request for specific educational training in sustainability issues. The gap that seems to occur between the consultancies and the construction trades can be bridged through the enforcement of education and training. Also, it appears that the experience gained from solving problems is not organised enough in a learning building process which allows solving problems associated with the performance of construction assets and constituent elements in a more systematic way. This could be the case for addressing life-cycle issues, and the re-use and recycling of materials. The need for training multi-skilled operatives should as well be considered with respect to new organisational forms and sustainability processes (COM, 2007).

Two of the project managers stated that their organizations were active in developing appropriate educational tools, in order to be able to communicate their incentives to all levels of staff and consultants. Whilst no specific description of those tools was given, such tools as collaborative engineering models, protocols and systems can focus on integral assessments of design through the different design phases. They must incorporate sustainability indicators in performance based strategies that match client requirements with assessed design performance (ASTM standards). Tools must be embedded in collaborative CAD environments, which all participants have, and should be accessible, by all actors in the process (Augenbroe and Pearce, 1998), which is often limited. Yet most of the project managers surveyed did not seem to have indicative educational tools and processes. According to literature the problem is that the actual standardisation process is very much fragmented and adapting very slowly to technological progress and market development (COM, 2007). There is a need to see how it could evolve more rapidly towards a set of standards integrating the various aspects of sustainable development and benefiting from new scientific and technical knowledge. When the standardisation process cannot deal correctly with innovative technologies, alternative paths need to be explored to back-up performance and support market development without compromising on safety and responsibility issues.

6.4. Assessment, Measuring and Reporting

Project managers lack a sustainability management model/framework which ensures that the project is managed to include environmentally sustainable practices in the design, construction and operational phases of the project. As suggested, a model/framework must take into account the social and economic aspects of the project performance as well as environmental, and provide management with a tool to measure, drive and reward outstanding behaviour on the project (Griffiths, 2005). Evaluation models and methods should be applied, despite some dimensions of sustainability which are not easily quantifiable (COM, 2007). Most project managers were aware of the limitations of the LEED rating system. That is why they often tried to encompass additional measurements immediately available to them through local sustainability codes, as well as national standards when dealing with other states (in the US each state has each own industry codes). The intent to achieve more and do better is there. Yet it is the guidance that is lacking, sometimes resulting in project managers developing their own systems even within the same organization. The construction industry has been classed as under-performing in each of the key sustainability theme groups: environmental, social and economic (CIRIA, 2001), and this was borne out by the responses of the project managers in the survey.

Some organizations had official sustainability checklists to control the quality of their internal possesses. Those that did not were not able to assess the accurate implementation of sustainability principles in their processes and outcomes; neither were they able to obtain homogenous results within the organization, amongst the different project managers. The environmental aspects of sustainability were viewed only as they related to the life-cycle costs of the project and were not measured or assessed individually as to their impact on the 'ecological footprint', but rather as they rated on the LEED system and the local codes. Environmental and social sustainability remain largely separated from the traditional core business strategies and management systems, which are geared mainly towards financial performance indicators. Accordingly management tools are needed that help firms to integrate financial, environmental and social management systems (Bieker et al., 2002).

The project managers perceived that clients identified costs as the primary factor influencing decision-making. Initial costs and life-cycle costs have to be assessed when measuring the economic aspect, as well as operational costs. However, some project managers expressed the view that clients often made their decisions based on the initial up-front costs only. It seems common in literature that many key decisions are taken on the basis of the lowest costs instead of on quality, safety and environmental criteria, and life-cycle costs. Although most project managers indicated that the percentage of public clients asking for sustainability-related goals to be met was higher than that of the private sector, yet the demand within the public sector for conventional projects was higher. Again cost was the primary reason, since public-sector project budgets were set and limited. With the actual tendering practices and separation of the budgeting functions within the public sector there is little incentive to propose solutions with a higher quality which match the customer's requirements. There is therefore a need to identify incentives to offer solutions at the advantage of both the clients and the industry.

Best practices that allow acceptance of the "Economical Most Advantageous Tender" (EMAT) and Life-Cycle Costing, and encourage the proposal of technological variants, would be a step forward (COM, 2007). The German DGNB rating system also addresses lower life-cycle costs as being a big parameter of the economic quality for sustainability (Bilfinger and Berger, 2008). Two project managers indicated that a further aspect in assessing economic sustainability in their projects was by identifying the economic stimulus the new construction brought to the region and/or the revitalization and re-use of the existing buildings. Social aspects were not separately measured since there were no set indicators on how to measure them. The DGNB system measures separately the socio-cultural quality, which incorporates social and cultural values, such as protection of health and comfort of inhabitants, the human surroundings and social and cultural values. In the DGNB system all three TBL pillars have the same weight, therefore giving them all the same importance. A smaller weight factor, but still of significance, is the "process quality" rating which includes quality of design and construction (Fraunhofer-Institut für Bauphysik, 2008; Bilfinger and Berger, 2008). These are standard measurements in the DGNB system that the survey results suggest the US-based practitioners might learn from in any process of re-evaluating the standards they currently use.

Some of the project managers stated that they were measuring their sustainable processes by the sustainable materials they were selecting for their projects; hence emphasising the need to focus on the processes themselves. The PMBOK Guide (PMI, 2008) states that projects are composed of two kinds of processes: project management processes and product-oriented processes. In order for a project to be successful, the project managers need to select appropriate processes within the Project Management Process Groups that are required to meet the project objectives (as indicated on Figure 6.1).

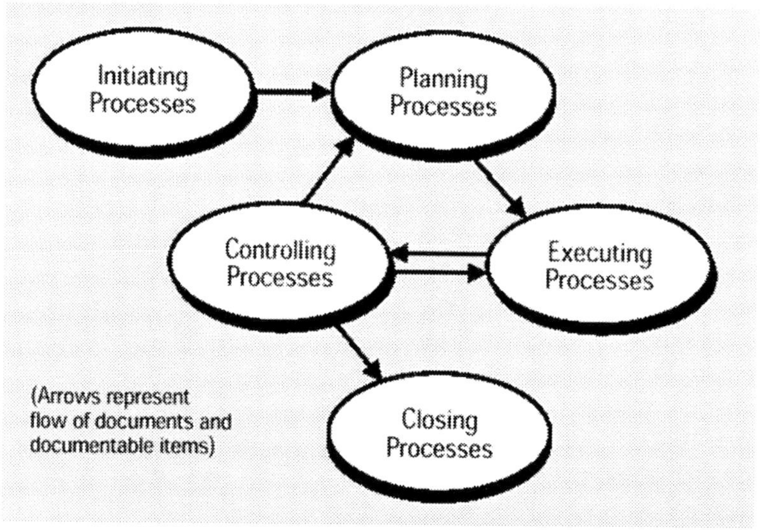

Figure 6.1. Project Management Process Groups (PMI, 2008).

Project management processes are concerned with describing and organizing the work of the project. Product-oriented processes specify and create the project's product. They are typically defined by the project life-cycle and vary by application area. Project management processes and product-oriented processes overlap and interact throughout the project. For example, the scope of the project cannot be defined in the absence of some basic understanding of how to create the specified product, as illustrated in Figure 6.2 (PMI, 2008).

None of the project managers surveyed was engaged in formal sustainability reporting. Reporting in public projects was done though government publications and progress reports by the ′government-client′. In the private sector reporting was mostly internal, amongst team members, excluding external stakeholders and community. Even though firms world-wide have taken their corporate citizenship seriously, many construction industry consultants do not uphold such a set of standards. In order to carry out proper reporting on sustainability issues, the management process and the reporting process should not be two separate things. An efficient management reporting system will only be generated when the two are merged. Managers need to understand that external as well as internal drivers play a vital role in the reporting process, with clear commitment the key to setting standards and making reporting attainable and measurable – as shown in Figure 6.3 (WBCSD, 2002).

To conclude this section, most project managers were aware of the TBL elements, but had never put them together in a single assessment model to measure sustainability. Rather, the components were arbitrarily selected in their checklists, which resulted in main elements been left out. Such elements being: communicating sustainability goals to stakeholders and communities in private projects, research for alternative development methods to reach sustainability goals, and formal sustainability reporting. Yet the main issue seems to be one of a lack of corporate governance. The absence of its active participation, and lack of understanding of the importance of setting corporate sustainability strategies as part of the core business to be followed by the entire organization, results in a fairly unstructured approach to sustainability in the project managers' organizations and subsequently variable end results in terms of delivering against the TBL.

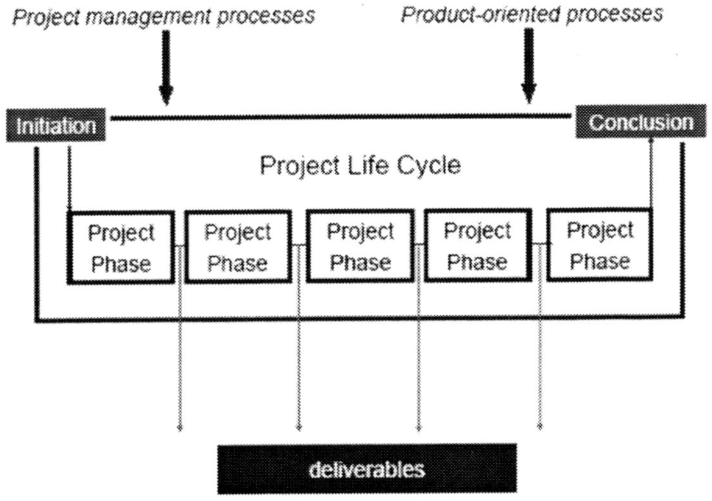

Figure 6.2. Project Management and Product-Oriented Processes (PMI, 2008).

LIVERPOOL JOHN MOORES UNIVERSITY

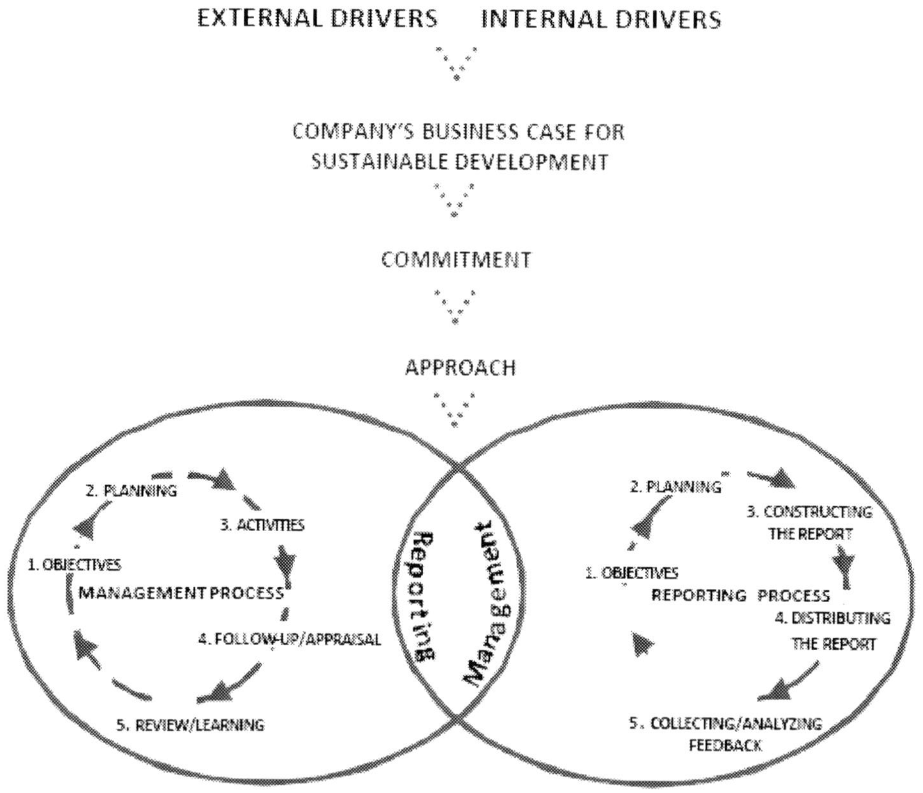

Figure 6.3. Toward an Integrated Management and Reporting (WBCSD, 2002).

7. EMERGENT ISSUES

This section presents a number of salient issues that emerged from the data which provide supplementary insight into the topic and enhance our understanding of how sustainability can better be strategically integrated into the core business processes – of which project management is one, of companies working in the construction sector.

7.1. Corporate Sustainability Company Strategies

The first emergent issue can be classed under the heading of corporate sustainability company strategies. Bieker et al., (2002) based on the work of Dyllick, Belz and Schneidewind (1997) derived four different types of strategies regarding corporate sustainability that can be applied to firms that engage in sustainability management. These four types are part of the ecological competition strategy – see Section 2.1 - and are as follows:

1. **Clean**: strategies the serve as a buffer, with the purpose to defend existing markets.

2. **Efficient**: strategies that address the environment, with the purpose to minimize costs related to environmental processes.
3. **Innovative**: differentiation strategies, with the purpose to increase sales that are related to environmental products.
4. **Progressive**: environmental market development strategies, with the purpose to differentiate sustainability-oriented firms and provide them with competitive advantage (Dyllick et al., 1997; cited in Bieker et al., 2002).

The results of the interviews with project managers indicated two major issues that affect the corporate sustainability strategies: costs and marketing. Even though in practice all four strategy types described above may overlap, the discussion will focus on strategy type 2 (Efficiency) and strategy type 4 (Progressive) and put them in context through a "sustainable cost strategy" and "sustainable market development". Additionally, the discussion will show the benefit of modifying the Corporate Sustainability Management Reference Model (CSMRM) applied in this research to incorporate these two additional strategies. The discussion draws heavily from Bieker et al., 2002, which also drew together the work of other authors in relation to linking environmental and social sustainability to business strategy.

7.2. Sustainable Cost Strategy

A company which follows the corporate sustainability strategy of efficiency will focus on environmental and social objectives that contribute to the reduction of their costs, thus aiming for measures that help to assess whether environmental and social standards are met in the most cost efficient way (Dyllick et al., 1997; cited in Bieker et al., 2002). In the environmental field this comprises the strategy of "eco-efficiency" (Schmidheiny, 1992; cited in Bieker et al., 2002). Its main objective is to minimise the cost-related ecological damage per product or service unit, typically realised by savings of materials, energy, water and waste. Measures would look at cost savings from pollution prevention rather than monitoring end-result solutions. The social field however, which covers the strategy of "social-efficiency", needs much more of a careful and aware management, and understanding of their employees is a prerequisite in order for appropriate measures to be taken (Bieker et al., 2002).

The CSMRM for cost efficient companies will focus on the internal objectives to optimise production processes. In the process perspective companies aiming for efficiency will implement objectives, indicators and measures in order to enhance process efficiency from a financial perspective as well as from an environmental and social point of view. Optimising the operating processes is the core, but innovation processes might get more important when a company realises that only through product innovation can it achieve production innovation (UBA, 2001: 579; cited in Bieker et al., 2002; PMI, 2004).

While an efficiency-based strategy would most probably focus on the process dimension, it might also consider supporting measures in the financial and development perspectives. In the financial perspective main objectives as well as lagging indicators would consider the costs of material, energy and water use. A ratio of turnover, earnings, or economic-value-added to material, energy and water use can express the objective to unhitch the resource use from the value creation of the company. Here firms would not only measure the actual disposal cost of waste but also add purchasing and handling costs of waste materials (EPA, 1995; cited in Bieker et al., 2002). In addition, costs can be saved for the company when realising cost reducing co-operations along their supply chain by using the concepts of life-cycle-costing (Schaltegger and Buritt, 2000: 109; cited in Bieker et al., 2002). In the learning perspective companies strive to enable their employees to deal with the natural resources as well as with their own manpower resources in efficient and saving ways. Training and education programs can make contributions to change behaviour as well as incentives for adopting more eco-efficient behaviour.

7.3. Sustainable Market Development

Similarly, a company which follows the corporate sustainability strategy of market development will focus on environmental and social objectives and measures that develop the political and societal framework of the competitive field. This is very pertinent to the construction industry where networks and personal connections often play a vital role in attaining work. Companies will aim at enlarging their existing markets for green and socially responsible products or even at creating completely new markets. Gaining maturity through practising the other strategies, such firms often have the experience that many process and product innovations do not pay off if the market is not yet ready for sustainability. To be able to better benefit from their pioneer position in sustainability know-how, these companies will try to influence the politics, the public and the consumers, in order to widen the competition fields. Therefore, they can use the strategies of getting more knowledge about ecological and social problems in their business areas, developing the public opinion by educating them in sustainability, developing the legislation by lobbying in a pro-sustainable way, developing the market in closer meanings by creating industry standards, resolving consumers and supporting push-strategies of the retailers (Dyllick et al., 1997: 78, 155; cited in Bieker et al., 2002).

A CSMRM for market developing companies will follow a strategy focused on the public and the politics, which will open a new perspective to control society-related objectives and measures. This new society perspective will focus on objectives, indicators and measures for the development of politics and the public as well as on research into solutions to sustainability-related problems. Leading indicators may be the expenses of public-relations work for sustainability, the number of educational projects and co-operations with non-governmental organisations, the educational level of the public measured by opinion research, the numbers of associations and panels the company is active as well as the number of supported research projects. Lagging indicators could be the measurable results of the research and co-operations projects, changed legislative frameworks, numbers of press releases in media, changed educational levels of the public and in the end savings or revenues realised in new or further developed markets (Bieker et al., 2002).

In the market perspective the main objectives are to develop existing markets or new markets in the context of sustainability. To realise first-mover-advantages, if markets have changed the capability of the company to produce sustainability-oriented innovative products in a sustainable way is critical. Therefore objectives and indicators of the innovative strategy type can be used. As such companies will need to think about the functions and needs behind their products and come up with new services to satisfy old needs (Hockerts, 1999a; Belz 1998; cited in Bieker et al., 2002). Process perspective objectives and indicators should ensure that the company has the capability to produce sustainably when the market development has been achieved. In addition supply chains used by the company will be tracked when companies advertise themselves as sustainable (Bieker et al., 2002) so methods and tools, such as Life-Cycle or Product-Line-Analysis, can help check the supply chains and be included in the CSMRM measures.

In the learning perspective the main objectives and indicators are also focused on creating the capability of the employees to act sustainably when the market has been developed. Because sustainable products and processes require more information and understanding, information sources and systems play an important role. Numbers of systems, suggestions for improvement, employees reached by training initiatives [etc.] can be indicators. The financial perspective takes into account the revenue made by sustainable products, but even more important is the financial potential of the companies´ products and services in the future when the markets are developed (Bieker et al., 2002). The CSMRM can be adopted accordingly to incorporate the intended strategies of each organization clearly and in detail. In order for those strategies to be implemented successfully, they have to become part of the core business processes rather than being seen as an additional, and perhaps optional, add-on.

8. Conclusions and Areas for Future Research

Perhaps the biggest challenge for humanity in the 21st Century is to build a sustainable society. During the last fifty years, the world has become more unsustainable. The planet is over populated, our natural resources have been severely degraded and the gap between rich and poor has increased dramatically. The challenge of building a sustainable society requires the adoption of a long-term view and the commitment and active participation of all members of society. In recent years many large companies worldwide have initiated sustainable development initiatives mainly to address the demands and expectations of government authorities, pressure groups, consumers, industry, religious associations and society at large. However, although most analysts state that these initiatives contribute to making their businesses more profitable many managers are not yet convinced of the validity of this argument. The reason is that most company sustainable development initiatives have been developed in isolation of business activities and are not yet directly linked to the business strategy of the organization. One way to strengthen the link that exists between sustainable development initiatives and the business strategy of an organization is to focus on the practices of the company in terms of the results of implementing sustainable development initiatives.

In discussing sustainability the concept of the "Triple Bottom Line" (TBL) of economic, environmental and social sustainability has emerged as the preeminent model for organizations to interpret sustainability. With this as the basis, the research presented in this chapter took an existing generic reference model whose structure incorporated the TBL principals – the Corporate Sustainability Management Reference Model (CSMRM), and derived a new evaluation model pertinent to the construction industry's requirements – the Sustainable Project Management Assessment Model (SPMA). The SPMA was used to evaluate how sustainability is applied through project management practices in consultancies in the construction industry. The research involved collecting data from ten senior project managers working in different organizations in the US. Due to the vast size and diversity of the country, the study conducted interviews with those working in only two neighbouring states, Illinois and Michigan, because they both have similar industry codes and regulations and alike climatic conditions. The research strategy was exploratory in nature, and all data were collected through in-depth telephone interviews.

Sustainable project management requires project managers to control and facilitate the project phases carefully in order to achieve sustainable results. Implementing sustainable project management practices ensures that a process will be followed and initiatives will be implemented during the delivery process to achieve measurable and reportable outcomes. In this chapter the importance of companies achieving sustainability has been stressed and discussed both on at the strategic and the project level. However, it is when sustainability management becomes part of the strategic focus that it brings maximum benefits to an organization. Hence, corporate governance plays an important role in setting and monitoring sustainability policies and practices that can offer a clear vision to all stakeholders.

The findings of this research were divided into the four groups of the SPMA. These are as follows:

Stakeholder Relations and Impacts: This emphasizes communicating sustainability goals and managing relationships between stakeholders. The participation of stakeholders in decision making processes and the impact sustainability has had on them.

Program Strategy and Operations: This refers to internal processes in regards to sustainability, the corporate strategy and the on-going operations strategy and planning of the organization.

Education, Research and Development: The emphasis here is on awareness, education and explanation of sustainability issues to project teams and stakeholders; in research and development of alternative solutions and sustainability methods; and promotion of innovation.

Assessment, Measurement and Reporting: Assessments are done on the economic, environmental and social aspects of the TBL. The use of a framework to measure, track and evaluate goal setting performance methodology, and reporting on all three levels of the TBL.

Taking each of four SPMA groups in turn; firstly, it was found that project managers did the bare minimum in terms of engaging the stakeholders and the communities in their projects. In public projects the involvement was greater than in private projects. This is not the desired as moving the construction industry towards sustainability will have to involve collaboration on the part of the stakeholders. Furthermore, sustainability requires working with community partners to increase awareness. A major obstacle which seems to have an impact in all four SPAM groups is a lack of corporate governance involvement. As such projects managers have no direction and they are left to devise their own frameworks or measuring standards for assessment. Stakeholders seemed to be the end beneficiaries of sustainable projects by reaping long term benefits, such as healthier environments and energy cost savings. Due to the lack of proper educational awareness, stakeholders and communities could not distinguish major differences between conventional versus sustainable projects. The information obtained from the media and other public sources seemed to form their opinions about sustainability.

The term "sustainability" meant different things to different project managers, confirming that it is still loosely perceived with no unifying definition. However, most project managers were aware of the three TBL components, but they did not use them all to assess and measure sustainability in their projects and practices. Environmental and economic aspects were more measurable and took precedence over social ones, which were harder to measure and were rather considered the effect of good practices. Even though LEED is the national US rating system for sustainability, most project managers recognised its limitations and were aware of the fact that it primarily encompasses environmental issues. Project managers had no awareness of other more holistic rating systems, such as the German DGNB, which is differentiated by clearly stating its inclusiveness of all the three TBL components of sustainability. In respect of stakeholders′ relations and interests, poor communication and lack of educational tools, can bring ambiguity, misunderstanding and can often result in mistrust among parties. This is a current area were improvement is needed as education and training on sustainability issues were directed by most organizations towards their own project team members and immediate stakeholders. There was no indicative training on sustainability issues for members of the construction teams, resulting in a gap between consultancies and the construction trades. One problem is that the actual standardisation process is very much fragmented and adapting very slowly to technological progress and market development. This hinders the development of innovative technologies and the seeking of alternative paths to be explored.

Very few organizations had official sustainability checklists to control the quality of their internal processes. The environmental aspects of sustainability were viewed only as they related to the life-cycle costs of the project. Environmental impacts were not measured or assessed individually as to their impact on the ′ecological footprint′, but rather as they rated on the LEED system and the local codes. To date environmental and social sustainability aspects remain largely separated from the traditional core business strategies and management systems, which are geared nearly solely towards financial performance. Clients identified costs as the primary decision-making factor, with initial costs and life-cycle costs having to be assessed when measuring the economic aspect of sustainability.

Observations by some project managers that sustainability processes are measured solely in terms of the use of materials leads to a further examination of the distinction of what the PMBOK Guide (PMI, 2004) describes as project management processes v. product management processes. Product oriented processes are typically defined by the project life-cycle and vary by application area. Project management processes and product-oriented processes overlap and interact throughout the project. None of the organizations surveyed was engaged in formal sustainability reporting. Reporting in public projects was done by the public client though government publications and project reports. In the private sector, reporting was mostly internal. Most project managers were familiar with the concept of the TBL, but they did not work within environments in which their project management systems operationalised the concept in a formal or a comprehensive way. Yet there was a clear desire for such a system and hence a role for corporate governance to establish and monitor a project management framework that incorporates the environmental, economic and social components of the TBL.

Hence, we return to the original research question, introduced in section 1.2: "How is the issue of sustainability applied through project management practices in the construction industry?" A summarised answer is as follows:

- In some cases project managers incorporate sustainability as part of their strategic goals and objectives, inform and educate the team players and stakeholders to the best of their ability, and satisfy the needs of their clients. By having their own internal tracking system they are able to keep sustainability goals and objectives in check for each of their projects. LEED and other local sustainability codes are followed to assure sustainable results for each project. Since in most organizations, corporate governance does not provide support or enforce sustainability practices, there are no standardized frameworks that could be followed. As such an informal approach to sustainability is taken in the strategic planning of the business.

Next, we revisit the research objectives (section 1.3) and draw some conclusions in relation to each one in turn:

- The first objective was to assess how, from the project managers´ perspective, their policies impact the stakeholders and communities. The findings indicate that their policies impact both stakeholders and communities by delivering both short and long term benefits. The correct implementation of sustainable policies on projects creates economic, social and environmental benefits for all stakeholder groups.
- The second objective was to evaluate how project managers define sustainability. A few defined it as meeting the needs of the present without compromising the ability of future generations to meet their own needs. But not all the definitions were consistent, indicative of the fact that not all project managers had the same understanding or definition of the concept.
- The third objective was to investigate if firms integrate sustainability into their core management systems. The research showed that sustainability has not been integrated by most firms into their core management systems, leaving project managers with the responsibility of developing their own assessment tools and methods as deemed appropriate.
- The fourth objective was to evaluate how sustainability is applied to construction projects. Sustainability has been applied mostly through the LEED assessment and the use of other local sustainability codes. Recycling and re-use of existing material and assessment of whole life cycle costs are other examples of sustainable applications to construction projects. Control checklists are also used to assure correct application of the standards set by each project managers and to educate team members to achieve delivery of sustainable results by all parties.
- The fifth objective was to explore to what extend participants are aware of the TBL components of environment, economic and social. All practitioners were aware of each of the three components but they did not typically integrate into one model to assess sustainability in their projects and practices.

- The sixth and final objective was to assess the validity of the Sustainable Project Management Assessment model (SPMA) and its applicability to the construction industry. The SPMA provides a useful framework for the construction industry as it uses all three components of the TBL and expands them into the areas of stakeholder relations, program strategy and operations, research and development, and measurement and reporting. These areas line up with the recommendations made by Agenda 21 on sustainability issues (CIB, 1999). Accordingly, all four areas of the SPMA are applicable to the way consultancies run their businesses and the practice areas they need to address; hence the model providing a framework by which sustainability can be assessed. The SPMA provides a structure for assessing sustainable project management practices in the construction sectors and for revealing the industries′ shortcomings. However, based on the emergent findings, the corporate sustainability strategies of cost and marketing are elements that could usefully be added under the Program Strategy and Operations area within the model.

In drawing these conclusions it must be stressed that this research had been limited to a small geographical area of the US and to a small number of consultancies in the construction industry. By its very nature it is exploratory and generalisations to a wider population would not be appropriate. Therefore further work is needed to validate the findings and build upon the research reported in this paper. For example, research could be conducted on US consultancy firms as well as construction firms that engage in international work, to see if these organizations. There are many other actors involved in construction projects, besides the project manager, hence further study could focus on project owners and other stakeholder groups, such as professional services and sub-contractors. Another suggested area of research could be on the integration of other emerging sustainability management systems into the core business processes. Again, the area of sustainability is so vast and many of the other findings in this research can offer guidance for further research in this field.

To conclude, the research reported in this paper indicates that achievement of sustainable project management in an organisation depends on the five key areas listed in table 8.1 below. Corporate governance is crucial followed by the implementation of the correct strategies, which include key sustainable development policies. These then have to be translated and integrated into the management systems of the company, and last but not least, the approach needs to be inclusive of all stakeholders. This finding is consistent with the assessment that was made by WBCSD (2001) and in same area order of importance.

Table 8.1. Successful sustainable development - Company context (WBCSD, 2001).

☑	CORPORATE GOVERNANCE
☑	STRATEGIES
☑	KEY SUSTAINABLE DEVELOPMENT POLICIES
☑	MANAGEMENT SYSTEMS
☑	STAKEHOLDER ENGAGEMENT

To move the sustainability agenda forward amongst practising project managers there is a need for knowledge dissemination. Enhancing awareness of all actors, stakeholders, industry players, and the public through access to the expertise found in local bodies of knowledge and at different institutions of higher learning, can contribute to education and awareness of sustainability issues. Also, partnering among institutions of higher education, and between the academic community and the industry, in order to leverage resources and expertise and generate a richer educational environment, which promotes development and innovation, can be a big contributor to the development of sustainable project management. At the end of the day, sustainability does not have to remain as part of a ´wish list´ of project managers but it can become part of the standard way of doing projects.

APPENDIX A: INTERVIEW QUESTIONS

Information about the organization:
How long do the projects typically last (in years)?
When have the majority of the projects you have described commence?

2007-Present			2004-06	2002-03	2001-02	<2000
What is your role in the project?			Programme Manager			
			Project Manager			
			Sponsor			
			Team Member			
			Other			
Please specify						
Are you LEED accredited?			Yes		No	
What types of projects have you mostly described?			Building			
			Infrastructure			
			Landscape			
			Other			
Please specify						
What is the approximate budget in average (in USD)?						
Nature of Business						
Type of Projects		Private	Public			
Size of Organisation	<10	11-50	51-100	101-500	>500	

Interview Questionnaire

Part One

Stakeholders and community

1. In your opinion how are stakeholders influenced by sustainable projects?
2. In your opinion do stakeholders see a difference between a ′green′ project and a conventional project?
3. In your opinion do stakeholders see benefits on ′green′ projects, and why? Can those benefits be categorized as short term, long term or both and why?
4. In your opinion, how does a sustainable project impact each community?
5. By employing sustainable practices what do you see are the benefits for each community? What are the advantages as well as disadvantages?

Part Two

Definitions of sustainable practices

1. How do you define sustainability?
2. Are you using LEED standards only?
3. How do you define the three dimensions of sustainability called the triple bottom line (TBL), which encompasses environmental, social and economic aspects?
4. Do you think LEED covers all three dimensions of the TBL?
5. Additional comments:

Part Three

Sustainability as part of the core management

1. Is sustainability considered on a project-by-project basis?
2. Does central management provide a sustainability framework that can be customized to the needs of each project?
3. Does corporate governance encourage and promote sustainable management practices?
4. Does your organisation have a corporate social responsibility (CSR) department?
5. Is there anyone in your organisation that is in charge and may be consulted on sustainability issues?
6. How often do you seek assistance from external consultants on sustainability issues?

Part Four

Sustainability in Projects

1. Do you have a set of standards on how to implement sustainability in your projects? Which sustainability guidelines do you follow on your projects? (i.e. LEED etc.)
2. Do you have a sustainability checklist to quality control the correct implementation of sustainable principles for each project?

3. Do you 'educate' your staff and consultants regarding sustainability issues to ensure that everyone has the same understanding, aims and goals?
4. Do you see a difference in sustainable practices between the private and the public sector? If so please elaborate how.
5. In view of the Triple Bottom Line (TBL):

   (a) Does your organisation address the environmental aspects of sustainability in projects? (i.e. energy, resources, impact etc.) Please explain.
   (b) Does your organisation address the social aspects of sustainability in projects? (i.e. health, comfort, contentment of occupants, functionality etc.) Please explain.
   (c) Does your organisation address the economic aspects of sustainability in projects? (i.e. high & stable economic growth of employment, inquiring costs, income/revenue, value etc.)
6. Is sustainability something your organisation practices as a standard and tries to educate the clients on or is it provided in response to the clients' demands only?

Part Five

Project life cycle

1. Are you, as a project manager, involved in early project decisions?
2. Do you typically carry the project through completion?
3. From your position as a project manager are you able to influence the client and team members on the decisions taken at the different project stages?
4. As a project manager, do you coordinate all the project actors such as owners, architects, engineers, general contractors [etc.] and links all of them together?
5. When working on a project do you focus on the individual stages only or do you consider all the stages of the project's life cycle and act accordingly?
6. As a project manager are you enforcing sustainable practices that affect the project's life cycle? If so, how?
7. When looking at costs, are you or the client are more concerned about the total life cycle costs or just focused mainly on the upfront costs?
8. How is reporting on sustainability done within your organization? Is there a difference in reporting between public and private projects?

APPENDIX B: SUMMARY OF KEY FINDINGS

participant code	impacts on stakeholders & community	sustainability definitions	integration to core management	sustainability guidelines for construction projects	awareness of TBL elements
A	The advantage is the pride pride that each community feels in their green design . It lets them know that a public body is sensitive to Green Issues and Awareness. The disadvantage is the lack of care the public takes of the facilities. The damage is significant and requires maintenance funds which may not be available.	Develop design features that are environmentally efficient and supportive	No	LEED standards, local codes	Medium
B	Improved health for our individual and our shared environments – now and for the future, increased awareness of the importance of our environment, hopefully a change in value systems, re-establishing a real sense of community and the character of place and a setting's natural systems	Living and thriving today without depleting systems for future life	Yes	LEED standards, local codes	High
C	Economic stimulus by using local resources and services, less waste in the waste stream, less demand for energy, healthier communities with less pollution and healthier employees. Disadvantage may be the naysayers don't want to participate and costs may be higher for some things	In architecture, I define sustainability as getting the most usable and efficient building while making the least impact on the planet's resources	No	LEED standards, local codes, has developed own checklist	High
D	Better neighbourhoods	Reusing existing materials	No	No	Low
E	Lesser energy and water usage are primary, higher initial costs are disadvantages	To do not compromise the next generation's ability to provide for themselves	No	Chicago Green Building	High
F	Greater sense of pride, global understanding of interrelatedness, promotion of sustainable practices in other communities	Environmental, social and economical sustainability in developments	No	Sustainability checklist, national and regional sustainability guidelines depending on the project location, for the landscape architecture projects is http://www.sustainablesites.org/, which is developing a very thorough set of guidelines specific to site development	High
G	Yes, at some degree, improved communities	Hard to define	No	LEED as guideline; some clients have their own set of design sustainable guidelines	High
H	One can only hope that having a sustainable building as a neighbour will help people see the advantages. Especially in the neighbourhoods of our affordable housing projects we hope that neighbours will see that it can be done on limited funds and hopefully they will hear from their new neighbours the benefits. The disadvantages may simply be the misunderstanding of these types of buildings and the impact and costs.	It is finding the best way to create a project that minimizes its impact on the environment within the limitations creating or operating that project	No	Depends on the project: LEED, City of Chicago Green Homes Checklist, and Illinois Department of Commerce and Economic Opportunities energy grant requirements.	High

(Continued)

J	Some sustainable practices encourage emerging markets and the development of new industries	Ideally, sustainability is about systems that are net neutral, so that they truly can be sustained indefinitely	Yes	LEED if the client desires to use it, but also our own system (based on LEED) as well as city and state standards, and other standards are referenced	High
K	Improves neighbourhoods, but many times people do not understand the difference and they don't appreciate it	By use of sustainable materials and practices	No	Mostly LEED standards	High

APPENDIX C: DETAILED INTERVIEW RESPONSES

Interview Responses	
Stakeholder Relations & Impacts	
Q-1	***Do you see a difference in sustainable practices between the private and the public sector?***
A	Yes. Private developers are striving for LEED certifications on their new buildings. They find that tenants will pay slightly higher rent to occupy a LEED certified building. In the Public sector, new schools, new libraries, new police stations etc are now going for Silver LEED certifications.
B	Both seem to focus strongly on energy efficiency and less on environmental impact of products, and air quality.
C	Yes, many of our public projects are required to follow LEED to get funding. Some don't take it very seriously and do the bare minimum to get certification. Some of our public clients are far more sophisticated and have their own requirements they want us to follow – such as colleges with their own environmental engineering programs. Most of the private clients don't want to pursue it unless it's something they can market and make money on.
D	Only have private clients
E	Private sector has to see more economic incentive. Public sector is willing to spend extra for green building.
F	N/R
G	Public clients typically have their own sustainable design guidelines; most private clients do not have the guidelines.
H	N/R
J	Yes, public sector projects are more open to sustainability, possibly due to available funding.
K	Public clients are geared more towards sustainability that private clients
Q-2	***In your opinion how are stakeholders influenced by sustainable projects?***
A	The public makes their desires know to the boards and commissions either through public meetings or by writing their commissioner.
B	Varies by stakeholder – ideally they buy in and spread the word and practices; at a minimum they push sustainability for promotional aspects.
C	They are forced to think about how they coexist with others, what their contribution is to the waste stream, and what their impact is on the environment.
D	They seem to be influenced by incentives to be 'green' and/or reductions in price or immediate gratification that comes from being green.
E	Many see green projects as desirable but more costly.
F	Media and policy
G	If the stakeholders are believers in sustainability, the project will likely moves forward with the sustainability goals better.
H	I think with all the hype of being green nowadays, it is easier to influence the stakeholders especially on commercial projects.
J	They benefit from improved operating costs and a healthier indoor environment. They also contribute to renewable and recycled markets.
K	Sometimes, depends on education and exposure they have.

(Continued)

Interview Responses	
Q-3	***In your opinion do stakeholders see a difference between a 'green' project and a conventional project?***
A	Yes. They tend to be better educated that the staff or commissioners.
B	They see the difference and understand it in varying degrees.
C	Yes, if they can be brought on board early enough to understand what they can do to make this a green project. They need to be educated that it isn't just a "green" construction – that the way they will use the building has a huge impact.
D	Yes. Conventional projects currently are seen as 'not expensive' – given the pricing of 'green products'. However, slowly they are seeing some benefits (where there are incentives to be sustainable, e.g. tax credits, discounts for incorporating green products, etc).
E	They see long term benefits of energy savings but not certain about the short term.
F	Yes
G	Sometimes
H	I think many commercial developers see being green as a way to one-up their projects from the competition, but now it has become almost too many doing that the effect is lost. Hopefully someday green will just be the way to go and will be the conventional project.
J	Yes, although the differences may be subtle. Operating costs may be the single largest difference.
K	Not immediate differences, some long term ones are more likely
Q-4	***In your opinion do stakeholders see benefits on 'green' projects, and why? Can those benefits be categorized as short term, long term or both and why?***
A	They tend to see the environmental and social benefits and reject the project cost issues.
B	Stakeholders see benefits, again to varying degree mostly based on their level of knowledge of sustainability. Benefits are short and long-term, architect needs to educate client on these. Not all clients are concerned about the long term benefits.
C	Yes, they see benefits such as less waste, less energy used, healthier employees, more productive employees (better day lighting and comfort), sales of their product or service can improve if they market their sustainability, economic gains in their community by using local resources. These can all be long term benefits
D	Yes they see the benefits in reduction of costs in utility bills or reduced costs in construction when re-using some existing conditions. Can those benefits be categorized as short term, long term or both and why? Short and long term since it effects their costs.
E	Yes both, but mostly long term
F	If they see the benefits, these stakeholders are able to understand short and long term benefits.
G	Sometimes; depending on the organization the stakeholders are from.
H	I think much of the commercial market is going green for the short term, whereas institutions and private parties are going green for the long term benefit economically and environmentally.
J	Some benefits are immediate and long term; others are long term and may include a long pay back period.
K	They understand better long term benefits but some communities see short term benefits because of immediate advantages (e.g. employability, recycling on construction sites etc.)

(Continued)

Interview Responses	
Q-5	***In your opinion, how does a sustainable project impact each community?***
A	I deal with the [ ] County Forest Preserve. So, we with our projects impact very directly on communities and the recreational public. With our projects we can educate the public on Green Issues. Our projects tend to have sustainable design components. The Forest Preserve needs to publicize this better.
B	Benefits are micro and macro – certainly sustainability benefits the occupants of a sustainable building and benefits our larger environment. Education and marketing can greatly extend these benefits.
C	Economic stimulation by buying local resources and using local labour, redevelopment (and revitalization) of older areas with existing infrastructure, less urban sprawl and inappropriate development of farmland.
D	Cuts down on energy usage; friendlier to environment; some projects incorporate recycled use of materials in the community (e.g. a demolished building)
E	Lesser energy and water usage are primary
F	There is typically a process related to sustainability and that investment and result is better understood within each community.
G	Socially, economically, and environmentally
H	One can only hope that having a sustainable building as a neighbour will help people see the advantages. Especially in the neighbourhoods of our affordable housing projects we hope that neighbours will see that it can be done on limited funds and hopefully they will hear from their new neighbours the benefits.
J	The immediate community of users sees the most tangible benefits; whereas the greater community benefits in a more measured smaller incremental way.
K	On labour, energy and resources
Q-6	***By employing sustainable practices what do you see are the benefits for each community? What are the advantages as well as disadvantages?***
A	The advantage is the pride that each community feels in their green design. It lets them know that a public body is sensitive to Green Issues and Awareness. The disadvantage is the lack of care the public takes of the facilities. The damage is significant and requires maintenance funds which may not be available.
B	Improved health for our individual and our shared environments – now and for the future, increased awareness of the importance of our environment, hopefully a change in value systems, re-establishing a real sense of community and the character of place and a setting's natural systems.
C	Economic stimulus by using local resources and services, less waste in the waste stream, less demand for energy, healthier communities with less pollution and healthier employees. Disadvantage may be the naysayers don't want to participate and costs may be higher for some things.
D	Better neighbourhoods
E	Lesser energy and water usage are primary, higher initial costs are disadvantages.
F	Greater sense of pride, global understanding of interrelatedness, promotion of sustainable practices in other communities
G	Yes; at some degree, Improved communities
H	See above for advantages. The disadvantages may simply be the misunderstanding of these types of buildings and the impact and costs. Too much hype leads to a misunderstanding of the main directive- you do it for the environment not to keep up with the Joneses.
J	Some sustainable practices encourage emerging markets and the development of new industries.

(Continued)

Interview Responses	
K	Improves neighbourhoods, but many times people do not understand the difference and they don't appreciate it.

Program Strategy & Operations	
Q-1	***How do you define sustainability?***
A	Develop design features that are environmentally efficient and supportive. The LEED movement has hightened this awareness in everything we do.
B	Sustainability means living and thriving today without depleting systems for future life.
C	In architecture, I define sustainability as getting the most usable and efficient building while making the least impact on the planet's resources.
D	Reusing existing materials
E	Sustainable practices do not compromise the next generation's ability to provide for themselves.
F	Environmental, social and economical sustainability in developments
G	Hard to define
H	It is finding the best way to create a project that minimizes its impact on the environment within the limitations creating or operating that project.
J	Ideally, sustainability is about systems that are net neutral, so that they truly can be sustained indefinitely.
K	By use of sustainable materials and practices
Q-2	***How do you define the three dimensions of sustainability called the triple bottom line (TBL), which encompasses environmental, social and economic aspects?***
A	Our awareness is 90% environmental and 10% economic. There is very little social dimensions at this point. With the new Obama emphasis the social component may grow. With a tight economy it is tough to worry about social features unless they are cost neutral.
B	Environmental aspects encompass everything in the natural world – air, water, soil, all living beings, etc. Social involves all aspects of interaction between natural living beings. Economic is currently the underlying thread that allows us to exchange goods and prosper.
C	First, I don't think of social aspects as limited to benefiting those using the building – I want to see benefits to society as a whole. Also, I want to see economic benefits beyond dollars in the pockets of the developer or building owner. The three are all tied together – I don't see a successful project unless you've addressed those as one issue. You have to use the best environmental practices; every built project needs to benefit society as a whole – preferably better a bad situation; the strongest projects use a combination of public and private funding to get the maximum involvement buy-in support from stakeholders.
D	I don't
E	Each aspect contributes to the overall impact of a project and with more and more focus on environmental aspects of a project, it is easier to tie the other two dimensions, particularly the social point, into evaluating success of the project.
F	-
G	-
H	I believe environmental is the key focus and social and economic aspects are the benefits.
J	Economic aspects are generally the easiest to "sell" to a client, if sufficient funding is available up front. Environmental aspects make sense to people but are difficult to quantify. Social aspects are the most abstract and most difficult to quantify.

(Continued)

Program Strategy & Operations	
K	-
Q-3	***Do you think LEED covers all three dimensions of the TBL?***
A	For our purposes it does.
B	Not very well.
C	I think LEED sets the standard for the bare minimum. There is a little attention to comfort and mechanical engineering efficiencies, but nothing to address architectural programming and good design. I think there is very little in LEED to encourage betterment of society (not just the environmental benefits, but the economic benefits and social issues that abound) and I think the only real economic impact is the financial benefits to the USGBC - for a piece of paper that says you jumped through the right hoops and wrote your check.
D	The economic dimension is not fully realized. The short term incentives are inadequate to entice many owners to go green. The higher initial costs are particularly harder on retail clients with short leases. Long term savings may be possible, but many of my clients don't have a life cycle of more than 5 to 7 years.
E	There does not seem to be direct coverage of all three dimensions in LEED certification. There is acknowledgment of social and economic ramifications, but there is virtually no credit tied directly to these issues.
F	It emphasises the environmental aspect more than the other two.
G	Yes
H	In most regards it covers the environmental, although some points that involve educating the users lead towards the social aspect. I do not feel any points are geared specifically towards the economic.
J	LEED more heavily favours environmental and economic benefits, although even these have a trickle down effect which impacts social aspects.
K	Not well, mostly environmental
Q-4	***Do you have a set of standards on how to implement sustainability in your projects?***
A	No. We derive sustainability items from our constant study and review of what others are doing. Working for Federal, State and Municipal agencies tends to focus on bottom line costs and very few projects are open to sustainability components unless they are high visibility projects.
B	We use LEED and others – not necessarily documented guidelines.
C	The company I work for uses LEED for standards and I have nothing formal or written, but I've been a project manager for 18 years. I've developed my own requirements and continually push for these with clients and team members. Typically clients don't even ask, they expect to get a more environmentally sensitive project.
D	No
E	No
F	Per the aforementioned QMS "sustainability checklist" these standards are considered as early as considering project pursuits for my firm.
G	Yes
H	There are no set standards other than if the owner chooses to obtain a rating through LEED or other rating system. Then that system will be the guideline.
J	Yes
K	Yes

(Continued)

Program Strategy & Operations	
Q-5	***Is sustainability considered on a project-by-project basis?***
A	Yes
B	No, it is always a goal of our design projects.
C	Yes
D	Yes
E	Only on client demand.
F	See earlier responses
G	Yes
H	Yes. It depends on the project type, the client's interests and knowledge of sustainability along with the funds available.
J	It is considered (to various degrees) in all projects
K	Yes
Q-6	***Does central management provide a sustainability framework that can be customized to the needs of each project?***
A	We are a small civil engineering firm. We each manage our own projects and develop a rapport with the client. There is no central management.
B	Yes
C	LEED only
D	No
E	No
F	See earlier responses.
G	Yes
H	No
J	Yes, a checklist has been developed that identifies relatively easy objectives and then notes other objectives that are likely based on project type.
K	No
Q-7	***Does corporate governance encourage and promote sustainable management practices?***
A	Yes
B	Yes
C	Yes, but many of us go beyond the minimum.
D	No
E	No
F	Yes, it seems more and more.
G	Yes
H	Encourage-yes; support- no. It tends to fall upon the project manager and the client and their goals.
J	Yes, including support of LEED accreditation by staff (mandatory at upper levels) and payment of exam fees upon successful completion, in house study courses etc.
K	Not always
Q-8	***Does your organisation have a corporate social responsibility (CSR) department?***
A	No
B	Not a formal department as we are a very small business

(Continued)

Program Strategy & Operations	
C	Not a department, but a designated person.
D	No
E	No
F	Yes
G	No
H	No
J	No
K	No
Q-9	***Is there anyone in your organisation that is in charge and may be consulted on sustainability issues?***
A	We have a LEED AP certified individual. I am trained and sensitive to sustainability issues.
B	Yes
C	Yes, both LEED and management issue (how we run our organization).
D	No
E	No
F	Within the firm there are numerous people who are identified as sustainable "leaders". Additionally, there is an internal "sustainability community" among many other design focus circles which confers typically on a monthly basis to exchange ideas.
G	Yes
H	The office has a sister company that does LEED/sustainability consulting both for the office and other companies.
J	YES, we have a partner company that focuses on sustainable design consulting
K	No
Q-10	***How often do you seek assistance from external consultants on sustainability issues?***
A	Often
B	We seek out experts on issues that we're not educated in – maybe once a month
C	Regularly meet with sales representatives and manufacturers to talk about their products, meet with other consultants as needed per project (such as a consultant who offers sustainability food service management to our clients).
D	Minimally at this time
E	Haven't yet
F	Very often as the need for a particular expertise, whether this stems from local issues, a specialized field or an aligning discipline.
G	No needs; internal resources are available
H	I have only sought the assistance of the consultants on our team, in large part the MEP engineers, but also have relied on manufacturers and also associations like the Air Barrier Association of America.
J	Frequently, especially for disciple specific aspects (mech., lighting, site, civil) or for specialized applications (PV, solar thermal, geo-exchange, wind turbine
K	Very often
Q-11	***Are you, as a project manager, involved in early project decisions?***
A	Yes
B	Yes
C	Typically, yes. Sometimes, we get a project after it's been through schematic design with others.

(Continued)

Program Strategy & Operations	
D	Yes
E	Yes
F	Yes
G	Yes
H	Not as much as I feel is necessary
J	Yes
K	Yes
Q-12	***Do you typically carry the project through completion?***
A	Yes
B	Yes
C	Yes
D	Yes
E	Yes
F	Yes
G	Yes
H	Yes
J	Yes
K	Yes
Q-13	***From your position as a project manager are you able to influence the client and team members on the decisions taken at the different project stages?***
A	Yes. I do it often because I seal the drawings.
B	Yes
C	Absolutely – I consider myself the major influencing factor.
D	Yes
E	Yes
F	More or less depending on project and project role.
G	Yes
H	Usually only later in the design phase which can be too late to influence major decisions, but I will take opportunities to influence the decisions I can.
J	Yes, to a degree depending upon budget and funding.
K	To a large degree yes
Q-14	***As a project manager, do you coordinate all the project actors such as owners, architects, engineers, and general contractors [etc.] and link all of them together?***
A	Yes
B	Yes
C	Yes
D	Yes
E	Yes
F	Ideally yes, but not always depending on project and project role.
G	Yes
H	This is usually shared with the partner-in-charge, while I will be more in touch with the engineers and team and contractors, the PIC will be as much involved with the owner.

(Continued)

Program Strategy & Operations	
J	Generally, yes.
K	Yes

Education, Research & Development	
Q-1	***Do you 'educate' your staff and consultants regarding sustainability issues to ensure that everyone has the same understanding, aims and goals?***
A	We train staff. We select sub-consultants that have the same or higher LEED awareness as ourselves if needed by the project.
B	Yes
C	Absolutely
D	We are only beginning this search and improving the knowledge
E	No
F	My firm is active in developing, innovating and implementing tools to create a vibrant sustainable practice and very good in communicating these initiatives to all level of staff and consultants.
G	Yes
H	To some degree yes, but often our consultants, especially MEP, are also educating us on issues as much of what they do is at the core of energy efficient operations.
J	Yes, we now incorporate a charter to define the project goals at the start of the project.
K	To some degree yes
Q-2	***Is sustainability something your organisation practices as a standard and tries to educate the clients on or is it provided in response to the clients' demands only?***
A	We ask up front. What are your design objectives? Lately the public clients want some environmental sustainable design. Bio-swales, prairie grass low maintenance recycled materials. Cost still is an overriding concern.
B	We practice sustainability as baseline criteria for our projects and continuously educate our clients on the value of sustainability.
C	Personally, many of us feel it's our duty to educate the client, but as a whole, I don't think the company pushes as hard as it should. We definitely use it as a marketing tool to get clients.
D	No
E	Client demand only
F	Sustainability is a standard
G	Can be both
H	I think the office would like to think it does, but other than a marketing statement, I don't feel the office walks the talk.
J	We try to incorporate this as a best practice in all of our projects, and as a function of corporate policy.
K	It depends on the project
Q-3	***Is there an awareness form your local bodies regarding sustainability tools and material?***
A	Very little
B	Mostly information on LEED and now Green Globes
C	Mostly LEED and sometimes they promote some of the local codes

(Continued)

Education, Research & Development	
D	It is directed more on energy initiatives
E	Some of the publications we get promote mostly LEED
F	Green Globes has an electronic system that helps keep track of sustainable design
G	Not that I am aware of
H	Maybe they do, but we are not aware of them
J	They promote primary the LEED and issue specifications on sustainable systems, more for awareness
K	Not much

Assessment, Measurement & Reporting	
Q-1	***Are you using LEED standards only?***
A	The LEED standards are being incorporated. We are more sensitive to local codes and permit regulations which are now incorporating LEED standards. It's not 100% yet but evolving.
B	No
C	Officially in the office, yes. Unofficially, I use Department of the Interior Standards relating to historic preservation on old buildings, whether they are historic or not. I also recommend the reuse of existing buildings rather than demolition to preserve embodied energy. I encourage environmental sensitivity in all team members and especially clients, whether we're using LEED or not. I insist on going beyond the bare minimum of number jumbling required by LEED. I use local materials unless absolutely necessary and I use materials with recycled content and that are recyclable. I've required some form of construction waste recycling (depending on processing and market availability) on my projects (while running my own company) since 1993.
D	No
E	No
F	The company maintains a "sustainability checklist" as part of its Quality Management System which is a dynamic tool, lasting the duration of the project and meant to be revisited at opportune points of project development. This tool references LEED standards, but assumes that LEED is only one baseline of sustainability standards.
G	Depending on the project.
H	No, we have also used a local green homes checklist developed for this region and followed certain standards for funding from the state.
J	No, others are used on a project by project basis.
K	Yes, with some local codes
Q-2	***Which sustainability guidelines do you follow on your projects? (i.e. LEED etc.)***
A	We follow LEED when we are able.
B	LEED, and other company guidelines.
C	At the office, we follow LEED. Although this isn't required for all projects, only if a client agrees to it. If a client doesn't plan to get a project certified, project managers don't necessarily follow common sense sustainability.
D	Have not had to use on a project yet.
E	Chicago Green Building

(Continued)

Assessment, Measurement & Reporting	
F	See earlier comments. Additionally, we review national and regional sustainability guidelines depending on the project location. Particularly helpful for the landscape architecture projects is http://www.sustainablesites.org/, which is developing a very thorough set of guidelines specific to site development
G	We try to apply good "sustainability design" practice; LEED provides some good guidelines. Some clients have their own set of design sustainable guidelines.
H	It depends on the project. I have followed LEED, City of Chicago Green Homes Checklist, and Illinois Department of Commerce and Economic Opportunities energy grant requirements.
J	LEED if the client desires to use it, but also our own system (based on LEED) as well as city and state standards, and other standards are referenced.
K	Mostly LEED
Q-3	***Do you have a sustainability checklist to quality control the correct implementation of sustainable principles for each project?***
A	No. We just indicate the work on as-builds. I do know that on LEED Silver buildings there are firms that are hired to keep track of all the voluminous documentation to certify their Silver building.
B	Yes
C	Officially, LEED only. I don't keep a checklist of my own.
D	No
E	No
F	See earlier comments.
G	Sometimes, depending on projects and clients
H	No
J	Yes, as part of our internal process.
K	No
Q-4	***In view of the Triple Bottom Line (TBL): Does your organisation address the environmental aspects of sustainability in projects?***
A	Yes. See response comments
B	Yes, we look at all aspects of products and systems that we use: what are the impacts of product components and production.
C	Yes, but we rely too heavily on LEED. We don't push sustainability unless a client wants LEED.
D	We are researching and becoming more knowledgeable about it.
E	Energy code compliance is the preliminary aspect addressed.
F	The understanding and incorporation of environmental aspects of sustainability have always been part of the firm's basis of design.
G	It is up to the designer or project managers.
H	We only address what can be addressed without adding cost or maintenance issues and only after making the client aware of these aspects. Otherwise, it is the owner who will direct the level of sustainability they wish to pursue.
J	Yes, many of our projects are for long term owners who have a vested interest in the life-cycle costs of the buildings we design for them.
K	Yes, more from the LEED standpoint.

(Continued)

	Assessment, Measurement & Reporting
Q-5	***In view of the Triple Bottom Line (TBL): Does your organisation address the social aspects of sustainability in projects?***
A	No. We deal with civil projects and they tend to be governed by standards.
B	Yes, we look at all aspects of products and systems that we use: are the companies socially responsible and how do they take care of their workers and communities.
C	As architects and engineers, I feel our company is very strong in our desire to address the social aspects of sustainability in the programming and design of the building as the right thing to do – despite LEED requirements. It's a matter of good design.
D	Minimally – on interior projects, for instance, we consider low or no VOCs.
E	No, not other that providing the usual components as design, these elements, as it pertains to sustainability are not expressly addressed.
F	Similarly the social and economic aspects go hand in hand with sustainability and good design.
G	It is up to the designer or project managers.
H	For certain projects more so. In particular, we do senior housing which can benefit from low VOC's and better indoor air quality, which we try to point out the advantages of that to our clients. However, this is often affordable housing and the funds are limited so we do what we can in that regard.
J	Yes, many of our clients serve the elderly and other populations with special needs and compromised health. Healthier environments are important fro residents and staff.
K	We assume that good design covers this aspect.
Q-6	***In view of the Triple Bottom Line (TBL): Does your organisation address the economic aspects of sustainability in projects?***
A	Yes. For example, we designed a 30 car parking lot using pavers. The bids came in too high for the public agency. We redesigned the project for recycled asphalt with regular asphalt as an alternate. The regular asphalt was \$80 per ton and the recycled asphalt was \$150 per ton. The public agency selected the recycled asphalt to broadcast its "green awareness".
B	Yes, we strive to look at long term costs not just initial cost.
C	Minimally, we leave most of this up to our clients, although we address increased cost of construction.
D	Yes
E	This is primarily seen as the determining factor. Cost and energy efficiency.
F	It is up to the designer or project managers, so it differs from project to project.
G	Yes as this is a vital part to both us and the client.
H	If the client can address the up-front costs of a more efficient mechanical system and lighting we will push that for our affordable housing projects since in the long run it benefits the tenants with lower utility costs.
J	Yes, but to a more limited degree. Life cycle and operational costs are considered to a greater degree.
K	We look at it from a life cycle perspective but many times upfront costs win.

(Continued)

Assessment, Measurement & Reporting	
Q-7	***When working on a project do you focus on the individual stages only or do you consider all the stages of the project's life cycle and act accordingly?***
A	All the stages are considered. Often I have to educate the contractor and subcontractor on why we are doing something. The low bidders tend to want to get done quickly and get out. We must insist on all the project elements being constructed because they tend to work in conjunction with each other.
B	We work hard to consider all stages of the project's life cycle.
C	I consider the entire project – my specialty has been historic preservation, so sometimes, I think of the project over many life spans.
D	When a client pays for full services, I look at the project being mindful of every cycle.
E	Try to look at all stages.
F	All stages
G	All stages
H	I prefer to consider the overall project and the process in making decisions.
J	We try to consider all the stages of the life cycle.
K	All stages
Q-8	***As a project manager are you enforcing sustainable practices that affect the project's life cycle? If so, how?***
A	See previous response.
B	Yes, we are working to develop maintenance and testing programs that ensure that our systems and materials are working as we intend and that they are maintained properly to ensure their long life and the health of occupants and maintenance staff.
C	Yes – by the quality of the materials selected, their lifespan, the economic stimulus to the region by the construction, but also by the redevelopment in a blighted area, the reuse and revitalization of existing buildings and the embodied energy they hold.
D	Not aggressively. Only beginning to put into project practice.
E	No
F	Yes, in design research which includes sustainability.
G	Yes, at design phase, coordinate with clients and consultants.
H	Yes, especially in construction when value-engineering becomes a problem and the team and owner begin to lose sight of why some decisions were made and the impact on the operations of the building. With affordable housing it can be a struggle to keep long term life cycle costs in mind when there are limited funds up-front.
J	Yes, by material selections (low maintenance, low-impact, renewable) and specifications.
K	Yes, by material selections and evaluation studies.
Q-9	***When looking at costs, are you or the client are more concerned about the total life cycle costs or just focused mainly on the upfront costs?***
A	Upfront costs because of the public sector's inability to get more funds from boards and commissions.
B	Clients are always more concerned about upfront costs!
C	Some clients are very concerned about life cycle costs – especially colleges who will have to maintain and use the building over many generations. Developers tend to focus on up-front costs because they're going to unload the building sooner.
D	Clients are mostly concerned about upfront costs.

(Continued)

Assessment, Measurement & Reporting	
E	Clients tend to focus on the upfront costs.
F	Total life cycle costs are always the higher focus although upfront costs sometimes win.
G	Upfront cost
H	As noted before, there is often a battle between up-front costs and life cycle. When changes start affecting the up-front costs it can be a battle to maintain the decisions based on the life of the project. The owners have good intentions, but have to stay within their funding.
J	Clients are often most concerned about up front costs; primarily due to extremely limited (finite) funds.
K	It depends on the client. Sometimes public clients look more at life cycle costs because they have to maintain the buildings, where private clients may be more interest at upfront costs, especially I the commercial sector.
Q10	***How is reporting on sustainability done within your organization? Is there a difference in reporting between public and private projects?***
A	There is not a formal reporting method. On public projects often the public entity issues publications which include the progress of a project.
B	For all projects reporting is done through meetings and memos.
C	A checklist many times serves as the report. On public projects often monthly meetings are held to inform the stakeholders and the general public.
D	On private projects is more of an internal review amongst the consultants and the client. On public project it would depend on the client, we might go through the same process but not with the client directly involved.
E	During meetings we assess the progress and record the meeting minutes. Unless we are aiming for LEED certification we do not have a checklist.
F	No formal reporting is done. On public projects government newsletters might be issued reporting the progress and milestones. During the planning and construction stages, monthly meetings are held, often open to the public.
G	No formal reporting method. A checklist might be used. On public projects sometimes quarterly meetings are held to inform stakeholders. On private projects the client will have to request it.
H	Checklists are used on reporting when the clients request it for either public or private projects. Public clients tend to inform their stakeholders as requested by the communities or general public, also for larger public projects governmental publications are issued.
J	No, we do not have a specific method of reporting. On LEED projects the clients see the checklist as requested. We do not have a comprehensive list of all the TBL components that we use. On public projects the stakeholders are usually informed through public meetings.
K	There are no real reporting standards. We have meetings and internal memos, but we are not encouraged by the company to take such measures. If we can get corporate governance involved into providing a sustainability management framework, incorporating the TBL principles, our jobs will become much easier, our projects can be evaluated more precisely and all of our staff will be more coordinated.

REFERENCES

[1] Addis, B. & Talbot, R. (2001). "Sustainable construction procurement: a guide to delivering environmentally responsible projects". *CIRIA C571*, London, CIRIA.

[2] Aguilera, R. V., et al., (2007). "Putting the S Back in Corporate Social Responsibility: A Multilevel Theory of Social Change in Organizations". *Academy of Management Review, Vol. 32, No. 3*, 836-863.

[3] Aikhafaji, A. F. (1989). A Stakeholder Approach to Corporate Governance. *Managing in a Dynamic Environment*. Westport, CT: Quorum Books.

[4] Allard, F., et al., (2004). "*A methodology to assess the sustainability of rehabilitations projects in urban buildings*". LEPTAB. La Rochelle: University of La Rochelle.

[5] Atkinson, G. (2000). Measuring Corporate Sustainability. *Journal of Environmental Planning and Management, Vol. 43*, No. 2, 235.

[6] Augenbroe, G. & Pearce, A. R. (1998). Sustainable construction in the USA; a perspective to the year 2010. *In L. Bourdeau (Ed.), Sustainable Development and the Future of Construction, Vol. 225*, Chapter 14, CIB.

[7] Berman, S. L., et al., (1999). "Strategic Stakeholder Management". *Academy of Management Journal, Vol. 42*, No. 5.

[8] Berthoin, A. A. (1992). *Corporate Social Performance*. Westview Press: Colorado.

[9] Bilfinger and Berger Associates, (2008). *Market potentials for sustainable design. HfT-IPM*, Stuttgart, 2008.

[10] Bieker, T., et al., (2002). "Linking Environmental and Social Sustainability to Business Strategy". *Institute for Economy and the Environment (IWÖ-HSG)*, 2002.

[11] Boswell, P. (2005). "Project Sustainability Management for Design-Built Projects". *Port Technology International, Vol. 26*, 3-17.

[12] Boswell, P. & Walker, L. (2004). Procurement and process design. *FIDIC and Lorna Walker Consulting Ltd.*, Geneva /London: 24 June 2004.

[13] Bourdeau, L. (1999). "Sustainable Development and the Future of Construction: A Comparison of Visions from Various Countries". *Building Research and Information, Vol. 27*, No. 6, 355- 367.

[14] Brite, J. (2009). "Value of the architect in sustainable design practice". *The News of America's Community of Architects, Vol.19.*

[15] Bronn, P. S. & Vidaver, C. D. (2009). "Corporate Motives for Social Initiative: Legitimacy, Sustainability, or the Bottom Line?" *Journal of Business Ethics, Vol. 87*, No. 1, 91.

[16] Bryman, A. & Bell, E. (2003). *Business Research Methods*. Oxford: Oxford University Press.

[17] Bryman, A. (2004). *Social research methods.* 2nd ed., New York: Oxford University Press.

[18] Brundtland Comisión, (1987). Our Common Future: The Brundtland Report. *World Council on Sustainable Development* (WCSD). Oxford: OUP.

[19] Burns, A. C. & Bush, R. F. (2000). *Marketing Research.* 3rd ed., New Jersey; Prentice Hall.

[20] Campbell, J. L. (2007). "Why Would Corporations Behave in Socially Responsible Ways? An Institutional Theory of Corporate Social Responsibility". *Academy of Management Review, Vol. 32*, No.2, 946-967.
[21] Carroll, A. & Buchholtz, A. (2006). *Business and Society: Ethics and Stakeholder Management.* 6th ed., Mason, OH: Thomson/South-Western.
[22] Center for Sustainable Innovation, (2006). *Corporate Sustainability Managements Reference Model.* CFSI, 2006.
[23] CIB Report, (1999). "*Agenda 21 on Sustainable Construction*". CIB Report, Publication 237, 1-119.
[24] CIOB, (2004). "*Corporate Social Responsibility and Construction*". Charted Institute of Building. Berkshire, 2004.
[25] CIOB, (2009). "*Sustainability and Construction*". Charted Institute of Building. Berkshire, 2009.
[26] CIRIA, (2001). "*Sustainable Construction Procurement*". A Guide to Delivering Environmentally Responsible Projects. CIRIA Guide C571. London: CIRIA, 2001.
[27] CIRIA Report, (1999). "*Standardisation and pre-assembly*: Adding Value to Construction Projects". CIRIA Report, No. 176, CIRIA, London,1999.
[28] COM, (2007). "*Accelerating the Development of the Sustainable Construction Market in Europe: Report of the Taskforce on Sustainable Construction*". Composed in preparation of the Communication: A Lead Market Initiative for Europe. 860 final.
[29] Denzin, N. & Lincoln, Y. (1994). *Introduction: entering the field of qualitative research. Handbook of Qualitative Research.* Thousand Oaks, CA: Sage.
[30] Donaldson, T. & Preston, L. E. (1995). "The Stakeholder Theory of the Corporation: Concepts, Evidence, and Implications". *Academy of Management Review, Vol. 20*, No.1, 71.
[31] Drucker, P. (1954). *The Practice of Management.* Harper and Row, New York, 1954.
[32] Egan, J. (1998). "Rethinking Construction". Report of the Construction Task Force on the Scope for Improving the Quality and Efficiency of UK Construction Industry, *Department of the Environment*, Transport and the Regions, London.
[33] Elkington, J. (1997). Cannibals with Forks: *The Triple Bottom Line 21st Century Business*. Oxford: Capstone.
[34] Elias, A. A. & Cavana, R. Y. (2003). *Stakeholder Analysis for Systems Thinking and Modelling.* School of Business and Public Management. Victoria University of Wellington New Zealand.
[35] FCGB, (2003). *Federal Commitment to Green Building: Experience and Expectations.* Office of the Federal Environmental Executive, December 2003.
[36] Figge, F., et al., (2002). "*Sustainability Balanced Scorecard.* Theory and application of a tool for value based sustainability management". Greening of Industry Network Conference. Gothenburg, 2002.
[37] Flyvbjerg, B. (2006). "Five Misunderstandings about Case Study Research." *Qualitative Inquiry, Vol. 12*, No. 2, April 2006, 219-245.
[38] Foddy, W. (1993). *Constructing questions for interviews and questionnaires, theory and practice in social research.* Cambridge: Cambridge University Press.
[39] Forsberg, K., Mooz, H. & Cotterman, H. (1996). *Visualizing Project Management.* John Wiley & Sons, New York, 298.

[40] Fraunhofer-Institut für Bauphysik, (2008). *From the energy evaluation to the assessment of the whole building performance*. 5th BMBF Forum for Sustainability, Berlin, 2008.

[41] Freeman, R. E. (1984). "Strategic Management: A Stakeholder Theory". *Journal of Management Studies, Vol. 39*, No.1, 1-21.

[42] Fugate, M. & Knapp, J. (1998). *The Development of Bodies of Knowledge in the Professions*. Appendix B in: Project Management Institute 1999. The Future of Project Management. Newtown Square, 101-113.

[43] Gardberg, N. & Fombrun, C. F. (2006). "Corporate Citizenship: Creating Intangible Assets across Institutional Environments". *Academy of Management Review, Vol. 31*, No. 2, 329-346.

[44] Global Reporting Initiative, (2006). *G3 Sustainability Reporting Guidelines*. GRI, Amsterdam, 2006.

[45] Graafland, J. & van de Ven, B. (2006). "Strategic and Moral Motivation for Corporate Social Responsibility" *Journal of Corporate Citizenship, Vol. 22*, 111-123.

[46] Graham, P., Coutts, G. P. L. & Hes, D. (2003). "What can the process of delivering sustainable buildings teach us about construction management education?" Paper presented at Working Together, 28th Annual Conference, *Australasian Universities Building Educators Association*, Geelong.

[47] Griffin, J. & Mahon, J. (1997). "The Corporate Social Performance and Corporate Financial Performance Debate". *Business and Society, Vol. 36*. 5-31.

[48] Griffiths, K. (2005). "Sustainability Champion, Northern Gateway Alliance; The Land Transport Management Act - Project Implementation". *Paper presented at Transit NZIHT 7th Annual Conference*, 2005.

[49] Hahn, T. & Scheermesser, M. (2006). "Approaches to Corporate Sustainability Among German Companies". *Corporate Social Responsibility and Environmental Management, Vol. 13*, No. 3, 121-181. -86-

[50] Hasegawa, T. (2002). Policy instruments for environmentally sustainable buildings. In T. D. Pettersen, (Ed.), *Proceedings of CIB/iiSBE international conference on sustainable building*. Oslo, Norway: EcoBuild.

[51] Hill, R. C., Bergman, J. G. & Bowen, P. A. (1994). "*A framework for the attainment of sustainable construction*." Sustainable Construction Conference Proceedings of CIB TG 16 Nov 6-9, 1994, Florida.

[52] Hill, R. C., Bowen, P. A. & Soboil, J. H. (1996). "Environmental Management Systems in the Attainment of Sustainable Construction in South Africa." *UNEP Industry and Environment, Vol. 19*, No. 2, 13-18.

[53] Hill, R. C. & Bowen, P. A. (1997). "Sustainable Construction: Principles and Framework for Attainment." *Construction Management and Economics, Vol. 15*, No. 3, 223-239.

[54] IUCN/UNEP, (1991). Caring for the Earth: *A strategy for sustainable living*. Switzerland: UNEP.

[55] Kahn, H. (1991). "Houses: A Synthesis of Traditional and Modernity." *Mimar Journal, Vol. 39*, MIT Press, Singapore.

[56] Jäger, P. & Hunziker, F. (2009). DGNB Seal of Quality: Sustainable in every respect. [online]. Available at: http://www.detail.de/artikel_dgnb-frank-peter-jaeger_ 23684_ En. htm [Accessed March 06, 2009].

[57] Jansen, M. C. (2001). Value Maximisation, Stakeholder Theory, and the Corporate Objectives Function. *The Monitor Group and Harvard Business School.*

[58] Jones Lang LaSalle, (2009). Perspectives on Sustainability: *Results of the 2009 Global Survey on Corporate Real Estate and Sustainability.* [online]. Available at: http://www.joneslanglasalle.com/Pages/ResearchDetails.aspx?ItemID=2834&ResearchTitle=Perspectives%20on%20Sustainability:%20Results%20of%20the%202009%20Global%20Survey%20on%20Corporate%20Real%20Estate%20and%20Sustainability&TopicName= [Accessed May 27, 2010].

[59] Kaplan, R. S. & Norton, D. P. (1992). "The balanced scorecard – measures that drive performance". *Harvard Business Review, Vol. 70,* No. 1, January-February, 71-79.

[60] Kearney, A. T. ISM, (2004). True and Profitable Sustainability Management: How supply Management is Key to Fulfilling a Promise. *The Institute for Supply Management,* USA., 2004.

[61] Kielstra, P. (2008). Going good: business and sustainable challenge. *The Economist Intelligence Unit,* special issue, 1-54.

[62] Kilbert, C. J. (1994). Establishing Principles and a Model for Sustainable Construction, in *Proceedings of the First International Conference on Sustainable Construction,* C. J. Kibert, ed., Tampa, FL, November 6-9, CIB TG 16.

[63] Kharbanda, O. P. & Pinto, J. K. (1996). What Made Gertie Gallop: *Learning from Project Failures? Van Nostrand Reinhold,* 368.

[64] Kotler, P. & Lee, N. (2005). *Corporate Social Responsibility, Doing the Most Good for Your Company and Your Cause.* Wiley, NJ: Hoboken.

[65] Lamb, R. B. (1984). *Competitive strategic management.* Englewood Cliffs, NJ: Prentice-Hall.

[66] Livingston, H. (2009). "How three large firms are tackling sustainability inside and out." *The News of America's community of Architects, Vol. 16.,* AIA.

[67] Loew, T., et al., (2004). The international discussion on CSR and sustainability and corresponding challenges for businesses and corporate reporting. Berlin: Future e.V./ Institut für ökologische Wirtschaftsforschung. [online]. Available at: http://www.ioew.de/home/download dateien/csr-end. [Accessed July 10, 2009].

[68] Machin, D. (2002). *Ethnographic Research for Media Studies.* London: Arnold.

[69] Malhotra, N. K. & Birks, D. F. (2000). *Marketing Research, An Applied Approach* (European ed.). Edinburgh: Pearson Education, Financial Times Prentice Hall.

[70] Marcoux, A. M. (2000). "Balancing Act" in J. R. DesJardins, & J. J. McCall, (eds.), *Contemporary Issues in Business Ethics.* 4th ed., Wadsworth, 92-100.

[71] Mason, J. (2002). *Qualitative researching.* 2nd ed., London: Sage Publications.

[72] McCartney, D. (2007). *Project Management and sustainable commercial buildings.* [online] Available at: http://www.yourbuilding.org/display/yb/Project+management+and+sustainable+commercial+buildings [Accessed April 4, 2009].

[73] Metcalfe, C. E. (1998). "The Stakeholder Corporation". *Business Ethics, Vol. 7,* No. 1, January 1998, 30-35.

[74] Morgan, G. & Smircich, L. (1980). 'The case for qualitative research.' *Academy of Management Review, Vol.5,* 491-500.

[75] Morris, P. (1994). *The Management of Projects.* Thomas Telford, London, 358.

[76] Morris, P. (2000). "*Researching the Unanswered Questions of Project Management.*" Project Management Research at the Turn of the Millennium. Proceedings of PMI Research Conference 2000, 21-24 June 2000, Paris, France, 87-101.

[77] Neuman, L. W. (2006). *Social Research Methods: Qualitative and Quantitative Approaches*. 6th ed., Allyn and Bacon, 2006.

[78] Ofori, G. (1998). "Sustainable construction: principles and a framework for attainment – comment." *Construction Management and Economics, Vol.16*, 141-145.

[79] Paech, N. & Pfriem, R. (2004). *Concepts of sustainability for companies. Theoretical demands and empirical trends.* Oldenburg, Germany: Oldenburg University.

[80] Phillips, R. (2003). *Stakeholder Theory and Organizational Ethics.* Berrett-Koehler Publishers, Inc.: San Francisco.

[81] PMI - Project Management Institute, (1999). *The Future of Project Management.* Newtown Square. 139.

[82] PMI - Project Management Institute, (2008). *A Guide to the Project Management Body of Knowledge.* 4th ed., Project Management Institute, USA.

[83] Ragin, C. C. (1994). *Constructing Social Research: The Unity and Diversity of Method.* Pine.

[84] Robson, C. (2002). *Real world research.* 2nd ed., Blackwell Publishing.

[85] Saunders, M., et al., (2003). *Research methods for Business Students.* 3rd ed., *Pearson Education Limited*, Harlow.

[86] Schaefer, K. (1994). Site Design and Planning for Sustainable Construction." *Sustainable Construction Proceedings of the First International Conference of CIB TG, Vol. 16*, November 6-9, 1994, Tampa: Florida.

[87] Shen, Y., L., et al. (2002). "Implementing of Environmental Management in the Hong Kong Construction Industry". *International Journal of Project Management, Vol. 20*, No. 7, 535-543.

[88] Shepard, J. & Greene, R. (2003). *Sociology and You.* Ohio: Glencoe, McGraw-Hill, A-22.

[89] Signitzer, B. & Prexl, A. (2008). "Corporate Sustainability Communications: Aspects of Theory and Professionalization". *Journal of Public Relations Research. Vol. 20*, No. 1, 1.

[90] Sternberg, E. (2000). *Just Business: Business Ethics in Action.* Oxford University Press.

[91] Sternberg, E. (2004). *Corporate governance: Accountability in the Marketplace.* 2nd ed., The Institute of Economic Affairs, London.

[92] The Economist, (2008). The driving motives for corporate sustainability. [online]. Available at: http://www.eon.businesswire.com/releases/economist/debate/prweb 1031214.htm-[Accessed on March 05, 2009].

[93] Turner, J. R. (1993). *The handbook of project-based management.* McGraw-Hill, London, 540.

[94] UNEP, (2006). *Innovating Financing for Sustainability*: Sustainability Managements and Reporting. Switzerland: IUCN/UNEP

[95] USGBC, (2009). US Green Building Council. [online]. Available at: http://www.usgbc.org [Accessed on March 20, 2009].

[96] Waddell, H. (2008). "Sustainable construction and UK legislation and policy". *Institution of Civil Engineers - Management Procurement and Law, Vol. 161*, No. 3, 127.

[97] Walker, A., et al., (2003). ESD initiatives for the master plan for the Kingston aged care centre development. *Unpublished report prepared for Hassell Architects*, Melbourne.

[98] Word Business Council for Sustainable Development (WBCSD), (2002). *Sustainable Development Reporting: Striking the Balance*. Atar Roto Presse SA, Switzerland.

[99] WCED, (1987). *Our Common Future*. Oxford University Press: Oxford.

[100] Wilson, M. (2003,). "Corporate sustainability: What is it and where does it come from?" *Ivey Business Journal, Vol. 2*, 1-5.

[101] WS Atkins Consultants, (2001). "*Sustainable Construction: Company Indicator*". CIRIA C563, London, CIRIA.

[102] Wyatt, D. P. (1994). "*Deconstruction; An environmental response for construction sustainability*". Sustainable Construction Proceedings of the First International Conference of CIB TG 16, November 6-9 1994, Tampa, Florida.

[103] Xing Y., et al., (2009). "A framework model for assessing sustainability impacts of urban development". *Accounting Forum, Vol. 33*, 209-224.

In: Project Management
Editor: Robert J. Collins, pp. 73-101
ISBN: 978-1-61761-460-6
© 2010 Nova Science Publishers, Inc.

Chapter 2

ASSESSING MODULARITY IN THE CONSTRUCTION PROJECT OF A NUCLEAR POWER PLANT

Franco Caron* ***and Monia Comandulli***
Politecnico di Milano, Department of Management, Economics and Industrial Engineering, Piazza Leonardo da Vinci 32, 20133 Milan, Italy
ABB, Process Automation Division, Via Luciano Lama 33, 20099 Sesto San Giovanni (MI), Italy

ABSTRACT

The world's current energy situation requires the use of a complex set of resources in order to satisfy the wide range of energy demand. Nuclear power should be seen not only as a possibility among other energy options, but also as a significant contribution to respond to the need for allowing a limited use of fossil fuels. In general, electrical energy projects are characterized by a highly dynamic and frequently unpredictable context. Plant modularity provides a high level of flexibility in the development of this kind of project. This means that, if flexibility is appropriately exploited, it is possible to change the course of the project in a favorable direction. In particular, focusing on project execution, building modularity into investments allows us to view investments as a sequence of expansion options. In this perspective, consistent with the real options framework, uncertainty can actually increase the value of the project as long as flexibility is preserved and investment not irreversibly committed. Furthermore, during plant construction, there are usually only cash outflows; in contrast, during construction of a modular plant cash outflows may be accompanied by cash inflows deriving from modules that have been completed and become operational. The chapter aims to estimate the value deriving for a project related to the realization of a nuclear power plant from the modularity exploited in terms of sequential options. A Monte Carlo simulation model has been developed in order to integrate discounted cash flow method and real options approach. Moreover, this model has general relevance: it can be used in order to evaluate complex modular power plant projects and then isolate the contribution of project flexibility, independently from the energy source. We demonstrate the utility of the

* Corresponding author: e-mail: franco.caron@polimi.it Tel: +39-02-2399-4064 Fax: +39-02-2399-4067

proposed model through the application to a real nuclear power plant project: we consider a III+ generation reactor, whose modularity allows for a high level of project flexibility and is associated with a number of options to expand equal to the number of units/modules that make up the plant. The example demonstrates the effectiveness of the proposed approach and provides illustrative numerical results.

1. Introduction

The availability of energy resources is of fundamental importance for society. An inability to access energy undermines the social and economic development of many regions, and also obstructs social, environmental and economic progress across the world. The main dilemma we are facing is that energy is a vital ingredient for growth, sustainable development and most economic activities, but the production of energy mainly through non-renewable sources together with its use contribute to global warming. The present challenge for the energy sector is how to address the growing demand for energy, limit the emission of greenhouse gases, and minimise the environmental impact, while at the same time reducing the costs of energy production.

The solution to this set of problems is the use of a complex set of resources in order to satisfy the broad range of energy requirements, taking account of the need for efficiency, reliability, feasibility and a limited use of fossil fuels. Moreover, all the energy options need to be kept open and developed. Sustainable development will depend both on the extensive use of existing efficient technologies, and on the development and commercialisation of innovative technologies.

We need to diversify the mix of energy sources particularly in two directions:

- the development of advanced and clean technologies such as renewable sources;
- the development of nuclear energy.

At present, Generation III nuclear reactors are available, while Generation IV models are still under development and will not be on the market until 2030. Generation III+ plants, be they *large reactors* (LR) or *small medium reactors* (SMR), present interesting development prospects, the former offering economies of scale, while by virtue of the modularity of the investment, the much smaller SMRs can take advantage of learning economies, reduced financial requirements, and greater flexibility in responding to market needs.

As a matter of fact, modularity, i.e., the possibility to divide the project output into more or fewer independent modules, is by definition an effective way of achieving a high level of project flexibility.

In the energy production industry, the increasing level of complexity and uncertainty in the business context requires a high level of adaptability to emerging changes. In general, project flexibility represents a typical response to uncertainty and complexity by developing the ability to react in the face of unanticipated events or conditions affecting the project.

In general, the need for flexibility [56, 57] derives from the fact that important decisions in projects are generally subject to incomplete information and emerging events changing the assumptions adopted at the project's early stage. The main requirements in order to achieve a high level of flexibility in the decision making process are:

- decisions should be sufficiently "robust" in order to minimize changes in previous decisions due to subsequent decisions or, in any case, to modify previous decisions at minimum cost;
- decisions should be postponed as long as the value of information remains high, in order to minimize the gap between the knowledge necessary to make the decision and the available knowledge;
- decisions should be taken considering the lead time necessary to implement the corresponding actions.

Large Engineering Projects (LEPs), like for instance power plants realization, represent a typical example of projects affected by a high level of complexity and uncertainty. In LEPs project effectiveness is a composite measure, combining economic performance, technical functionality, social acceptability, environmental acceptability, political legitimacy and economic development [48]. LEPs are not selected once for all, rather they are shaped progressively from an initial concept by the dialectical interaction of stakeholders [3, 48, 49]. As a result, projects interact with their complex and uncertain environment and adapt to the ongoing changes as strategic entities [2]. In particular, typical approaches aiming to improve project flexibility include: design robustness, redundancy, contingency planning, modularity, real options, etc. In particular, project flexibility is highly dependent on the degree of modularity. Advantages deriving from modularity are related to both project phases:

- project execution, e.g., in terms of investment flexibility;
- system operation, e.g., in terms of system availability.

Focusing on project execution, building modularity into projects allows to view investment as sequential options. In this perspective, consistent with the real options framework, uncertainty can actually increase the value of a project as long as flexibility is preserved and investment committed as late as possible.

Among the different types of real options, we can in particular identify expandability, the firm's ability to add capacity which is akin to a call option, and reversibility, the firm's ability to undo its previous investment which is akin to a put option. Since in Large Engineering Projects investments are normally irreversible, the expandability option should be exploited, since the opportunity to wait in order to learn more about the uncertain future increases the likelihood of project success [25]. Plant's modularity guarantees a high level of project flexibility, in the sense of being able to decide during the course of the project if and when to expand the plant's capacity, i.e., if and when to build another reactor identical to the one(s) already in operation. This means that during the construction phase, there are a series of decision-making gates when owners have to decide whether or not to invest in another module. With the development of the project, these decision-making gates are associated with an increasing level of information, which if appropriately exploited can result in an increase in the overall value of the project. Furthermore, modularity changes the nature of the construction phase. During plant construction, there are usually only outgoing cash flows. In contrast, during construction of a modular plant involving several modules, outgoing cash flows may be accompanied by incoming flows derived from modules that have been completed and become operational.

In this chapter we propose a model allowing us to assess and compare investment projects in the energy production industry. In particular, the model allows for the assessment of the economic and financial advantages that modularity may offer to a power plant construction project, independently from the technology used.

The second section introduces a general framework about real option analysis. The third section describes the cash flow model used to assess investment projects in the energy production industry and to estimate the real options value in the case of modular plants. The fourth section illustrates the nuclear power plant case. The fifth section highlights the comparison between a configuration based on a Large Reactor and a configuration based on a set of modular Small Medium Reactors. In the sixth section an estimate is given of the sequential expansion options comprised in the modular configuration based on SMRs. Finally some comments are given.

2. Real Options

The choice between various alternatives and the decision to proceed in the construction of an energy production plant is a capital budgeting project. In the literature, there are numerous studies that compare different technologies for the production of electrical energy using the Levelized Cost valuation model, a particular approach to discounted cash flow (DCF), which assuming an economic profit of zero allows us to establish the best alternative by calculating the Levelized Unit Electricity Cost (LUEC) of each technology [27, 29]. This methodology presents some limitations, associated mainly to the difficulties in effectively incorporating risk in the LUEC. As a result, the traditional DCF model has been preferred, which, when integrated with Monte Carlo simulation, can take account of and also assess uncertainty [58, 59].

DCF alone, however, is not able to register the contribution of project flexibility, especially that linked to capital intensive projects [24, 45, 55, 67]. There are two principal means to assess projects subject to risk in which project flexibility plays an important role: one is *decision analysis* (in particular Decision Tree Analysis – DTA) and the other *real option analysis* (ROA), which derives from the option pricing approach. The first procedure is more general than the second [62] and allows risk to be introduced by defining a probability for each output (i.e. for each payoff associated to the terminal nodes). As this is an exhaustive methodology, the size of the problem must be limited [41]. In contrast, ROA is more easily adapted to complex situations.

The option pricing approach originates in two methods proposed by Black-Scholes-Merton to assess put and call financial options [6, 46]. ROA was originally proposed by Myers in 1977 [54] and Ross in 1978 [60], but became popular with the works of Myers [55] and Kester [39] in 1984. Both the decision analysis method and real option pricing theory were applied for the first time to the assessment of oil and gas investments [62].

The estimate of the contribution of project flexibility in a capital budgeting project requires a different assessment rule than DCF: *expanded net present value* [67]. This method enriches the NPV derived from the application of traditional DCF with the value of the option that depends on management's opportunities to make decisions and influence project progress and which can be measured with real option analysis. ROA does not replace DCF, but represents an extension [41]. When a project presents a null option, the DCF and the ROA coincide.

Use of ROA is appropriate when management has ample room for intervention and there is a high level of uncertainty. Moreover, the contribution provided is particularly significant in those situations in which the NPV is very low and tending to zero. ROA can also be attractive for managerial reasons, as the approach encourages managers to break down the investment project into components at least partially independent [11]. In this way, managers are encouraged to think about the project in a proactive and creative way, and consider how project value can be increased through flexibility [17].

A model to assess real options presupposes the use of one of the following methods: *partial differential equation* (PDE), *lattices* and *Monte Carlo simulation*. However, a PDE approach may not provide a closed analytical solution [61], is not suitable for the assessment of American options and does not aid the introduction of uncertainty [25, 41]. The best known PDE approach is based on the Black-Scholes formula [6]. Lattices are more flexible than PDE, but are difficult to control with a large number of stochastic variables [22, 63, 66]. The most flexible tool (and, consequently, the one used in this chapter) is the Monte Carlo simulation [21, 41] (see figure 1), even if this approach also has some difficulty in analysing American options in which the type of decision and the best decision time have to be determined simultaneously. The literature offers various optimisation algorithms to overcome this problem. Barraquand and Martineau [4], for example, developed a model to assess American options which can take account of various sources of uncertainty regarding the value of the underlying asset. Grant et. al. [34] introduced into the Monte Carlo simulation the possibility to exercise the option prior to the maturity date, so combining the simulation, which follows a forward logic, with dynamic programming, based on a backward logic. Longstaff and Schwartz [43] proposed an assessment method using regression based on the least squares method. Broadie and Glasserman [13] assessed American options on the basis of a 'high estimator' and a 'low estimator' the average of which constitutes a robust estimate of the value of the option. Tseng and Barz [68] looked at the case of an energy production plant using a stochastic model and proposing a means of calculation combining forward simulation and backward dynamic programming.

Starting from the various studies on the assessment of modularity, particularly the work of Moel and Tufano (2000) [51], and the literature dealing with the energy sector [59], above all nuclear energy [10, 32], we have developed a model that combines DCF and ROA based on Monte Carlo simulation.

For example, Gollier in 2005 [32] developed a model based on a backward logic in order to optimize the investment strategy of a nuclear plant project in which the optimal starting construction time of each modular unit depends on the uncertainty of a single parameter (the price of electricity) that varies randomly in time. The flexibility value is derived by comparison between the modular project and the investment project in an LR unit.

Compared to Gollier's study [32], the model presented in this chapter is based on different assumptions aiming to adhere more closely to the actual managerial decision making process, based on a sequence of decision steps each concerning a single modular unit.

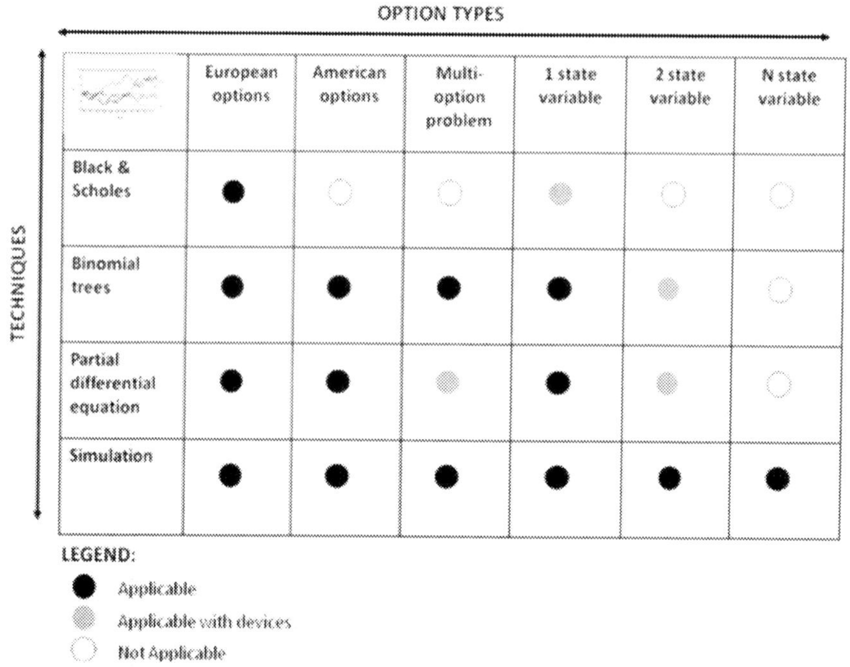

Figure 1. Techniques to asses different types of options.

In particular the model focuses mainly on the construction phase that plays a critical role in the investment project. During the construction phase, for instance, the expenditure profile, possible construction delays, the mix of financing sources, and the learning economies are assessed as elements that may significantly influence the construction of the plant. Unlike Gollier's approach, the model sets a maximum time limit of the option to expand, beyond which the benefits resulting from the learning economies, in terms of reduction of costs, are lost. To ensure greater reality, the model also considers the cost investment variability over time, assuming a high correlation between the price of the materials requested to build the plant and the price of electricity.

Moreover, particular emphasis is given to the financial aspects of the project, which are of particular importance from the investor's point of view and often used as comparison criteria between two profitable investments. For instance, the model considers the effects of self-financing cash flow deriving from early deployed units already operative. The uncertainty regarding the price of electrical energy during the plant life cycle is also described in a different way from Gollier's approach. Instead of using a simple random fluctuation model, the *"mean reverting with jump diffusion"* model is applied. In this way, the model provides a more realistic definition of the electricity price profile, taking account of possible shocks that can result in sharp positive and negative variations in price.

Finally, unlike in the Gollier's study, the comparison with the LR is not used as a benchmark to determine the modularity value. The model proposed is based on the comparison of two identical projects, one of which is not flexible. This non-flexible case derives from the same modular project (and therefore has similar costs) and assumes that the construction strategy cannot be modified, just as for a LR.

The goal of the model is to highlight the modularity/flexibility advantages. Sometimes these advantages materialize as the possibility to optimize the construction strategy, sometimes as the possibility to react quickly to market changes, and sometimes as the possibility to limit potential losses. In aiming to optimize the whole investment strategy, Gollier does not take account of this last point, which, on the contrary, is included in our model. Assuming the decision to build the first unit is taken irrespective of its profitability at the beginning of the planning horizon, the model developed in this chapter aims at analyzing how a modular investment can be adapted through flexibility to different situations, so allowing management to address critical contexts or to exploit the maximum advantage from positive opportunities.

3. The Model

The model proposed can be used to assess and compare alternative investments for electrical energy production, independently from technology used (be it nuclear or not) and configuration adopted (be it modular or not). It is divided into two main blocks:

- the DCF model to calculate *operational free cash flow* (OFCF) and determine the profitability of the investment;
- the ROA model to determine the value of the sequential options linked to a modular configuration.

The DCF model, in turn, comprises three sub-models concerning respectively:

- the construction phase;
- the operating phase;
- the trend over time of the price of electrical energy.

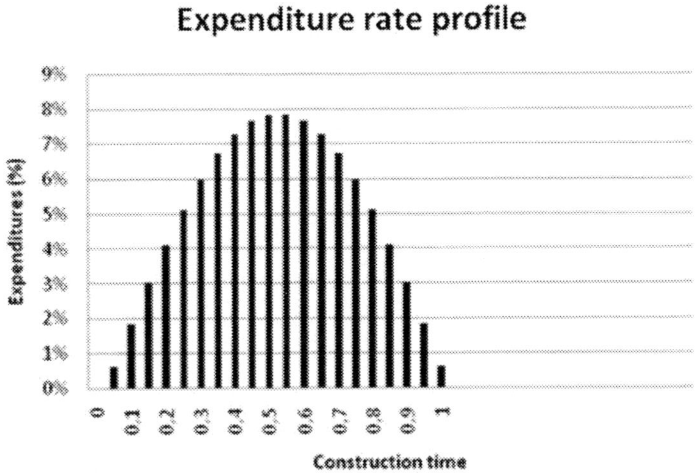

Figure 2. Expenditure rate during the construction phase.

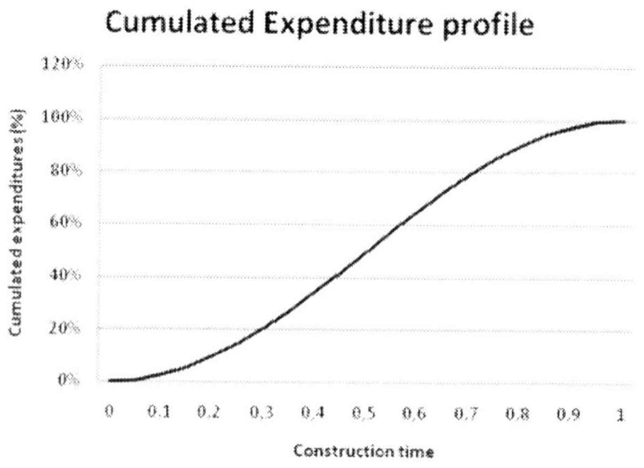

Figure 3. "S" curve of the cumulated expenditure during construction.

The DCF model places particular emphasis on the construction phase, during which management has the greatest influence on project development. This is not the case during the operating phase, when external variables, like the electricity price, play a predominant role.

In the construction phase, expenditure is modelled with a flexible "**S**" curve (see figure 2 and figure 3), whose parameters, total duration and total expenditure, can vary independently of each other, so creating situations in which just one or both parameters increase.

The curve's adaptability allows different types of delay in construction phase to be modelled. Such delays can lead to an increase in the actual construction duration and, possibly in expenditure (i.e. non-recoverable delays), or merely contribute to an increase in expenditure (recoverable delays), assuming that by increasing the resources available it would be possible to complete construction within the deadline. The additional expenditure is considered proportional to the delay, involving costs related to labour and construction equipment. Initially, each delay is considered to be potentially recoverable. Distinction between the two types of delay is based on the maximum expenditure rate that is acceptable to investors. If, in the case of a delay, an attempt to complete construction on time determines an expenditure rate less than that acceptable by investors, the delay will be considered recoverable and additional resources (and corresponding costs) will be allocated to the project in order to finish within the deadline. Otherwise, the delay will be considered non-recoverable and will be added to the time required to complete construction. Overall, the various types of delay that the model can manage are as follows:

- a non-recoverable delay without additional expenditure. Such a delay increases the construction time, postponing cash in-flows, but does not cause any additional costs (see figure 4a);
- a recoverable delay. Such a delay does not increase the construction time, and therefore does not influence cash in-flows, but requires that more resources are put in place and the corresponding additional costs are spread over the remaining duration of construction (see figure 4b);
- a non-recoverable delay with additional expenditure. Such a delay increases the construction time, postponing cash in-flows, and causes additional costs (see figure 4c).

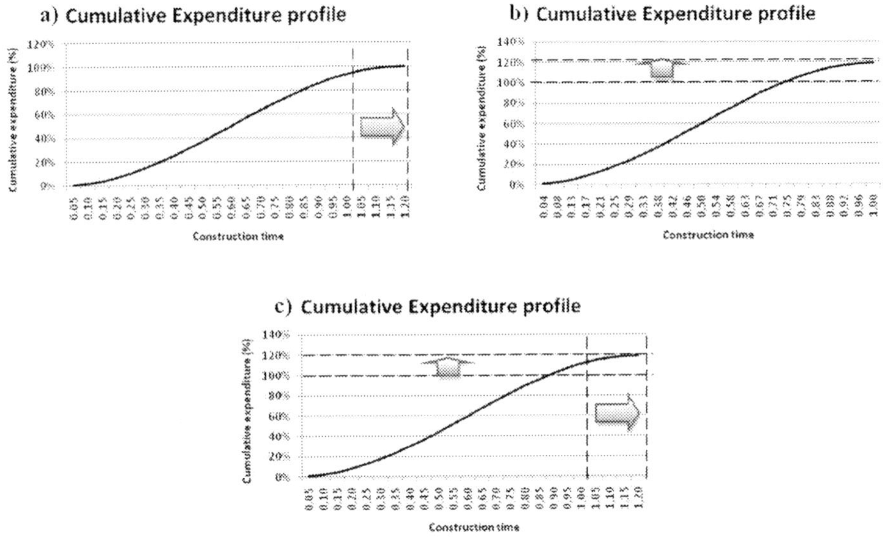

Figure 4. Different types of delay during construction: a) non recoverable delay without additional expenditure; b) recoverable delay with additional expenditure; c) non recoverable delay with additional expenditure.

When comparing investment alternatives, a simulated delay during the construction phase presents the same characteristics in all the alternatives considered.

The model considers three sources of funding:

- equity;
- debt;
- self-financing.

Assumptions about the mix of equity and debt are adopted at the beginning of the simulation process in terms of the ratio between them. Debt is paid back when the plant comes into operation, following a leveraged buy-out scheme: interest on the debt matured during the construction phase (interest during construction – IDC) is capitalised, i.e. increases the debt contracted during construction and is payable once the plant comes into operation.

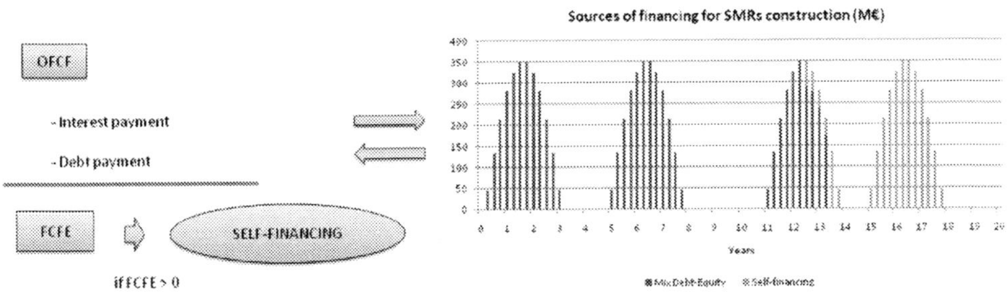

Figure 5. Mix of funding sources for a modular project comprising four modules, where OFCF indicates Operative Free Cash Flow and FCFE Free Cash Flow to Equity.

Self-financing is possible only for modular plants, as it exploits the cash flows from previously constructed modules. Self-financing has a greater weight the longer the time lapse between the construction of the modules, and, in particular, has a greater impact on the last modules. Firstly, the investment is funded via cash flows deriving from the previously built modules, if these are available and are generating positive cash flows. The part of the investment not covered by self-financing is then divided between equity and debt according to the desired mix. Self-financing plays a positive role, as it allows the amount of debt to be reduced, thus also lowering the IDC necessary to finance the investment (see figure 5).

The model of the operating phase considers the elements that determine the cash flow. Operating revenues depend on the quantity of electrical energy supplied to the network and are calculated considering both the capacity factor, a parameter which takes account of the plant's availability factor, and the load factor, related to the quantity of energy that can be transmitted to the electricity network. Operating costs increase over time in line with nominal inflation, which is country-specific as is the level of tax.

Account is also taken of the possibility that there is a plant breakdown during operation resulting in a temporary interruption of electricity production and an increase in costs determined by the necessary repairs, i.e. materials and labour costs (see figure 6). A breakdown during the operating phase presents the same timing and characteristics in all the investment alternatives considered.

Finally, the analysis of the trend over time of the price of electrical energy is based on a "*mean reverting with jump diffusion*" model (see figure 7), comprising the following three components [7, 8, 9]:

1. Geometric Brownian Motion (GBM), which describes the volatility of the price of electrical energy around the equilibrium value;
2. Mean Reversion, which describes the 'force' that tends to bring the price of electrical energy back to the equilibrium value after it moves;
3. Jump Diffusion Process, which describes the effect of unexpected and very large increases or decreases in the price of electrical energy.

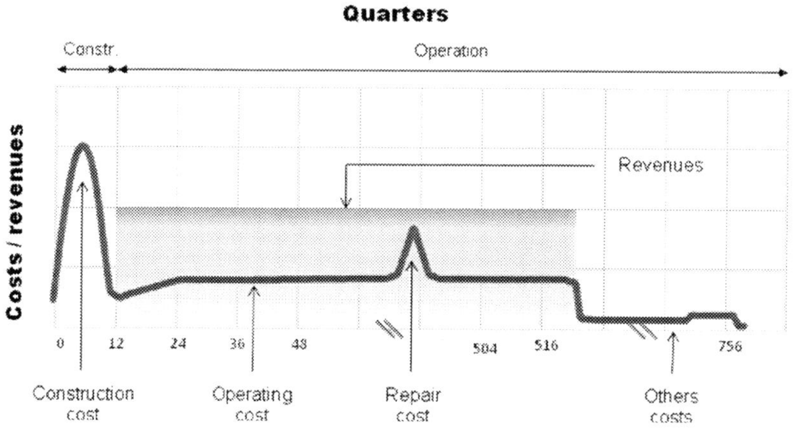

Figure 6. Costs tied to a nuclear power station.

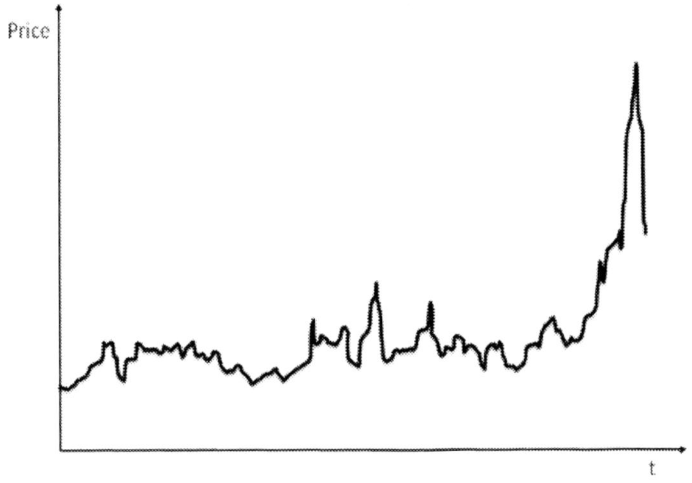

Figure 7. Example of a typical trend in the price of electrical energy.

Parameters	Definition	Value
P(t=0)	Electricity price at initial time t=0	99.07 [€/MWh]
Volatility	Expected price variability over time	14.31%
Mean reversion speed	Speed at which prices revert to equilibrium value	51.13%
Mean reversion level or Long run mean price	Equilibrium price	88.81 [€/MWh]
Drift component	Electrical energy price drift	0.65 [€/quarter]
Jump size	Maximum expected size of jumps, expressed in percentage terms of the price recorded in previous period	40%
Standard deviation of jump	Dispersion of jumps around their mean value	10%
Jump occurrence	Average jumps frequency over a predefined period of time	0.02 [jumps/quarter]

Figure 8. Parameters of the mean reverting with jump diffusion model.

In the case illustrated below, the parameters describing these three components (see figure 8) are derived from the historical trend of prices in a European country market.

The DCF model, comprising the three sub-models related to construction, operations and electricity price trend respectively, allows us to assess and compare alternative technologies and plant's configurations for electrical energy production; for instance it allows us to compare a nuclear Large Reactor with a set of modular Small Medium Reactors offering the same level of overall capacity.

The DCF model has been extended adding a ROA block able to assess the value of the American sequential options made possible by the modular configuration of the plant. In order to strictly isolate the value of the sequential options during the construction phase, we have introduced a benchmark characterised by the same operational features of the modular configuration in terms of costs, capacity, availability, service continuity, etc. but without the sequential options. So, the ROA block requires the comparison between two alternative configurations:

- a modular configuration without sequential options;
- a modular configuration with sequential options.

In the latter case, at each simulation iteration, the decision corresponding to each option to expand capacity is taken based on the foreseen trend of electricity price. The value of the option is derived by comparing the NPV of the investment when management choices can influence project development, i.e. with sequential options, and the NPV of the same investment when it is assumed that management cannot intervene, i.e. without sequential options [44].

The first configuration, i.e. modular without sequential options, representing the benchmark against which the value of modularity in terms of sequential options is measured, is given by a set of modules strictly built in series without any time lapse between the end of the construction of one module and the beginning of the next, i.e in a staggered stand alone mode. In this construction strategy it is assumed that, as for a LR project, management cannot exploit the options linked to the possibility to postpone the expansion of capacity.

The second configuration, i.e. the modular configuration with sequential options, after the start of the construction of the first module generates the option to invest in the second module. In this way, when each module has been constructed, the owner can decide whether to increase the plant's capacity or stop at the capacity level reached, based on the foreseen trend of the electricity price. Note that construction of the first module initiates at the beginning of the planning horizon. A further assumption is that the construction of different modules cannot overlap, i.e. the modules are realised in series with the possibility of a time lapse between the end of the construction of one module and the beginning of the construction of the next.

Since the value of each individual option should take account of the value of the subsequent options, the ROA model considers at each iteration just one decision-making process involving the whole number of options present in the project. Within this process, the model calculates the NPV of all the possible construction strategies in terms of if and when exploiting the available options. Consequently, the model may be computationally demanding. For example, with three modules, each with an option that can be exercised at three possible instances in time, the exhaustive approach adopted calculates 39 distinct NPVs. As the number of modules and the number of decisions instances in time increase, so the number of NPVs increases considerably.

At each simulation iteration, providing the NPV is positive, the strategy that gives the largest NPV is that giving the greatest value to the sequential options. This value is obtained as the difference with respect to the NPV of the corresponding modular configuration without sequential options and provides an estimate of the maximum value for the options, i.e. a kind of upper limit for the value of exploiting modularity in terms of sequential options. However, the proportion of this value that can be effectively harnessed depends on management's ability to analyse the context and exploit the greater information content that becomes available as the project progresses.

The general structure of the model is given in figure 9.

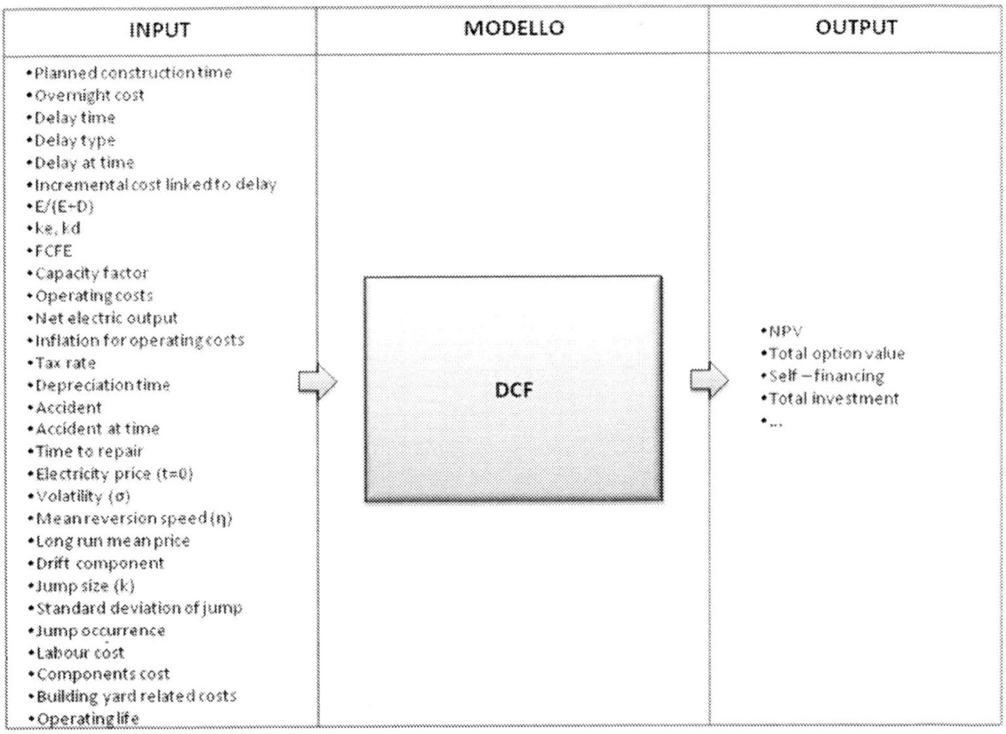

Figure 9. Inputs and outputs of the model.

4. Application of the Model to a Nuclear Power Plant

The model proposed has been applied to a nuclear power plant case, based on the IRIS nuclear reactor. This is a small, III+ generation modular reactor with a completely integrated primary system.

The application of DCF model allows us to give evidence of economical and financial advantages and disadvantages of SMRs (i.e. a nuclear modular configuration with sequential options) with respect to LRs (i.e. a nuclear monolithic configuration). As monolithic configuration we chose an AP1000 reactor, a III+ generation LR using the same technology as IRIS.

Below, we describe the main model assumptions considering the different sub-models, i.e. construction, operation and electricity price trend, respectively.

In order to make the comparison between IRIS and AP1000 we chose to consider the following alternatives:

- a configuration based on a 1005 MWe AP1000 LR;
- a configuration based on 335 MWe IRIS SMRs built on the same site.

The comparison assumes the same 'theoretical' capacity for the two plants. The capacity is theoretical, as the modularity of the IRIS reactor means that installed capacity (i.e. the number of reactors) can be limited if during construction the investment proves to be unbeneficial. The installed reactors could, nevertheless, begin operation and generate cash flows. In contrast, once construction of the AP1000 reactor has begun, everything must be completed and full capacity installed in order for operation to begin and cash flows to be generated. Consequently, if it should prove unbeneficial to invest in further SMR units, the comparison would be carried out in any case, but with a lower capacity for the IRIS reactor compared to the AP1000.

Construction of the AP1000 and the first IRIS module starts at the beginning of the planning horizon, irrespective of their expected profitability, while the construction strategy adopted for the subsequent SMR units, depending on the trend of the electricity price (see figure 10), assumes that the individual modules are constructed in series, so exploiting their operational autonomy (i.e. in a stand-alone mode). Specifically, we assume that there is no time overlap between the construction of the modules, i.e. a module can only be built if the previous module has been completed. As exploitation of modularity in terms of sequential options means that investment for each module can be postponed, there may be a certain time lapse following completion of the previous module before investors may decide to build the next reactor.

Each single SMR can be built in about 3 years. Therefore, if we use the construction strategy illustrated above, the overall electrical energy production capacity is made available gradually. Given the strong focus on the construction phase, the unit time period considered in the model is three months.

An AP1000 reactor can be built in 5 years. Thus, although it takes less time to build a single IRIS unit than to build an AP1000, if we use the construction strategy illustrated above, the full modular plant will be completed later.

AP1000 and IRIS have different overnight costs. Furthermore, the single SMR modules may have different overnight costs. In particular, we have to consider that SMRs cannot benefit from the traditional economies of scale (typically associated to LRs), but can take advantage of the economies of learning that derive from the construction of different modules in the same time and place, but also from the simultaneous construction of individual units at different sites. The learning effect is due to the scalable nature of the investments in SMRs. The benefits of the learning effect result in increasing efficiency and decreasing duration of the construction phase due to the experience acquired both by subcontractors and equipment suppliers [47]. A reduction in the overall cost of construction of the plant can therefore be realised as far as the number of modules built increases. The assumed loss of economies of learning (and, consequently, the increase in the SMR overnight cost) is linearly proportional to the time lapse between the completion of one unit and the start of the next, taking into account the number of years requested in order for all economies of learning to be lost (about ten years). Moreover the model allows to assume a given probability of delay during construction both for LR and SMR. While the type and the time entity of delay is the same for both reactors (see section 3), the corresponding cost differs, as the cost of investment for AP1000 and IRIS is not the same. A potentially recoverable delay could be managed in different ways in the LR and SMR cases, as it depends on the additional cost and the acceptable expenditure rate, which differ in the two cases examined. So it is possible that the same delay could be managed as recoverable for one type of reactor and as non-recoverable for the other type.

As for the operation phase, the model assumes a duration of 40 years both for IRIS and AP1000.

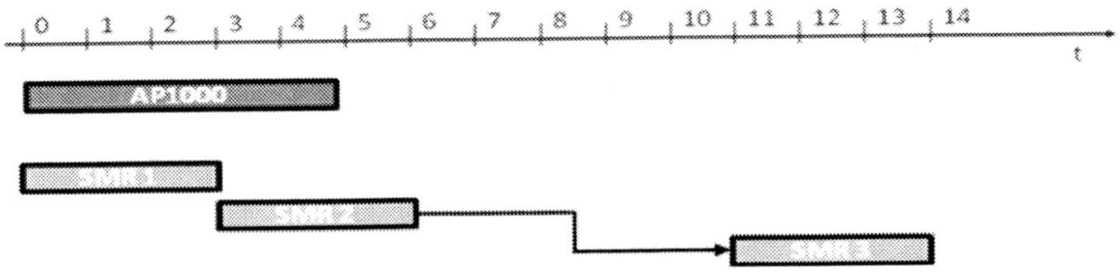

Figure 10. Example of the construction strategy for the SMR.

The operating costs differ for IRIS and AP1000 (see figure 13) and include the following items: fuel cost, operation & maintenance cost, decommissioning & decontamination (D&D) sinking fund, and repair costs of any fault during the operating period. All operating costs increase with inflation. The D&D sinking fund is taken as 20% of the construction cost, and therefore varies with the overnight cost.

The model assumes as an example of major fault the Steam Generator Tube Rupture (SGTR) and assumes it can occur only once in the lifetime of a power station. For IRIS reactors we assume that a possible breakdown at a given time would affect just one of the operating modules. Indeed, a modular plant (if it includes more than one unit) can continue to supply electrical energy to the distribution network, because even if a module is shut down as a result of the breakdown, the others can continue to operate, as they are constructed as stand-alone units. The overall result is that, despite the breakdown, a modular plant can nevertheless exploit at least part of its generating capacity and so guarantee continuity of supply to the electrical energy network. When rupture involves the AP1000 reactor, however, the continuity of supply to the electrical energy network is compromised. We assume that the probability of a SGTR for either power plant is that of the AP1000 (10^{-3} accidents per year). Repair costs differ from IRIS and AP1000 and fall in the same quarter in which the fault occurs.

The time required to undertake repairs varies for the LR and the SMR. The following considerations led us to assume a shorter average repair time for the IRIS reactor compared to the AP1000:

- to repair a steam generator (SG), even the traditional type, the primary circuit must be shut down and partially emptied. With a traditional type reactor, the time to open the pressure vessel (which is a significant percentage of the overall time required) would be saved, however this cannot be compared with the time required for start up/restart, meaning the penalisation for the IRIS reactor is limited;
- if there is a pipe fault with an obstruction of the split or damaged pipes, the primary circuit of the IRIS reactor could be kept closed and it would not even be necessary to empty it partially, as it would be sufficient to empty the secondary circuit to gain access to the pipes;
- in the worst-case scenario of a SG replacement, the time required for an IRIS reactor would be less than for an AP1000, as the SG is modular and, unlike traditional types, is easily dismantled and assembled; this would mean a considerable saving in time and money.

During the overall project life cycle at each quarter the price of electrical energy is estimated based on a 'Mean reverting with jump diffusion' model. With regards the capacity factor, a constant load factor of 100% is assumed, as nuclear power stations are base-load plants. Consequently, reactor performance depends exclusively on the availability factor, which is taken as constant throughout the lifecycle of the plant.

The AP1000 overnight cost at the beginning of the planning horizon is assumed about 2700 €/kWe, corresponding to a NOAK reactor in single unit configuration. Starting from this value, the AP1000 overnight cost during the overall planning horizon is calculated at each quarter as a function of the foreseen electricity price. The ratio between the variation in the price of the electrical energy and the variation in the overnight price is defined through a factor which considers the weight of electrical energy in determining the price of materials and the incidence of the latter on the total overnight cost. A delay of three months has been introduced between the variations in the price of energy and the corresponding variations of the overnight cost. The total overnight cost for the LR is given from the value corresponding to the quarter in which construction begins, since most of the costs are committed in the early phase of the project.

The overnight cost for each IRIS module is obtained at each quarter from the value of the AP1000 overnight cost by applying a cost factor (specific for each single unit) that considers the following aspects: loss of economies of scale, economies of learning, presence of more than one unit on the same site, modular design and intrinsic design features [10]. As for the LR, the total overnight cost for each SMR module is given from the value corresponding to the quarter in which construction begins, since most of the costs are committed in the early phase of the project.

As for the application of ROA model to the IRIS reactor, it allows us to asses modularity in economical terms as comparison between a nuclear modular configuration with sequential options and a benchmark configuration, represented by a modular configuration without sequential options.

The main assumptions used in applying the ROA model to the case under examination can be summarised as follows:

- the project without sequential options used as a benchmark consists of three modules built in series and completely identical to the modules of the project with sequential options; construction of the first module starts at the beginning of the planning horizon; the subsequent modules are built in series without any time lapse between them (see figure 11);
- the investment exploiting sequential options comprises three modules, of which the first is again constructed at the beginning of the planning horizon, irrespective of the expected profitability; therefore, this plant's configuration has two options for expansion – linked to the second and the third modules – respectively; the first option always exists (as the first reactor will be constructed regardless of the expected NPV), while the option involving the third module only exists if the second module is built;
- the lifetime of each option is taken to be 10 years; i.e. once a module has been completed, there is a 10 years period during which the investment in the subsequent module can be postponed or even cancelled; during this period there is a linear loss over time in the economies of learning;

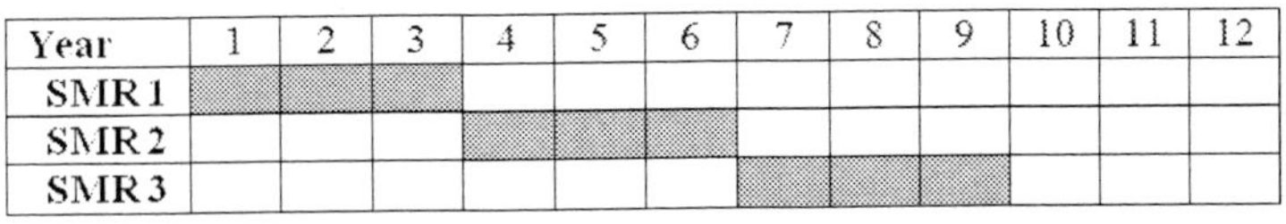

Figure 11. Benchmark construction strategy.

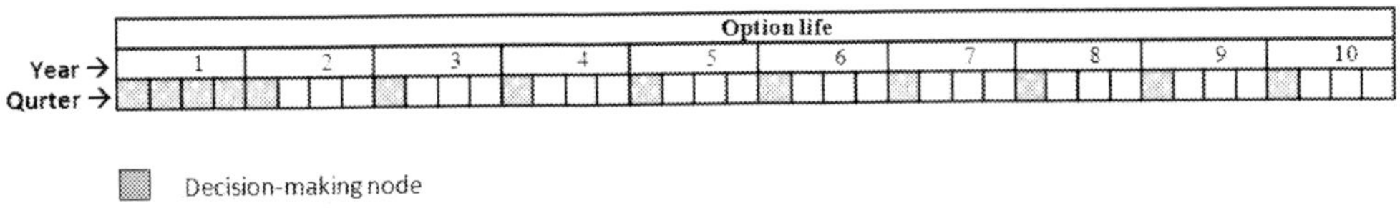

Figure 12. Decision-making nodes along the option life.

- it is assumed that within the lifetime of each option, the decision-making nodes are positioned at the beginning of each quarter for the first year and from year to year subsequently (see figure 12).

In the simulation process, the overall time horizon considered varies from iteration to iteration, depending on any construction delays, on how many SMR modules are built, and on the time lapse between the end of the construction of one module and the start of the next.

Figure 13 and 14 summarise the inputs and the outputs of the model respectively.

Deterministic inputs

Input	Value	Source
AP1000 Net electric output	1005 MWe	[1]
IRIS Net electric output	335 MWe	[18], [19]
AP100 Construction time	5 years	[69]
IRIS Construction time	3 years	[20], [23]
Labour cost/overnight cost	41%	[53]
Building yard related cost/overnight cost	15%	[53]
SMR 1 Cost saving factor	1,40	[10]
SMR 2 Cost saving factor	1,20	[10]
SMR 3 Cost saving factor	1,13	[10]
LR steam generator cost	38,46 mln€	[53]
SMR steam generator cost	19,23 mln€	[53]
Electrical energy influence on material	50%	[5]
Material influence on overnight cost	48%	[53]

Stochastic inputs

Input	Distribution	Distribution's parameters	Source
Tax rate	Uniform	Min value 32%, max value 38%	-
Inflation for operating cost	Triangular	Min value 1,5%, max value 4%, most likely value 3%	[26], [38]
kd	Triangular	Min value 5%, max value 13%, most likely value 8%	[1], [23], [37], [40], [50], [64], [65]
ke	Uniform	Min value 12%, max value 15%	[1], [37], [40], [50]

Figure 13. (Continued)

Stochastic inputs			
Input	**Distribution**	**Distribution's parameters**	**Source**
E/(E+D)	Triangular	Min value 30%, max value 60%, most likely value 50%	-
Availability factor AP1000	Triangular	Min value 80%, max value 100%, most likely value 93%	[18], [69]
Availability factor IRIS	Triangular	Min value 90%, max value 100%, most likely value 95%	[18], [27]
Delay time	Uniform	Min value 1 quarter, max value 4 years	-
Delay in quarter #	Uniform	All AP1000 and 1st IRIS unit common construction quarters	-
AP1000 O&M cost Fuel cost Operating cost D&D sinking fund	 Uniform Uniform Uniform	 Min value 5,3, max value 6,5 €/MWh Min value 5,8, max value 7,0 €/MWh Min value 1,1, max value 1,3 €/MWh	[10], [27]
IRIS O&M cost Fuel cost Operating cost D&D sinking fund	 Uniform Uniform Uniform	 Min value 5,3, max value 6,5 €/MWh Min value 5,3, max value 6,5 €/MWh Min value 5,3, max value 6,5 €/MWh	[10], [27]
Depreciation	Triangular	Min value 13, max value 20, most likely value 15 years	[30], [35]
Accident	Histogram	Probability of accident 10^{-3}	[69]
Accident in quarter #	Uniform	All AP1000 and IRIS common operative quarters	-
AP1000 time to repair	Uniform	Min value 35, max value 60 days	[33]
IRIS time to repair	Uniform	Min value 25, max value 50 days	-
Linear lost of economics in # years	Triangular	Min value 4, max value 7, most likely value 6 years	-

Variable inputs within the timeframe of each iteration			
Input	**Estimation model**	**Model's parameters**	**Source**
Electricity price cost	Mean reverting with jump diffusion	P(t=0) = 99,07 €/MWh	-
		Volatility = 14,31%	-
		Mean reversion speed = 51,13%	-
		Long run mean price = 88,81 €/MWh	-
		Drift = 0,34 €/quarter	-
		Jump size = 40%	-
		Standard deviation of jump = 10%	-
		Jump occurrence = 0,02 jump/year	-
		Jump: binary variable that defines the presence of jump according to the probability of occurrence (P) as defined by "Jump occurrence" $Jump = \begin{cases} 1, & P = 5 \cdot 10^{-3} \\ 0, & P = 1 - (5 \cdot 10^{-3}) \end{cases}$	-

Figure 13. (Continued)

Variable inputs within the timeframe of each iteration			
Input	**Estimation model**	**Model's parameters**	**Source**
AP1000 overnight cost	Mean reverting with jump diffusion	P(t=0) = 2700 €/kWe	[10]
		Volatility = 3,43%	-
		Mean reversion speed = 51%	-
		Long run mean price = 2700 €/kWe	-
		Drift = 6,13 €/quarter	-
		Jump size = 10%	-
		Standard deviation of jump = 2%	-

Figure 13. Inputs to the model and corresponding values.

Output	Description
AP1000 NPV	NPV of the LR
Total AP1000 investment	Overall investment used to construct the LR
IRIS NPV	NPV of the modular configuration with sequential options
SMR 1 NPV	NPV of the first unit of IRIS modular plant with sequential options
SMR 2 NPV	NPV of the second unit of IRIS modular plant with sequential options
SMR 3 NPV	NPV of the third unit of IRIS modular plant with sequential options
IRIS modular plant without sequential options NPV	NPV of modular plant without sequential options
SMR 2 NPV without sequential options	NPV of the second unit of the modular plant without sequential options
SMR 3 NPV without sequential options	NPV of the third unit of the modular plant without sequential options
IRIS total investment	Overall investment used to construct the modular plant with sequential options
Total self-financing value	Amount of the overall investment financed through the cash flow generated by early deployed units
Self-financing % on total IRIS investment	Percentage of overall investment that is financed through cash flow generated by early deployed units
Starting SMR 2 construction after # quarters from SMR 1	Temporal delay between the end of the construction of the first unit of IRIS reactor and the beginning of the construction of the second unit in the modular configuration with sequential options
Starting SMR 3 construction after # quarters from SMR 2	Temporal delay between the end of the construction of the second unit of IRIS reactor and the beginning of the construction of the third unit in the modular configuration with sequential options
Option value related only to the second module	Advantage, in financial terms, that is linked to the second unit thanks to modularity
Option value related only to the third module	Advantage, in financial terms, that is linked to the third unit thanks to modularity
Option total value	Advantage, in financial terms, that is linked to the nuclear plant thanks to modularity: "Option value related only to the second module" + "Option value related only to the third module"

Figure 14. Outputs from the model.

5. Comparison between Large Reactor and Small Medium Reactors

As for the comparison between LR and SMR, IRIS results less profitable than AP1000 (see figure 15).

Note that the NPV is obtained without considering the possible effects of operational modularity, which should have a positive impact (i.e. increasing availability, continuity of supply to electrical energy grid, etc.) on the overall profitability of the IRIS reactor.

Furthermore, the AP1000 can achieve a higher maximum NPV (€4590,97 million vs. €4480,15 million) but also greater losses than the SMR (€1285 million vs. €975 million). This latter aspect, in particular, underlines how the options inherent in the construction of an IRIS allow to avoid the worse situations and limit possible losses. Also the variance of NPV, and hence the riskiness to invest in the AP1000 reactor, is greater that the variance of IRIS NPV.

Although the SMR is characterised by a greater cost/kWh, the average investment necessary to realise an LR or an SMR based configuration comprising three modules is similar (see figure 16).

This means that, despite of a less NPV expected value the IRIS alternative has a lower degree of variability due to the scalable nature of the investment; when the context is such that the nuclear plant investment becomes not profitable, the higher IRIS intrinsic flexibility allows the project to best adapt to external scenarios e.g. by postponement and/or deletion of the investment in the subsequent planned modules. This higher adaptability to the context is not possible for the AP1000 reactor. In order to generate cash inflows it is necessary to complete the construction phase, and this means to spend all or more of the scheduled budget against a lower foreseen income.

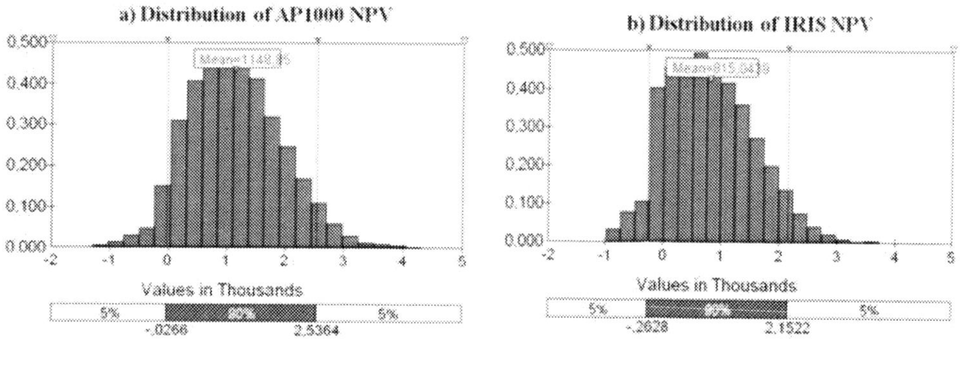

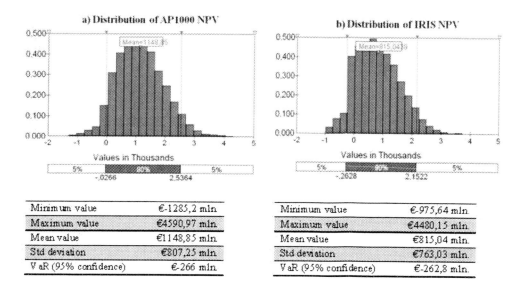

Minimum value	€-1285,2 mln
Maximum value	€4590,97 mln
Mean value	€1148,85 mln
Std deviation	€807,25 mln
VaR (95% confidence)	€-266 mln

Minimum value	€-975,64 mln.
Maximum value	€4480,15 mln.
Mean value	€815,04 mln.
Std deviation	€763,03 mln.
VaR (95% confidence)	€-262,8 mln.

Figure 15. Comparison between the AP1000 NPV (a) and the IRIS NPV (b).

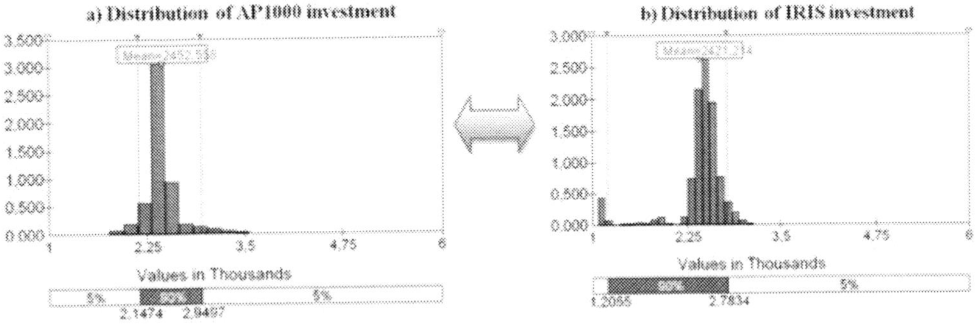

Minimum value	€1776,81 mln.
Maximum value	€5701,39 mln.
Mean value	€2452,56 mln.
Std deviation	€235,17 mln.
VaR (95% confidence)	€2147,4 mln.

Minimum value	€1072,75 mln.
Maximum value	€3238,01 mln.
Mean value	€2421,21 mln.
Std deviation	€357,02 mln.
VaR (95% confidence)	€1205,5 mln.

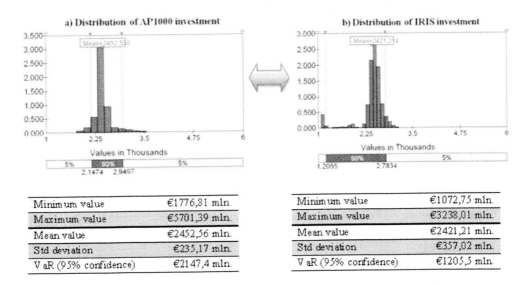

Figure 16. Comparison between the AP1000 investment (a) and the IRIS investment (b).

This is mainly due to economies of learning. For the same reason the IRIS maximum value of investment is meaningfully less than the AP1000 one. Furthermore, while for the construction of an LR, the investment must be entirely funded with debt and equity, construction of an SMR based configuration can be funded up to a considerable level (as much as 13%) using flows of self-financing (see figure 17).

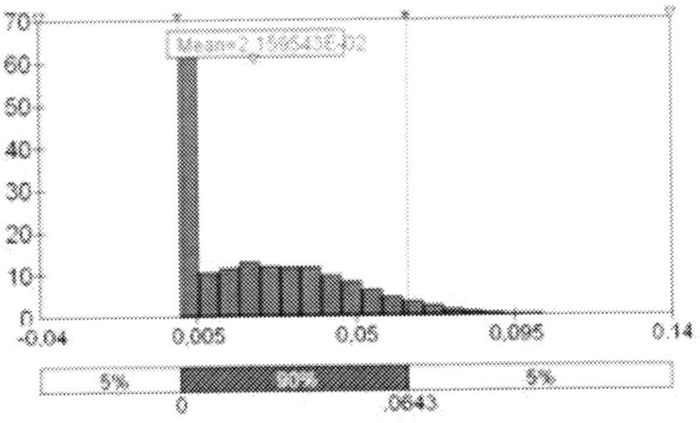

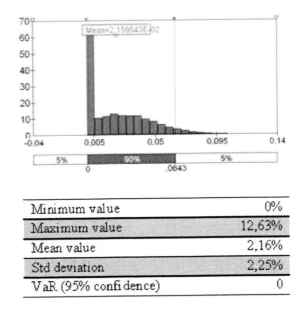

Minimum value	0%
Maximum value	12,63%
Mean value	2,16%
Std deviation	2,25%
VaR (95% confidence)	0

Figure 17. Distribution of IRIS self-financing % on total IRIS investment.

6. Assessment of the Sequential Options Value

The ROA model highlights that in the presence of high uncertainty in the external variables, particularly regarding the trend in the price of electrical energy, the sequential options linked to the plant's modularity assume a significant overall value, approximately €14 million (see figure 18). If the uncertainty in the price of electrical energy falls, then also the value of the options diminishes.

In fact, the value of the total option can reach very high levels if external conditions are not favourable and the expansion options are not exercised, so avoiding a dramatic project failure.

The first option contributes 66% and the second 33% of the total value of the sequential options, indicating that the value of the options falls as project progresses and uncertainty about the remaining work diminishes.

From the comparison between the NPV distribution of the modular configuration with sequential options and the NPV distribution of the modular configuration without sequential options, we obtain a more detailed analysis of the two alternatives.

As we can see in figure 19, the difference between maximum values of NPV is negligible. On the contrary, there is a significant difference in the minimum values of NPV, since project flexibility may be decisive in limiting project losses in case of non favorable contexts. Due to the same reason, also NPV VaR at 95% confidence level is quite different between the two cases.

Isolating the NPV distribution related only to the second and third module (since the first has the same impact in both configurations i.e. with and without sequential options), the expansion options associated to the second and third modules reduce significantly the impact of uncertainty on the project performance. Indeed, by postponing and/or possibly cancelling the investment the negative tail of the NPV distribution can be eliminated (see figure 20), in this way eliminating or at least reducing possible project losses.

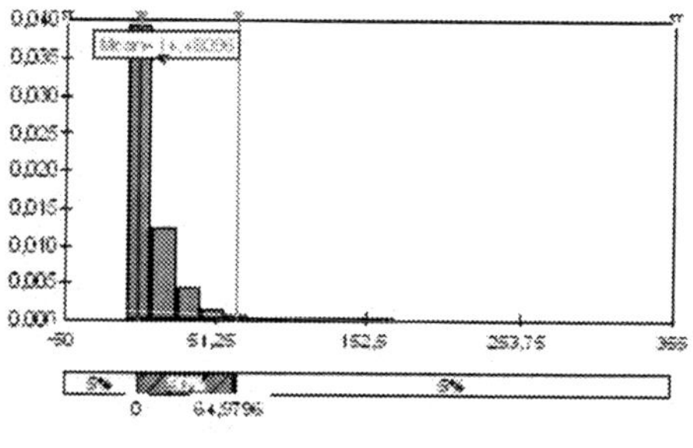

Minimum value	€0 mln.
Maximum value	€351,76 mln.
Mean value	€14,48 mln.
Std deviation	€32,87mln.
VaR (95% confidence)	€0 mln.

Figure 18. Value of the sequential options.

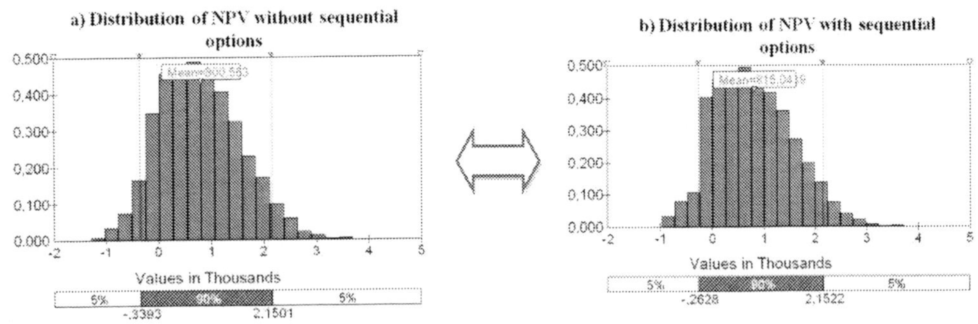

Minimum value	€-1282,6 mln.
Maximum value	€4480,15 mln.
Mean value	€800,56 mln.
Std deviation	€775,55 mln.
VaR (95% confidence)	€-339,3 mln.

Minimum value	€-975,64 mln.
Maximum value	€4480,15 mln.
Mean value	€815,04 mln.
Std deviation	€763,03 mln.
VaR (95% confidence)	€-262,8 mln.

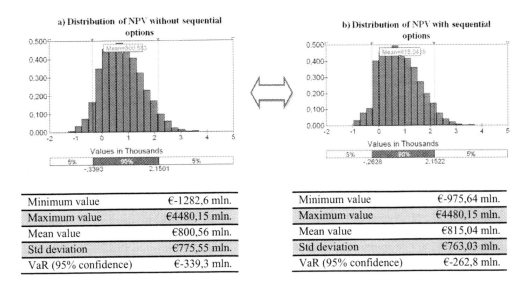

Figure 19. Comparison between the NPV of the modular configuration without sequential options (a) and the NPV of the modular configuration with sequential options (b).

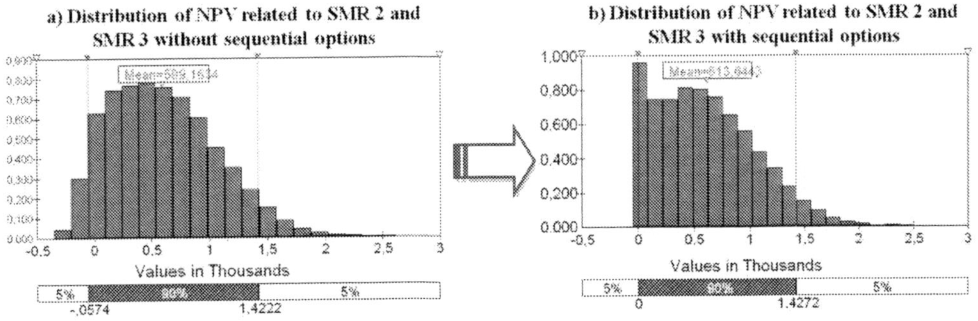

Minimum value	€-351,76 mln.
Maximum value	€2916,74 mln.
Mean value	€599,16 mln.
Std deviation	€461,13 mln.
VaR (95% confidence)	€57,4 mln.

Minimum value	€0 mln.
Maximum value	€2916,74 mln.
Mean value	€631,64 mln.
Std deviation	€448,51 mln.
VaR (95% confidence)	€0 mln.

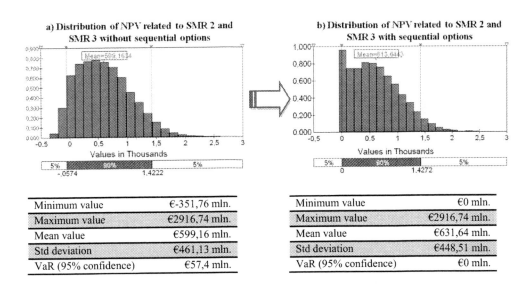

Figure 20. NPV distribution related to second and third module without sequential options (a) and with sequential options (b).

On average, the 13% of the investment was covered by auto-financing deriving from modules already operating, so reducing the risk exposure for investors.

The main parameters that have an impact on the value of the sequential options are the price of electrical energy and, consequently, the overnight cost, which is correlated to the energy price. These two parameters define, respectively, the cash flow during the operating phase and the cost of investment, confirming the analogy with the general assessment of options based on the comparison between the value of the underlying asset (i.e. the project cash flow) and the corresponding strike price (i.e the overnight cost).

Financial aspects also influence the value of the options, albeit to a lesser extent. The cost of the debt capital, the cost of the equity and the funding mix would appear to be particularly significant. Sensitivity analysis of these parameters reveal that their impact on the overall value of an option is less than that generated by the price of electrical energy.

On the other hand, the overall project profitability is mainly influenced by the cost of debt, the cost of equity and the postponement decisions. This latter parameter, in particular, allows us to justify *a posteriori* the model's focus on the construction phase.

7. CONCLUSION

A DCF model has been proposed for the evaluation and comparison of alternative investment projects in the energy production industry, considering both production technology and a plant's configuration. The model is made up of three sub-models related to construction phase, operation phase and the trend of electricity price respectively. The model focuses in particular on the construction phase in which relevant decisions are taken influencing the project development. The model takes account of the expenditure profile during construction, possible delays, economies of learning, and moreover, possible flows of self-financing.

The model has been extended to estimate the value of project flexibility deriving from the plant's modular configuration in terms of sequential options. The total option value is determined as the difference between the NPV of the modular project with sequential options and the NPV of a similar, modular project without sequential options. In the latter case, management cannot decide whether and when to invest and therefore has no opportunity to influence project development. In estimating the maximum value of the sequential options, all the possible construction strategies for the modules are considered. However the proportion of the value that can be effectively harnessed depends on management's ability to exploit the greater information that becomes available as the project progresses.

Application of the model to a nuclear power plant reveals that in conditions of high uncertainty concerning the context variables, modularity plays a significant role and can eliminate possible losses by allowing for the postponement or cancellation of at least part of the investment.

Overall, therefore, we can claim that within a dynamic and variable context such as electrical energy production, the modularity of the IRIS reactor offers significant opportunities. Indeed, in addition to the operational value of modularity, the SMR offers the advantages of its small size, the economies of learning, the possibility to adapt to change in the context, the opportunity to make a gradual investment (attractive when financial resources are limited), and the chance to exploit cash flows from self-financing, implying a reduced financial burden.

Even if the average NPV of the LR is above that of the SMR based configuration, the latter presents less risk, measured for instance by the standard deviation of the NPV.

Further research could allow us to integrate the results obtained about sequential options during construction with the estimate of the advantages deriving from modularity during the operating phase in terms of availability, service continuity and adaptability to demand variations.

8. List of Main Abbreviation and Acronyms

D	Debt
D&D	Decommissioning & Decontamination
DCF	Discounted Cash Flow
DTA	Decision Tree Analysis
E	Equity
FCFE	Free Cash Flow to Equity
GBM	Geometric Brownian Motion
IDC	Interest During Construction
kd	Cost of debt
ke	Cost of equity
LEPs	Large Engineering Projects
LRs	Large Reactors
LUEC	Levelized Unit Electricity Cost
mln	Million
NOAK	N^{th} of a Kind
NPV	Ney Present Value
O&M	Operation & Maintenance
OFCF	Operative Free Cash Flow
PDE	Partial Differential Equations
ROA	Real Option Approach
SG	Steam Generator
SGTR	Steam Generator Tube Rupture
SMRs	Small Medium Reactors
Std	Standard
VaR	Value At Risk

9. References

[1] Alemi, M. (31 October 2007). Nuclear renaissance: small reactors may become an investor play. *New Energy Finance*.

[2] Arrto, K., Kujala, J., Dietrich, P. & Martinsuo, M. (2008). What is project strategy? Int. *J. Proj. Manage*, *26*, 4-12.

[3] Arrto, K., Lehtonen, M., Aaltonen, K., Aaltonen, P., Kujala, J., Lindemann, S. & Murtonen, M. (2009). Two types of project strategy- empirical illustrations in project risk management. *IRNOP IX*, October 2009. Berlin.

[4] Barraquand, J. & Martineau, D. (1995). Numerical valuation of high dimensional multivariate American securities. *Journal of Financial and Quantitative Analysis*, *30(3)*, 383-405.

[5] Benecchi, L. (23 February 2008). *All'acciaio serve il nucleare*. Il sole 24 Ore.

[6] Black, F. & Scholes, M. (1973). The Pricing of Options and Corporate Liabilities. *J. Political Economy*, *81*, 637-659.

[7] Blanco, C., Choi, S. & Soronow, D. (2001). *Energy Price Process Used for Derivatives Pricing & Risk Management.* Commodities Now. March, 74-80.

[8] Blanco, C. & Soronow, D. (2001a). *Mean Reverting Process - Energy Price Processes Used For Derivatives Pricing & Risk Management.* Commodities Now. June, 68-72.

[9] Blanco, C. & Soronow, D. (2001b). *Jump Diffusion Processes - Energy Price Processes Used for Derivatives Pricing & Risk Management.* Commodities Now. September, 83-87.

[10] Boarin, S. & Ricotti, M. (2010). *INCAS Integrated model for the competitiveness Analysis of small-medium sized reactors.* IAEA Internal document.

[11] Brabazon, T. (1999). Real options: Valuing flexibility in capital investment decisions. *Accountacy Ireland, 31(6)*, 16-18.

[12] Brennan, M. J. & Trigeorgis, L. (2000). *Real Options, in: Project flexibility agency and competition.* Eds. M. J. Brennan, & L. Trigeorgis, Oxford University Press.

[13] Broadie, M. & Glasserman, P. (1995). Pricing American-style securities using simulation. *Journal of Economic Dynamics and Control, 21*, 1323-1352.

[14] Broadie, M. & Glasserman, P. (1998). *A Stochastic Mesh Method for Pricing High-Dimensional American Options.* Working Paper.

[15] Broadie, M. & Detemple, J. (1997a). Recent Advances in Numerical Methods for Pricing Derivative Securities, in: *Numerical Methods in Finance*, eds. L. C. G. Rogers, & D. Talay, Cambridge University Press.

[16] Broadie, M. & Detemple, J. (1997b). The Valuation of American Option: Valuation on Multiple Assets. *Mathematical Finance, 7*, 241-286.

[17] Browman, E. H. & Moskowitz, G. T. (2001). Real options analysis and strategic decision making. *Organization Science, 12(6)*, 772-777.

[18] Carelli, M. D. (2003). IRIS: A global approach to nuclear power renaissance. *Nuclear news, 46(10)*, 32-42.

[19] Carelli, M. D., Petrović, B., Čavlina, N. & Grgić, D. (September 2005). IRIS (International Reactor Innovative and Secure) – *Design Overview and Deployment Prospects.* Nuclear Energy for New Europe 2005. Bled (Slovenia).

[20] Carelli, M. D., Conway, L. E., Oriani, L., Petrović, B., Lombardi, C. V., Ricotti, M. E., Barroso, A. C. O., Collado, J. M., Cinotti, L., Todreas, N. E., Grgić, D., Moraes, M. M., Boroughs, R. D., Ninokata, H., Ingersoll, D. T. & Oriolo, F. (2003). The design and safety features of the IRIS reactor. *Elsevier Journal*, 151-167.

[21] Cobb, B. R. & Charnes, J. M. (2007). Real option valuation. *2007 Winter Simulation Conference*, Washington DC, USA.

[22] Copeland, T. & Antikarov, V. (2001). *Real Options: A Practitioner's Guide.* New York, Texere LLC.

[23] DGEMP. Les statistiques. L'énergie nucléaire. [online] (2008). Available from: http://www.industrie.gouv.fr/energie/sommaire.html.

[24] Dixit, A. K. & Pindyck, R. S. (1994). *Investment under Uncertainty.* New Jersey University Press. New Jersey.

[25] Dixit, A. K. & Pindyck, R. S. (2000). Expandability, reversibility, and optimal capacity choice, in: *Project flexibility, agency, and competition*, eds. M. J. Brennan, & L. Trigeorgis Oxford University Press.

[26] European Commission. *Statistics database.* [online] (2008). Available from: http://epp.eurostat.ec.europa.eu, 2008.

[27] Feretic, D. & Tomsic, Z. (2005). Probabilistic Analysis of eletrical energy costs: Comparing production cost of gas, coal and nuclear power plants. *Energy policy*, 33.

[28] Floricel, S. & Miller, R. (2001). Strategizing for anticipated risks and turbulence in large scale engineering projects. Int. *J. Proj. Manage*, *19*, 445-455.

[29] Fraser, P. (2003). *Power Generation Investment in Electricity Markets*. OECD/IEA.

[30] Gallanti, M. & Parozzi, F. (2006). Valutazione dei costi di produzione dell'energia elettrica da nucleare. *Tecnologia*, *3*, 60-70.

[31] Gargiulo, M. (2008). The strcture of the Matisse model. *Modelli tecnico-economici e scenari per l'energia e l'ambiente*, Rome.

[32] Gollier, C., Proult, D., Thais, F. & Walgenwitz, G. (2005). Choice of nuclear power investments under price uncertainty: Valuing modularity. *Elsevier Journal*, *27*, 667-685.

[33] Gonyeau. *Operation of a nuclear power plant*. [online] (2009). Available from: www.nucleartourist.com/operation/sg-mod1.html.

[34] Grant, D., Vora, G. & Weeks, D. (1997). Path-dependent options: Extending the Monte Carlo simulation approach. *Management Science*, *43*, 1589-1602.

[35] Harding, J. (2007). *Economics of New Nuclear Power and Proliferation Risks in a Carbon-Constrained World*. Nonproliferation Policy Education Center.

[36] Hellstrom, M. & Wikstrom, K. (2005). Project business concepts based on modularity – improved manoeuvrability through unstable structures. *Int. J. Proj. Manage*, *23*, 392-397.

[37] IEA. (2006). *Energy Technology Perspectives 2006*. [E-pdf]. Available on: http://www.enea.it/com/web/convegni/work180906/ExecutiveSummery.pdf.

[38] ISTAT. Informazione, dati e analisi sull'inflazione. [online] (2008). Available from: http://www.istat.it.

[39] Kester, W. C. (1984). Today's Options for Tomorrow's Growth. *Harvard Business Review*, *62*, 153-160.

[40] Keystone Center. *The Keystone Center Joint Fact-Finding On Nuclear Power*. [online] (2009). Available from: www.keystone.org.

[41] Kodukula, P. Dr. & Papudesu, C. (2006). *Project Valuation Using Real Option - A Practitioner's Guide*. J. Ross Publishing.

[42] Kolltveit, B. J., Karlsen, J. T. & Gronhaug, K. (2004). Exploiting opportunities in uncertainty during the early project phase. *Journal of management in engineering*, October.

[43] Longstaff, K. J. & Schwartz, E. (2001). Valuing American options by simulation: A simple least-squares approach. *The Review of Financial Studies*, *14(1)*, 113-147.

[44] Mason, S. P. & Merton, R. C. (1985). The role of contingent claims analysis in corporate finance. Recent Advance in Corporate Finance, in: *Recent Advances in Corporate Finance*, eds. E. I. Altman, & M. G. Subrahmanyam, Irwin.

[45] McDonald, R. & Siegel, D. (1984). The value of waiting to invest. *Quarterly Journal of Economics*, *101*, 707-728.

[46] Merton, R. C. (1973). The Theory of Rational Oprion Pricing. *Bell J. Economics and Mgmt. Sci.*, *4*, 141-183.

[47] Miller, K. (2005). IRIS - Economic review. *International Congress on Advances in Nuclear Power Plants*, Seoul. [E-pdf]. Available from: www.icapp2005.org.

[48] Miller, R. & Lessard, D. (2000). The strategic management of large engineering projects, *shaping institutions*, risks and governance. MIT.

[49] Miller, R. & Lessard, D. (2001). Understanding and managing risks in large engineering projects. Int. *J. Proj. Manage*, *19*, 437-443.

[50] MIT. (2003). *The Future of Nuclear Power*. An Interdisciplinary MIT Study.

[51] Moel, A. & Tufano, P. (2000). Bidding for the Antamina Mine: Valuation and Incentives in a Real Option Context, in: Project flexibility, agency, and competition, eds. M. J. Brennan, & L. Trigeorgis, Oxford University Press.

[52] Morris, P. W. G. & Jamieson, A. (2005). Moving from corporate strategy to project strategy. *Proj. Manage. J*, *36(4)*, 5-18.

[53] Mycoff, C. W. & Locatelli, G. (2007). *Parametric Mathematical Modular Model To Compute Economic Differences In The Capital Cost Between Sites With Gen III+ Reactors And SMRs.*

[54] Myers, S. C. (1977). Determinants of Corporate Borrowing. *J. Financial Economics*, *5*, 147-175.

[55] Myers, S. C. (1984). Finance Theory and Financial Strategy. *Interfaces*, *14*, 473-487.

[56] Olsson, N. O. E. (2006). Management of flexibility in projects. Int. *J. Proj. Manage*, *24*, 66-74.

[57] Olsson, N. O. E. (2008). External and internal flexibility – aligning projects with the business strategy and executing projects efficiently. Int. *J. Proj. Org. Manage*, *1(1)*, 47-64.

[58] Rode, D., Fishbeck, P. & Dean, S. (2001). Monte Carlo Methods for appraisal and valuation: A Case Study of a Nuclear Power Plant. *Journal of Structured and Project Finance*, *7*, *3*, 38-48.

[59] Roques Fabien, A., Nuttall William, J. & Newbery David, M. (2006). *Using Probabilistic Analysis to Value Generation Investments under Uncertainty*, MIT Institute.

[60] Ross, S. A. (1978). A Simple Approach to the Valuation of Risky Income Streams. *J. Business*, *51*, 453-475.

[61] Schwartz, E. S. & Trigeorgis, L. (2004). Real Options and Investment Under Uncertainty: *Classical Readings and Recent Contributions*, MIT Press.

[62] Smith, J. E. & McCardle, K. F. (1998). Valuing oil properties: integrating option pricing and decision analysis approaches. *Operations Research*, *46(2)*, 198-217.

[63] Smith, J. E. (2005). Alternative approaches for solving real options problems. *Decision Analysis*, *2(2)*, 89-102.

[64] The Royal Academy of Engineering, (2004). The cost of Generating Electricity. [E-pdf]. Available from: http:// www. raeng. org. uk/ news/ publications/ list/ reports/ Cost _Generation_Commentary.pdf.

[65] The University of Chicago, (2004). The Economic Future Of Nuclear Power. [E-pdf]. Available from: http://nuclear.energy.gov/np2010/reports/NuclIndustryStudy-Summary.pdf.

[66] Trigeorgis, L. (1993). The nature of options interactions and the valuation of investments with multiple real options. *Journal of Financial and Quantitavive Analysis*, *28(1)*, 1-20.

[67] Trigeorgis, L. (1995). Real Options in Capital Investment: *Models, Strategies, and Applications*, Greenwood Publishing Group.

[68] Tseng C. L. & Barz, G. (2002). Short-term generation asset valuation: a real option approach. *Operations Research, 50(2)*, 297-310.
[69] Westinghouse, (2007). AP1000. *Ready to Meet Tomorrow's Power Generation Requirements Today.*

LIVERPOOL JOHN MOORES UNIVERSITY
LEARNING SERVICES

In: Project Management
Editor: Robert J. Collins, pp. 103-120

ISBN: 978-1-61761-460-6
© 2011 Nova Science Publishers, Inc.

Chapter 3

The Project Management Consultant – Developing the Consulting Plan

Margaret R. Lee
Blackburn College, Carlinville, Illinois, USA

Abstract

Following some basic steps, the project manager can move from organizational project management into the field of project management consulting. This requires the development of a solid business plan for the proposed consulting business. The first step is self-assessment of consulting competencies. This includes an evaluation of personal competencies using the Compleat Consultant Assessment, developing a matrix of consulting skills and a SWOT analysis of personal strengths and weaknesses, followed by action items for improvement. An examination of preferred consulting approach and the reasoning behind selecting the process consulting approach, along with a discussion of personal assumptions and beliefs should follow. The next step deals with the development and operationalization of the mission and values for the proposed consulting business. This discussion leads to an analysis of consulting methods and techniques, consulting focus, and the development of a personal philosophy of consulting and underlying reasons for the consulting focus chosen. Next is the development of a marketing strategy which should focus on several marketing activities (not sales), and include the specific market niche, value proposition, and branding. As an important next step in marketing includes strategies regarding establishing value-based fees and proposed attraction and retention of talent must be developed. Finally, the implementation plan should include discussions on sustaining revenue, developing a clientele or stable group of clients, and potential challenges to the implementation plan and action item(s) to overcome weaknesses.

Introduction

The consulting world can be a very competitive and difficult environment regardless of the classification of the consultant or the management issues involved. The constant pressure of marketing one's self, self-development to remain current, travel demands, difficult work-life balance, and legal/financial stress portray a work environment that is certainly not easy. Bennett (2005) reported that consulting salaries had decreased or not made projections in 2004-2005 and Greiner and Poulfelt (2004) indicate a future growth rate of less than ten percent for management consulting. Yet the world of management consulting still remains magnetic and mesmerizing to many because of the ability to work for oneself and potentially make a large salary.

One key to success in the world of consulting is to prepare and follow a business plan. Waters (1988) repeats the sage advice that "If you don't know where you're going, any road will take you there" and suggests the best defense to becoming lost on that road is to write a business plan. The business plan provides the opportunity to identify goals and develop strategies to meet those goals. The plan plays an important role in the success of any new or small business, and is a tool that can help a business achieve or surpass its goals (Hormozi, Sutton, McMinn, & Lucio, 2002). Research shows that businesses that write business plans are generally more successful than those that do not (Crawford-Lucas, 1992, and Orser, Hogarth-Scott, & Riding, 2000).

The first step for the business plan is a self-assessment of consulting competencies. This includes an evaluation of personal consulting competencies, including the Compleat Consultant Assessment, a matrix of consulting skills and a SWOT analysis of personal strengths and weaknesses, followed by action items for improving these competencies. An examination of consulting approaches and the reasoning behind selecting a particular process consulting approach, along with action items for improving and a discussion of personal assumptions and beliefs should follow.

The next step deals with the mission, values and ethics of the proposed consulting business, and the operationalization of the mission, values, and ethics statements. This discussion leads to an analysis of consulting methods and techniques, consulting focus and personal philosophy of consulting and underlying reasons for the consulting focus chosen.

Essential to the business plan is a marketing strategy for the consulting practice. Marketing services to provide distinctive, competitive services involve unique marketing strategies. The marketing strategy focuses on several marketing activities (not sales), and includes specific market niche, value proposition, and branding. Strategies regarding fees are part of marketing, so establishing value-based fees and proposed attraction and retention of talent are required. Finally, the marketing plan is synthesized from various marketing theories and practices of established, successful consultants, and provides the detail necessary to implement the plan into the overall business plan.

A business plan is not complete without an implementation strategy by which to move forward. The implementation plan includes discussions on sustaining revenue, developing a clientele or stable group of clients, and potential challenges to the implementation plan and action item(s) to overcome weaknesses.

Consulting Competencies

Bobrow (1986) recommends that the new consultant begin with self-analysis. An internal assessment of the consultancy's strengths and weaknesses are necessary for developing a business strategy (McLarty & Robinson, 1998).

The first step is a self-assessment of consulting competencies. This includes an evaluation of personal competencies, including an overview and review of the results of the Compleat Consultant Assessment, developing a matrix of consulting skills and a SWOT analysis of personal strengths and weaknesses. A major part of self-awareness is the ability to identify action items for improving competencies, and these should be included. Understanding different consulting approaches and then selecting the appropriate approach is an important step in self-discovery. Again, action items for improving the competencies necessary to be a successful process consultant are a necessary part of self-awareness. Added to the mix are personal assumptions and beliefs that underlie the existing and developing competencies and the approach chosen for the consulting practice.

Overview and Evaluation of Personal Consulting Competencies

Begin by reviewing previous career work, management and project management experience, including any teaching or facilitation experience. According to a study done by Mahan, Halverson and Harty (1971) teaching was one of several effective activities for external consultants working with educators, along with evaluating and reassuring, procuring, and disseminating information.

The Compleat Consultant Assessment Tool

The ability to self-assess is crucial to the consultant for continual self-development and growth. Williamson and Buehler's (1998) Compleat Consultant instrument is a tool that provides a diagnostic profile of the behaviors that are important to the success of a consultant. The tool presents six primary roles (Grounded Expert, Trusted Advisor, Business Driver, Insightful Observer, Committed Partner, and Change Leader) and their accompanying competencies based upon the work and activities of a consultant. The basis of the model is that the consultant plays many roles, and roles are situational in consulting work. The more able the consultant is to develop the competencies for all roles, the more successful the consultant will be (Williamson & Buehler, 1998). The tool allows for self-examination of the roles and competencies based upon the rankings of the behaviors. Completing this profile will provide insights into the primary role strengths that will enhance the project management consulting business. When taking the assessment, many of the competencies necessary for the roles needed for a consultant will be exposed. Areas needing development and that are consistently weak areas when managing projects and leading teams will also be exposed.

The Compleat Consultant for HR ad OD Professionals Development Guide– Self Assessment tool is published by Linkage. It can be ordered online through Linkage.

The Consulting Skills Matrix

The consulting skills matrix is a tool that enables the consultant to determine existing skills and abilities (Lewin, 1995) that will be valuable in a consulting practice. The most commonly used skills will be clearly reflected on the matrix. The Compleat Consultant tool adds to the matrix by indicating some of the weaker areas. Project management skills (Project Management Institute, 2007) primarily show under Skills and Abilities.

To develop the matrix, consider what skills and abilities would be important to the consulting business. Reference professional organizations for lists on competencies. Explore similar consulting firms' web sites for ideas on skills. Place these under the "Skills and Abilities column." List experience by industry, using the resume or curriculum vitae as a guide. Include volunteer work, as it often is directly related to the skills and abilities necessary for consulting. Table 1 is an example of a consulting skills matrix for a project manager with experience in the banking, insurance and educational areas, plus volunteer experience.

The results will indicate those areas in which the project manager tends to use these skills and has the most experience. The matrix also shows those areas in which the project manager has the least experience and fewest skills.

Table 1. Example of a Consulting Skills Matrix.

Skills and Abilities	Industry			
	Banking Industry	Insurance Industry	Educational Institutions	Volunteer Organizations
Management Skills	X	X		X
Team/Unit Management		X		X
Strategic Planning		X		X
Coaching		X	X	
Instructional Design		X	X	
Training/Teaching		X	X	X
Curriculum Development		X	X	
Virtual Experience		X		
Training Assessment		X		
Writing		X	X	X
Customer Service	X	X		
Planning a Project		X		X
Project Execution		X		X
Project Monitoring and Control		X		X
Reports and Executive Summaries	X	X		X
Communication Skills	X	X	X	X
Leadership Skills	X	X		X
Problem Resolution	X	X		X
Negotiation Skills	X	X		X

SWOT Analysis for Consulting Competencies

The SWOT (acronym for strengths, weaknesses, opportunities, and threats) analysis is a tool by which an organization or individual can assess its situation to create a strategy that will improve its competitive advantage (Thompson, Strickland, & Gamble, 2005). Presented as a chart, the SWOT analysis provides an objective, rational snapshot. As an in-depth analysis, this tool allows the organization or individual to draw conclusions that can create strategic actions, but relies upon objectivity and realism in creating and reviewing the SWOT. The need for the consultant to conduct a SWOT is important to the development process of the practice (McLarty & Robinson, 1998).

Like the Compleat Consultant, the SWOT analysis provides motivation to analyze strengths and weaknesses (internal-organizational), but also opportunities and threats (external-environmental) that will enable the project manager to formulate a successful strategy for a project management consulting practice. Coupling the SWOT analysis with the Consulting Skills Matrix allows for the further definition of the strongest skills and abilities, although the Consulting Skills Matrix does not provide an avenue for identifying weaknesses, opportunities or threats.

Table 2. Example of a SWOT Analysis.

Strengths • Communication skills, both oral and written • Instructional Design and curriculum development experience in two industries • Training/Teaching experience • Project Management experience, skills and competencies for both volunteer and industry projects • Leadership skills • Problem Resolution and Negotiation skills • Self-starter and continuous learner	Opportunities • The trend for educational facilities to increase online programs • Greater awareness of the trend toward virtual project management • The current lack of individuals consulting in e-leadership and virtual project management • Chance to help project managers in e-leadership and virtual project management • Opportunities may exist in corporations to provide e-leadership and virtual project management training or coaching
Weaknesses • Relationship Building, team building, coaching • Training Assessment • Assuming others understand • Driving too hard/fast • Lack of contacts and vendors who can currently provide virtual project management and e-leadership courses • Lack of contacts and connections at universities	Threats • Current financial situation (self and country) • Ability of educational institutions to afford consulting help • Inability to be able to find the necessary courses for the curriculum and having to write them

To develop the SWOT chart, make four quadrants, and label them "Strengths," "Opportunities," "Weaknesses," and "Threats." Drawing from the Consulting Skills Matrix, locate the columns with the most check marks. In our example, the Skills and Abilities of "Teaching/Training," "Writing," "Customer Service," "Reports and Executive Summaries," "Communication Skills," "Leadership Skills," "Problem Resolution," and "Negotiation Skills" have three or four checkmarks, indicating strengths. The same activity is completed for Skills and Activities with only one or two skills to indicate weaknesses on the SWOT. Reviewing the results of the Compleat Consultant Assessment tool, strong areas indicated for the example consultant were Grounded Expert, Trusted Advisor, Business Driver and Committed Partner. Areas needing development were Insightful Observer and Change Leader. These results are incorporated into the SWOT analysis text. The following SWOT analysis (Table 2) shows the quadrants for the same project manager with experience in the banking, insurance and educational areas, plus volunteer experience.

Action Items for Improving Competencies

These three tools, the Compleat Consultant Assessment, consulting skills matrix and SWOT analysis, enable the project manager to recognize weaknesses and design a self-development plan to continue to improve on these competencies. Action items for improving weaker competencies include keeping these competencies at the top of the list when interacting with people and leading projects. The use of 360 reviews and requesting feedback to improve skills are good tools to continually improve weak competencies. Books on all types of personal improvement processes are available. The continued use of these tools will provide direction for self-development to be able to achieve the level of consulting that will utilize strengths, minimize weaknesses, and recognize opportunities and threats to build a successful consulting practice.

EXAMINATION OF THE CONSULTING APPROACH

There are several styles of management consulting. The "diagnosis" style or "doctor-patient" (Canback, 1998, Part one) involves the consultant performing an assessment or investigating problems within an organization. With the "coaching" style of consulting, the consultant works directly with the leader of the organization to overcome management or communication problems. Both of these styles do not require industry-specific knowledge and are, therefore, somewhat generic. The "expert" consultant helps an organization (in an industry in which the consultant has expertise) develop a strategy for success. This is also called purchase-of-expertise (Canback, 1998, Part one) and requires less hands-on, interpersonal work than any of the other styles.

The emphasis of consulting has changed from just solving problems to helping clients diagnose problems, learn and change by themselves, in addition to analyzing client problems and providing recommendations (Werr, Stjernberg, & Docherty, 1997). The "process" style involves facilitating (Canback, 1998, Part one) strategic planning to help the organization discover the solution to a problem, and requires that the consultant have expertise in the industry. Cooke (1997) presents the role of helping as action-based, with every intervention making a difference. Using a process consulting approach, he suggests, does not necessarily make one a process consultant. Process consulting, instead, simply describes a mode of practice in which the relationship (but not dependency) with the client is structured by the consultant. Cooke suggests that process consulting recognizes three principles: that the client knows more than the consultant ever will; that the client must have ownership of the activities; and that the consultant should help the client solve their own problem(s).

According to Turner (1982), there are eight fundamental objectives of consulting: provide information, solve problems, diagnose, recommend, implement, build buy-in, help the client learn how to resolve future problems, and improve organizational effectiveness. These activities, however, must be tempered by the ability of the process consultant to help the client "own" the problem and be actively involved in the development of the solution, in addition to offering expertise and diagnosing any problems (Schein, 1990). The process consultant facilitates strategic planning to help organizations discover the solution to a problem, with the client contributing expertise (Canback, 1998, Part one). Consultants with industry-specific experience are considered more valuable than with firm-specific experience (Richter & Schmidt, 2006).

The international peripatetic consultant (Weiss, 2006) travels from place to place working for short periods of time. For work as an international peripatetic consultant, Smith (2000) provides guidelines for the consultant for conducting international consulting.

Harris (2001) suggests that consultants should understand their motivations, attitudes and aptitudes to be successful. The consultant's personal assumptions and beliefs should be explored through self-reflection before continuing with the consulting planning process.

Mission, Values and Ethics Statements

The Mission Statement

A mission statement should clearly describe the buyers' needs, customer groups, market segments, and how (method, resources and/or technology) the organization is going to satisfy these needs (Thompson, Strickland & Gamble, 2005). A good mission statement should showcase a limited number of goals, focus on the company's policies and values, and define the company's industry, products, applications, competence, and market segment (Kotler & Keller, 2007). An example mission statement for a curriculum consulting project management business was written as:

Our mission is to assist educational facilities in strategically planning a curriculum for virtual project management and e-leadership development.

Value and Ethics Statements

The consultant should also provide value statements for the client, including experience, quality of work, issue resolution and opportunity management, and be quantifiable (Parker, (2003). For the same consulting firm as above, the value statement would read:

> *Our value to you*
> *We will assist you, in an objective, independent and knowledgeable manner, in establishing a scholar-practitioner educational program that will align with the strategic direction of your organization to provide a distinctive, competitive curriculum in virtual project management and e-leadership studies.*

The ethics statement is the consultant's promise to maintain the highest level of integrity when dealing with the client. The importance of integrity is underscored by Maister (2005), who states that the best consultants with the highest profits are those who have high values, stands and principles. The Institute of Management Consultants Code of Ethics (IMC, 2005) lists the moral expectations for the client and for the consultant and can be used as validation of behaviors (Lewin, 1995). Using an ethics statement as part of your business plan and marketing pieces is a good way to highlight this important element of the business. Again for the proposed curriculum consulting practice, the ethics statement might read:

> *Our work ethic*
> *We are committed to quantifiable, quality consulting practices and to providing on time, in budget, and in scope deliverables. We will maintain the highest level of integrity in all our dealings. We pride ourselves on being customer-centered. Our priorities are to listen to your needs and provide outstanding service.*

Operationalization of Mission, Values and Ethics Statements

Frye (2003) presents nine suggestions for service: (1) Make service visible, (2) Provide more than the required or expected, (3) Minimize inconvenience for the client, (4) Think in terms of clients for life, (5) Every consultant is responsible for marketing, (6) Look the part, (7) Actively seek feedback, (8) Cultivate a quick response mode, and (9) Train clients to expect good service. The client needs to know and understand what it is that the consulting firm will be able to do to assist them. The explanation of how the mission and values should be operationalized is found in the listing of services for the consulting practice. These services should reflect the mission, value, and ethics statements. An example of how these can be operationalized is found in the listing of services for the consulting practice. Such a listing, for our example consulting firm, is found below.

Our services

As the field of project management evolves into virtual work environments, scholar-practitioners who have professional and academic experience will be on the forefront of building a better understanding and application of the theories and practice that will help project management thrive. OUR EXAMPLE Curriculum Consultants reflects a research-based, strategic vision for the advancement of virtual project management by assisting educational facilities to build a curriculum for virtual project management and e-leaders.

To assist your institution in developing a specialized virtual project management and e-leadership curriculum, we will:

- facilitate strategic planning
- empower your educators to contribute their expertise
- assist in incorporating appropriate academic research and managerial practices in the development of the new curriculum
- collaborate on planning the new curriculum
- work with your team to analyze existing course offerings
- recommend courses and learning paths
- assist in resolving issues and capitalizing on opportunities
- assist your educators in managing the development and implementation of the curriculum
- coach your leaders to maintain and sustain the curriculum

Our team's qualifications include high-level experience and advanced education in virtual project management and e-leadership, and we are available virtually and/or in-house.

CONSULTING METHODS AND TECHNIQUES

Somewhat similar to project management, Lewin (1995) suggests that project scope, proposal, and planning are important elements to follow for successful consulting. Lewin introduces seven phases for consulting projects: initiating, analyzing, design, selecting, modifying, implementing, and reviewing. These are very familiar to the project manager. Project management process groups are: initiating, planning, executing, monitoring and controlling, and closing (Project Management Institute, 2004). The project management knowledge areas are the management of integration, scope, time, cost quality human resource, communications, risk, and procurement (Project Management Institute, 2004). Block (2000) suggests five phases for the consulting project: entry and contracting, discovery and dialogue, feedback and decision to act, engagement or implementation, and extension, recycle or termination. These, too, are similar in focus.

Many resources are available to help navigate successfully the development of a consulting practice. Among these are other individuals who are involved in similar types of consulting. Forming alliances, according to Lewin (1995), can be valuable to the consultant, especially for the new consultant. Another resource is individuals in the industry. Using the services of other consultants to help with the consulting practice during the development of the business strengthens these relationships. The "use of consultants increases as entrepreneurs/business owners progress through the business life cycle, moving from the discovery phase through to an established/operational business" (Klyver, 2008, p. 181). The Internet is also a resource for discovering successful techniques and methods, and networking with other project managers who have consulting experience. Performing a search on the Internet using the proposed consulting focus and the word "consultant" or "consulting" will bring up references that might be useful. If, after changing search words, very few results surface, this may be an indication of the need for further research into the area of consulting being proposed.

Process consulting is a tool to help clients accomplish goals, by helping the team help itself. Techniques that can be used by the process consultant include: listen, ask questions, help the team solve its own problems, don't make judgments, and concentrate on the way the team works, rather than what it is working on (Anonymous, n.d.). Werr, Stjernberg and Docherty (1997) found that a strong tendency to emphasize learning for the client, with transfer of knowledge and skills, indicated a process approach versus an expert approach to consulting. Chrusciel's (2004) study relates the fact that many organizations expect the consultant to not only institute change, but also invoke collaboration and facilitate learning in the organization (role of the consultant as a teacher). The process approach assumes that the consultant will also work as a coach and expert when needed, so this experience will be helpful.

Philosophy of Consulting and the Consulting Focus

Strategy planning is considered one of the strongest areas of consulting work, as indicated by George Braxton Bennett, of Braxton Associates, Inc. (Washburn, 1982). It is important that the consultant is skilled and competent in helping the clients contribute their insights and expertise to the development of the project or process that is being worked on, as client participation in gathering and analyzing data will be invaluable to the process (Harrison, 1989). Understanding the underlying reasons for the chosen consulting focus will provide the basis for a strong philosophy for the consultant.

Marketing

To market, one must create need. Marketing, or the strategy behind selling, is actively promoting and publicizing the value proposition of the consulting business – why the buyer needs and should hire the specialized consulting services (Weiss, 2001). Sales, on the other hand, involve direct activities, the actual service provided to the client (Greiner & Poulfelt, 2004). The consultant should not only understand the role of marketing, but also marketing techniques (Lewin, 1995). Marketing involves creating and promoting the value proposition, and conducting marketing plan activities that focus on awareness building and establishing qualifications.

Marketing is often considered a difficult process, so consultants are advised to build a marketing plan and follow it, or delegate marketing to someone else (Waters, 1988). The marketing plan or strategy is an important part of the business plan and is comprised of activities that reinforce each other to publicize and promote the value proposition of the consulting business. The marketing process involves many activities such as market research, product planning and public relations, all of which require a process and strategy (Smith, 1990).

Chiaqouris and Wansley's (2003) study identified several guidelines to help organize a new company's marketing plan - develop a well-defined mission statement, develop a marketing plan, establish brand identity, vary the market research program, and over-invest in marketing. This section of the business plan focuses on many of these marketing activities (not sales), and includes information on market and market niches, the value proposition, and branding. Strategies regarding fees are part of marketing, so discussions follow on establishing value-based fees and how a compensation package could be leveraged to attract and retain key talent. The actual marketing plan is synthesized from various marketing theories and the marketing practices of established, successful consultants and provides the detail necessary to implement the plan into the overall business plan.

Markets and Market Niches

For those considering building a consulting practice, Boroian (1987) suggests that a market must exist or the new consultant will need to educate potential clients to build a market, and that this market must be broad-based enough to support the practice. McLarty and Robinson (1998) suggest that the new consultant define the current issues and needs of the marketplace, and then select a target market based on the analysis of environmental forces and influencing factors. Boroian (1987) compares specialization in consulting to specialization in medicine and suggests that within the specialization the consultant can find many ways to diversify and offer services that are directly transferable to a specific niche. Jansen (2003) suggests that differentiating a firm's consulting services provides clients with a better reason to select that firm over others. Alexis (2008) indicates that some organizations are increasingly utilizing consulting services to assist in strategic planning, technology, organizational structure, financial management, fundraising and outsourcing. This is the result of increased external pressure for change, fewer internal resources available, more regulations, and institutional politics. Canback (1998, Part two) suggests that fundamental shifts in the economy have raised transaction costs and increased the demand for external consultants.

Value Proposition

Traditionally, companies focused on the value their organization could get from the client relationship (income, acquisition, retention). Today competition has changed the focus to how the company can provide value to the customer (Payne, 2004). Payne suggests that creating customer value is a key source of competitive advantage, but identifying what is meant by customer value and how consultants propose to deliver it is rarely communicated clearly.

The value proposition can include the target customer, benefits and price (Payne, 2004) or it can simply include the customer and the intended client's outcome (Weiss, 2001). Frye (2003) suggests the value proposition must support a specific market niche. The purpose of the value proposition is to target the customer and explain the benefits of doing business (Tilton, 2008). The focus of the value proposition needs to be on what the client sees as valuable, not what the consultant does or what the consultant wants to achieve, the consultant's agenda, or the consultant's services.

The value proposition, when written correctly, should clearly communicate what is meant by customer value and how the consultant proposes to deliver it. The value proposition for the consulting practice whose mission statement was used as an example above may be:

> *"For universities that need to establish a virtual project management and e-leadership program, we assist in strategically establishing a distinctive, competitive curriculum."*

Branding

Consistency in using the value proposition will help build and manage the consultant's brand. The key to brand building is also consistency (Bliss & Wildrick, 2005). Zednik and Streginger's (2008) quantitative study of brand management models offered by consulting firms, advertising agencies and market research companies showed that the major objectives of brand management models were (1) brand positioning, (2) determining brand value and strategy, and (3) brand communication. The brand, generally, is an abbreviated version of the value proposition and should be concise, crisp, memorable and effective (Weiss, 2001). For the example consulting business, the brand could be: "Leading E-Leadership Education."

Weiss (2001) suggests putting the brand on email, letterhead, promotional materials and presentation slides used in public speaking and teaching. Using the brand as part of the e-mail signature file (Weiss, 2006) can promote consistency and build brand awareness. Consistency in using the brand, like the value proposition, can play an important role in marketing the consulting business. The payoff of effective branding can be huge for the consultant, where the client's decision to buy services is often linked to intangibles (Bliss & Wildrick, 2005).

Establishing Value-Based Fees

Using value-based fees, instead of an hourly or project-based fee structure, provides a fair and equitable fee arrangement for both the consultant and the client (Weiss, 2001). To be able to establish value-based fees, the focus must be on the value of the outcome of the consultation (ROI), not amount of time involved, tasks performed or deliverables. The value of the consulting service should be established together with the client based on the value of the consulting experience to the organization.

Compensation Package to Attract and Retain Key Talent

Any partnership compensation should be structured as an equity ownership. Attracting and retaining talent for the consulting firm could be from contacts at the businesses where the consultant has had work. Should the need for administrative, hourly employees exist, Weiss (2006) strongly suggests using a payroll service.

Table 3. Example of a Marketing Plan.

Goal Category	Strategy	Date – Development	Date – Implementation	Cost	Measurement	Rank	Active/ Passive (A/P)
Relationships	Professional associations related to project management, e-leadership, e-business.				Number of referrals from association relationships Number of proposals produced	5a	A
Relationships	Professional associations for top level individuals (Lewin, 1995) in academia				Number of referrals from association relationships Number of proposals produced	5b	A
Credibility, visibility	Interviews (radio, TV, magazine, newspaper)				Hits on Web site or calls following interviews Number of proposals produced	7	A
Credibility, visibility	Web site with on-line newsletter				Number of hits on Web site that result in contact Number of proposals produced	10	P
Credibility, visibility	Publish professional journal and magazine articles, position and white papers				Number of contacts from writings, number of interviews, etc. from writings. Number of proposals produced	6	P
Credibility, visibility	Public speaking - Seminars*				Number in audience, number of speaking requests Number of proposals produced	2	A
Credibility, visibility	Publish book				Number of books sold Number of proposals produced	8	P
Alliances and Networking	Reciprocal web links with other curriculum consultants and associations				Number of hits on Web site(s), number of contacts and proposals produced	9	P
Alliances and Networking	Visiting professor opportunit-ies, teaching				Number of proposals produced	3	A
Referrals	Sponsorship				Number of referrals Number of proposals produced	4	P
Referrals	Referral request system				Number of referrals Number of proposals produced	1	P
Referrals	Cold call letters with follow-up call				Number of responses Number of proposals produced	12	A
Products	Books, article reprints, checklists, CDs, audio-tapes				Number of items sold Number of proposals produced	11	P

* - Waters (1988) suggests that research has proven teaching seminars as the second most effective way to reach prospective clients.

** - A sponsor is a person who refers clients to the firm, such as an executive of the local Chamber of Commerce or vendors (Norris, 1987).

Marketing Plan

The actual marketing plan is synthesized from marketing theories and the marketing practices of established, successful consultants. It provides the detail necessary to implement the marketing strategies into the overall business plan. Bobrow (1986) suggests using a table for mapping the marking strategy that includes columns for the marketing goal, strategies for the goal, dates, cost, measurement of the results, and ranking for each goal. Weiss (2001) suggests that successful consultants implement in both active and passive marketing as income-producing techniques. Combining these suggestions, the preliminary marketing plan table (sans dates and cost) for the hypothetical consulting firm used as an example in this chapter might look like the following (Table 3).

The marketing plan is synthesized from various marketing theories and practices of established, successful consultants. It provides the detail necessary to implement the plan into the overall business plan. However, marketing involves more than just a plan. Marketing activities (not sales), such as determining the specific market niche, developing a value proposition, and branding should be incorporated into the overall business plan. Strategies regarding value-based fees are part of marketing, as is the proposed attraction and retention of future talent for the consulting practice. Marketing strategies that promote the consulting business will enable it to fulfill its mission.

IMPLEMENTATION PLAN

The full business plan for the new consulting firm will include the marketing plan, an operational/management plan, financial statements, startup expenses and capitalization, and financial plan. Implementation of the plan should be according to an established timeline. Careful planning is fundamental to the success of the business (SBA, n.d.), but implementing the plan according to an established timeline is essential to growth. Also important to the plan are systems for sustaining revenue and sustaining clientele. The potential challenges to implementing the plan are important to systematically developing a successful strategy for the business. Review of the SWOT analysis can provide insight into external and environmental threats. The consultant's personal approach drives the business plan and the implementation of it and must be realistic.

Sustaining Revenue

Long-term relationships with clients are recommended over single projects for sustainability of revenue (Poulfelt, Greiner, & Bhambri, 2005). With sixty percent of consulting revenues originating from exiting or former clients (Poulfelt, Greiner, & Bhambri, 2005), the long-term client is essential to sustainability. The consultant should work to establish long-term relationships with clients by periodically following up on the project(s) and regular communications.

Market expansion should evolve through the relationships established from existing consulting accounts. Cheung (2002) suggests that academia may be perfect springboard for a complementary specialized consulting business, so contacts within the academic community should be considered. Should more revenue by required, expanding to provide businesses assistance in the consultant's area of expertise may be a possibility.

Sustaining Clientele

Consultants should attempt to deal with the highest level of decision-maker in the organization. It is at this level that the consultant is able to provide the best value to the organization (Nadler, 2005). Weiss (2001) also suggests that the consultant always deal with the principal of the organization, and bi-annually review the clientele list to remove the lower fifteen percent of the clients.

Nadler (2005) suggests that pressure on boards and shareholder demands has caused boards to look to outside consultants for guidance and expert help. Becoming familiar with board members and joining the professional associations they are involved with may allow the consultant to build and sustain board-level clientele.

Potential Challenges to the Implementation Plan and Action Items

Understanding the world in which the decision-maker must operate is key to the success of the consultation (Nadler, 2005). Alexis' (2008) study posits that organizations require that consultants have strong technical skills, knowledge and experience; the ability to define their approach and the project's scope; the ability to make recommendations; and familiarity with the industry. Failures by consultants include inaccurate definition of the problems, poor communication, poor understanding of client and consultant expectations, inadequate project investigation, impractical recommendations, and the consultant's lack of preparedness and familiarity with decision-making processes (Alexis, 2008).

Following the established seven phases for consulting projects (initiating, analyzing, design, selecting, modifying, implementing, and reviewing), the project manager consultant can blend project management skills and consulting to provide exceptional service. The marketing plan will provide the structure for marketing the business, and the full business plan (which includes the operational plan, financial statements, startup expenses and capitalization, and financial plan) can provide the road map.

CONCLUSION

The evaluation of personal consulting competencies and examination of consulting approaches are exercises that strengthen the goals of the consultant. This, in turn, assists the development and the operationalization of the mission, value, and ethics statements for the consulting practice. This discussion leads to an analysis of consulting methods and techniques, consulting focus and an understanding of the consultant's personal philosophy and underlying reasons for the consulting focus.

As the business plan begins to emerge, the marketing strategies and services to provide distinctive, competitive services are developed. The marketing strategy focuses on marketing activities including definition of the specific market niche, value proposition, branding, establishing value-based fees and proposed attraction and retention of talent, and a plan for marketing the business. Incorporating consulting theories and the best practices of successful consultants, implementation for the business plan and for sustaining revenue, developing clientele, and potential challenges should be addressed. The business plan plays an important role in the success of any new consulting business, and revolves around the consultant's personal approach, which must be developed and evaluated as part of the planning process.

REFERENCES

[1] Alexis, M. (2008). Tips for a more successful higher education-consultancy relationship. *Diverse Issues in Higher Education, 25(6)*, 18.

[2] Anonymous. (n.d.). Process consulting for change management and organizational effectiveness. *Toolpack Consulting.* Retrieved on February 15, 2009, from http://www.toolpack.com/process.html.

[3] Bennett, J. (2005, September 22). Setback in consulting salaries. *Accountancy Age*, 2.

[4] Bliss, J. & Wildrick, M. (2005). How to build a personal brand. *C2M: Consulting to Management, 16(3)*, 1-5.

[5] Block, P. (2000). *Flawless consulting: A guide to getting your expertise* used (2nd ed.). Danvers: MA: Jossey-Bass.

[6] Bobrow, E. E. (1986). Grand strategies for marketing small consultants. *Journal of Management Consulting, 3(1)*, 37-43.

[7] Boroian, D. D. (1987). Leverage in a specialty consulting practice. *Journal of Management Consulting, 3(3)*, 42-46.

[8] Canback, S. (1998, Part one). The logic of management consulting: Part one. *Journal of Management Consulting, 10(2)*, 3-11.

[9] Canback, S. (1998, Part two). The logic of management consulting: Part two. *Journal of Management Consulting, 10(3)*, 3-12.

[10] Cheung, S. (2002, October, 25). The academic consultant--Why start a consultancy? *Science Career Magazine.* Retrieved on January 11, 2009 from http://sciencecareers.sciencemag.org/career_magazine/previous_issues/articles/2002_10_25/noDOI.17644875736485445495

[11] Chiaqouris, L. & Wansley, B. (2003). Start-up marketing. *Marketing Management, 12(5)*, 38-43.

[12] Chrusciel, D. (2004). Consultant as teacher or teacher as consultant: What is the relationship? *Leadership & Organization Development Journal, 25(7/8)*, 663-677.

[13] Cooke, B. (1997). From process consultation to a clinical model of development practice. *Public Administration & Development, 17(3)*, 325-340.

[14] Crawford-Lucas, P. A. (1992). Providing business plan assistance to small manufacturing companies. *Economic Development Review, 10(1)*, 54-58.

[15] Frye, E. T. (2003, September). Service as a value proposition for ESAs. *Perspectives, 9*, 73-80 Retrieved on February 15, 2009, from http:// www. aesa. us/ Pubs/ AESA% 20Perspjournal%202003.pdf#page-81.

[16] Greiner, L. E. & Poulfelt, F. (2004). *Handbook of management consulting: The contemporary consultant*. Mason, OH: South-Western.

[17] Harris, C. (2001). Consulting and you. *Consulting to Management, 12(1)*, 45.

[18] Harrison, M. I. (1989). Diagnosis and planned organizational change. *Journal of Management Consulting, 5(4)*, 34-42.

[19] Hormozi, A. M., Sutton, G. S., McMinn, R. D. & Lucio, W. (2002). Business plans for new or small businesses: Paving the path to success. *Management Decision, 40(7/8)*, 755-763.

[20] Institute of Management Consultants USA (IMC). (2005, February 3). IMC USA Code of Ethics. Retrieved on February 23, 2009, from http://imcusa.org/?page=ETHICSCODE

[21] Jansen, J. (2003). Ways smaller firms can gain clients. *C2M: Consulting to Management, 14(2)*, 1-4.

[22] Klyver, K. (2008). The shifting consultant involvement. *Journal of Small Business and Enterprise Development, 15(1)*, 178-193.

[23] Kotler, P. & Keller, K. L. (2007). *A framework for marketing management* (3rd ed.).Upper Saddle River, NJ: Prentice-Hall.

[24] Lewin, M. D. (1995). *The overnight consultant.* NY: John Wiley and Sons.

[25] Mahan, J., Halverson, P. & Harty, H. (1971, March). *Teachers and external curriculum consultants: Can they function effectively together?* Paper presented at the ASCD Annual Meeting, St. Louis, MO.

[26] Maister, D. (2005). Professionalism in consulting. In L. Greiner, & F. Poulfelt, (Eds.), Handbook of management consulting: The contemporary consultant (23-34). Mason, OH: South-Western.

[27] McLarty, R. & Robinson, T. (1998). The practice of consultancy and a professional development strategy. *Leadership & Organization Development Journal, 19(5)*, 256-263.

[28] Nadler, D. A. (2005). *Consulting to CEOs and boards*. In L. Greiner, & F. Poulfelt, (Eds.), *Handbook of management consulting: The contemporary consultant* (151-171). Mason, OH: South-Western.

[29] Norris, D. B. (1987). A marketing checklist for consultants. *Journal of Management Consulting, 3(3)*, 47-51.

[30] Orser, B. J., Hogarth-Scott, S. & Riding, A. L. (2000). Performance, firm size, and management problem solving. *Journal of Small Business Management, 38(4)*, 42-58.

[31] Parker, S. L. (2003). Understand what your clients value. *Consulting to Management – C2M, 14(1)*, 25-29.

[32] Payne, A. (2004, September 4). The value creation process in customer relationship management. *My Customer.com*. Retrieved on February 15, 2009, from http://mycustomer.com/download/5077/bt-028.pdf

[33] Poulfelt, F., Greiner, L. & Bhambri, A. (2005). The changing global consulting industry. In L. Greiner, & F. Poulfelt, (Eds.), *Handbook of management consulting: The contemporary consultant* (3-22). Mason, OH: South-Western.

[34] Project Management Institute. (2004). *A Guide to the project management body of knowledge: PMBOK guide* (3rd ed.). Newton Square, PA: Project Management Institute.

[35] Project Management Institute. (2007). *Project manager competency development framework* (2nd ed.). Newton Square, PA: Project Management Institute.

[36] Richter, A. & Schmidt, S. L. (2006, October). Antecedents of the performance of management consultants. *Schmalenbach Business Review, 58*, 365-396.

[37] Schein, E. H. (1990). A general philosophy of helping: Process consultation. *Sloan Management Review, 31(3)*, 57-64.

[38] Small Business Administration (SBA). (n.d.) Manage your business from start to finish. *Small Business Planner*. Retrieved February 20, 2009, from http:// www. sba. gov/ smallbusinessplanner/index.html

[39] Smith, A. W., Jr. (2000). Making Globalization Work. *Consulting to Management, 11(1)*, 1-3. Retrieved on February 15, 2009, from http:// 222. imcusa. org/ resource/ collection/ 89E9353A-415C-42CD-B8AA-8F466CCCCFD7/11.1_2000_Smith_-_Making _Globilization_Work.pdf.

[40] Smith, B. P. (1990). Marketing of management consulting. *Journal of Management Consulting, 6(1)*, 34-40.

[41] Thompson, A., Strickland, A. & Gamble, J. (2005). *Crafting and executing strategy: Text and readings* (15th ed.). New York: McGraw-Hill.

[42] Tilton, S. (2008, April 3). How to write effective value propositions. *Marketing Communications.* Retrieved on February 16, 2009, from http://www.salesvantage.com /article/1304/How-to-Write-Effective-Value-Propositions

[43] Turner, A. N. (1982). Consulting is more than giving advice. *Harvard Business Review, 60(5)*, 120-129.

[44] Washburn, S. A. (1982). Five perspectives on consulting today. *Journal of Management Consulting, 1(1)*, 7-19.

[45] Waters, B. G. (1988). How to market a consulting practice. *Journal of Management Consulting, 4(3)*, 53-58.

[46] Weiss, A. (2001). *The ultimate consultant: Powerful techniques for the successful practitioner.* SanFrancisco: Jossey-Bass/Pfieffer.

[47] Weiss, A. (2006). *Million dollar consulting toolkit.* Hoboken, NJ: John Wiley & Sons.

[48] Werr, A., Stjernberg, T. & Docherty, P. (1997). The functions of methods of change in management consulting. *Journal of Organizational Change Management, 10(4)*, 288-298.

[49] Williamson, S. A. & Buehler, M. L. (1998). *The compleat consultant for HR and OD professionals: Self-management assessment, worksheet, and development plan.* Burlington, MA: Linkage.

[50] Zednik, A. & Strebinger, A. (2008). Brand management models of major consulting firms, advertising agencies and market research companies: A categorization and positioning analysis of models offered in Germany, Switzerland and Austria, *Journal of Brand Management, 15(5)*, 301-311.

In: Project Management
Editor: Robert J. Collins, pp. 121-135
ISBN: 978-1-61761-460-6
© 2011 Nova Science Publishers, Inc.

Chapter 4

THE IMPACT OF PROJECT DURATION ON IT PROJECT SUCCESS FACTORS

Deborah H. Stevenson and Jo Ann Starkweather
Northeastern State University

ABSTRACT

Common to periods of economic downturn, many companies seek to reduce budgets, cut costs and minimize the risk of project failure. In line with these initiatives, we have seen many firms over the last few years shorten project timelines, in an effort to heighten control over project outcomes, providing more accountability and sustainability in an uncertain business environment. While much has been written regarding measures of project success and the incidence of project success or failure throughout the years, the corporate landscape has now significantly changed, giving rise to new assessments and determinants of project success or failure.

This study is composed of 2 phases, whereby IT recruiters were asked to identify a set of criteria best indicative of successful project managers, Composed into the Hiring Criteria Index, these criteria, along with questions regarding measurements of project success, project duration and perceptions of short term or long term project success were sent by questionnaire to 3,258 IT managers and executives nationwide. Respondents were asked to identify, on a 10 point Likert scale, what percentage of projects were considered successful across 5 measures of success: Cost, On Schedule, Quality1 (Met Tech Specs), Quality2 (Met Client-Defined Business Requirements) and Client/User Satisfaction. Results indicated that respondents achieved greater than 70 % of project success, as measured across all five factors. However, when assessing the relationship between these measures of success and project duration, respondents indicated that they experienced more success for short term projects (i.e. projects a year or less in duration), as measured by all indicators, except Client/User Satisfaction. It appeared that the ability to satisfy the customer was unaffected by length of project cycle. Of those measurements of success that appeared to be associated with shorter project durations, On Schedule and Quality2 – Met Client-Defined Business Requirements, were indicated to have the strongest relationship to successful short term projects.

Introduction

Critical to the success of a corporation is the success of its individual projects. Much has been written on project success rates and failures and those criteria thought to be most valued in the deployment of a product that is thought to be a success by not only the client, but stakeholders and project team alike. Over the years, the goal remains the same – identify the best combination of criteria that will increase the chances of success for projects undertaken. In today's global economy this task becomes a significant challenge, as project costs skyrocket, committed project resources fall by the wayside and many good projects end up being shelved for better times. One way to counter these effects is to convert longer term projects into short term ventures with specific, early deliverables that are visible and measurable.

Literature Review

Success. Project management professional journals are rife with articles that have as their focus, "success." It is, after all, the bottom line for eventual assessment of a given project. The difficulty inherent in such a wealth of scholarship on success is the lack of cohesion one finds in perusing such a plethora of articles. Conceptually, there appears to be a collective sense of what is meant when it's stated that a project was successful. Operationally, however, there is virtually no agreement on whether who, what, when, why, or how becomes the criterion for success. The following discussion will highlight the contributions of some of the oft-cited scholarship on success. The articles included in this review are by no means exhaustive, rather the intent is that they be representative of the trends in project management scholarship.

The best place to start a review of project management success criteria would be with the tried and true *Iron Triangle* (time, cost, specifications). If the project were completed within the specified timeframe, within the budget parameters, and the technical specifications were achieved—the project was a success. The primary reason for the initial use of the triangle is that these metrics were readily available. However, it's important to note that there has never been an argument against these criteria as important benchmarks when measuring project success—they're still used today. Consider, for example, that the infamous Standish Group Reports are based on assessments of an IT project's performance on the iron triangle benchmarks. Despite consistent improvements in success rates over the decade from 1994 – 2004, more recent data indicate some regression. Specifically, "32 percent of IT projects were delivered on time and within budget. However, 44 percent were 'challenged,' which means they were late, over budget, and/or missed meeting performance requirements. In addition, 24 percent failed, were cancelled, or never used…this is the highest failure rate in over a decade" (Larson and Gray 2011:4). Thus, what has changed over time is not the import of the iron triangle, but the breadth of critical success factors considered, the variable definitions of success factors by different stakeholders, the question of whether process or product success is paramount, and most recently the recognition of the strategic import of project management. No longer relegated to the periphery of the company--those *free spirits* in R & D-- project management has become ubiquitous throughout the organization.

Among the early contributors to the CSF (critical success factor) genre, Wateridge (1995, 1998) incorporated the work of Morris and Hough (1987) and Turner (1993) in his two year compilation of data based on an extensive questionnaire and in-depth interviews from a broad spectrum of participants in 12 IS/IT projects. Collectively, the group ranked the following six criteria as most important for success:

- Meets user requirements
- Achieves purpose
- Meets timescale
- Meets budget
- Happy users
- Meets quality

When the data were analyzed separately for users and then for project managers, significantly different perceptions emerged. Users gave top priority to the criteria of "Meets user requirements," (96%), "Users are happy (with system)" (69%), and "Achieves purpose" (65%). The group of project managers gave top priority to "Meets user requirements," (81%), "Meets time" (71%) and "Meets budget" (71%). Project managers' assessment of the importance of "happy users" yielded a mere 35%. Although this is significantly below the priority assigned by the users, it is actually the highest priority assigned to happiness by project managers. The other two 'happiness' criteria (happy team, happy sponsor), shared the lowest success priority assigned by project managers at 27% each (Wateridge 1998). Using the 1990s scholarship of Wateridge as illustrative of PM research during this period, the import of recognizing perceptions of success as variable (depending on the constituency polled), and the introduction of 'soft' success factors (happy users) are indicative of the middle stages of conceptual maturation for PM "success."

A second theme pursued over the last two decades is that of identifying critical success factors within various stages of the project life cycle. Early research by Slevin and Pinto (1986) resulted in the construction of a 10-factor (50 item) Project Implementation Profile (PIP). Subsequent research by Pinto and Prescott (1988) analyzed responses from over 400 PM professionals with the goal of determining which factors were deemed critical to success within a given project stage. Pinto and Prescott hypothesized that all 10 factors would be significant predictors of success in each of the life cycle stages by virtue of their appellation as a *critical* success factor. Several additional hypotheses suggested various clusters of factors that would be stronger predictors of success within particular stages. For example, Project Mission and Client Consultation were hypothesized as dominant CSFs in the conceptual phase of the project while Client Acceptance and Client Consultation were the dominant CSFs in the termination stage. One controversial result of this research was the finding that the Personnel factor was not a significant predictor of success in any of the project life cycle stages. In the midst of vigorous scholarly debate taking exception to this conclusion, work by Belout (1998) challenged the findings of Pinto and Prescott on conceptual, methodological, and statistical grounds. Still later, Belout and Gauvreau (2004) attempted a retest of the conclusion that the Personnel factor was a non-significant contributor to project success. Belout and Gauvreau stated that despite finding a "link" between Personnel and Success via a statistically significant correlation ($r = .377$) , subsequent regression analysis did not reveal a statistically significant contribution by Personnel to the dependent variable Success. The author's discussion of this finding pointed to a lack of consensus on a definition of effectiveness in HRM, along with the vagueness of HRM objectives and varied interpretations of HR practice (2004:8) as potential explanations for the lackluster performance of the Personnel factor.

Despite the disappointing performance of the Pinto and Prescott Personnel factor, several scholars have addressed the importance of human resource management as a determinant of project success using alternative operationalizations for the HR concept. Both conceptually and empirically, many researchers have defined the competencies and attributes of the project manager as an important dimension of human resource management and determinant of project success. For example, just prior to the 21st century, Belzer declared that "Project management (was) still more art than science" (2001). She stated that the *soft skills* of the project manager were the missing link—the answer to the question, "What makes a project manager successful?" Belzer offered a list of 7 attributes critical to PM success (communication, organizational effectiveness, leadership, problem solving and decision-making, team building, flexibility and creativity, trustworthiness). Chief among this list was communication which was comprised of a wide range of skills including: convey complex ideas easily, clearly articulate what must be accomplished, keep the team moving toward a common goal, foster an environment that allows team members to communicate openly/honestly, admit their own mistakes without losing respect, negotiate, listen, and facilitate. More recently, research has enumerated PM critical competencies associated with project success as perceived by IT executives (Stevenson and Starkweather 2010). In support of Belzer's conclusion, results by Stevenson and Starkweather empirically affirmed the import of several dimensions of PM communication as correlates of project success. Factor analysis and reliability analysis resulted in the development of a 6-item Critical Competency Index comprised of: Leadership, Ability to Communicate at Multiple Levels, Verbal Skills, Written Skills, Attitude, and Ability to Deal with Ambiguity and Change. Narrowing the focus to the impact of PM leadership style on project success, Turner and Muller offer a comprehensive review of the literature assessing the link between different styles of leadership and the project environment (2005). In addition to finding that the most effective leadership style differs across project life-cycle stages and that multi-cultural projects are enhanced by specific leadership styles, one study linked the project manager's perceptions of success with his/her leadership style. "[There is] a significant relationship between the leader's perception of project success and his or her personality and contingent experiences. Thus the inner confidence and self-belief from personal knowledge and experience are likely to play an important role in a manager's ability to deliver a project successfully" (Turner and Muller 2005:59; from Lee-Kelley, et al. 2003).

In 1996, Belassi and Tukel began an empirical trend that continues today—that of grouping critical success factors and explaining the interaction between them. The six groups of factors included Project factors, Project Manager factors, Team, Organization, and Environment factors. The authors concluded that the presentation of individual factors within labeled factor groups "presents the factors in a more systematic way…(and) helped respondents understand the overlooked dimensions of project success such as project attributes and project environment" (1996:149). Scholarship by Cooke-Davies identified factors critical to project management success, critical to success on an individual project, and factors that lead to consistently successful projects (corporate success). Regarding project management success, a detailed analysis of 136 European projects isolated correlates to on-time performance and on-cost performance. Several of the on-time correlates were related to risk management, including company-wide education, assigning ownership of risk, maintenance of a risk register, and up-to-date risk management plan. Project duration was also correlated to on-time performance with a recommendation that a project or project stage be limited to 1 year (2002:186). Correlates to on-cost performance included limiting changes to scope "through a mature scope change control process and maintain(ing) the integrity of the performance measurement business (2002:186). In terms of individual project success, Cooke-Davies cites "The existence of an effective benefits delivery and management process that involves the mutual cooperation of project management and line management functions" (2002:188). In his discussion of this factor, Cooke-Davies suggests that the failure to account for benefits (what stakeholders hoped to achieve through the project) may actually be semantically masked or subsumed under project purpose or goals. In any case, the author emphasizes the necessity of PM and Operations Management cooperation. Finally, at the corporate success level, critical success factors included:

- portfolio management practices that thoughtfully apportion enterprise resources across projects in a manner that enhances corporate strategy and business objectives
- 'line of sight' feedback on project performance via metrics at the project, program, and portfolio levels
- feedback and education mechanisms that combine explicit and tacit knowledge.

More recently, research by Fortune and White formalize the "framing of project critical success factors by a systems model" (2006). Following a review of 63 articles offering lists of variables described as critical success factors, Fortune and White developed a formal systems model that included 60 different individual factors. Advantages noted to the systems approach included the ability to measure relationships between factors and the recognition of the process as dynamic rather than static. The authors concluded that the ability of the Formal Systems Model to distinguish between successful and unsuccessful projects "can facilitate the human and organizational aspects of systems development projects… if used in planning and implementation phases" (2006:63).

Emphasizing the impact of organizational characteristics on project success in recent scholarship, three examples are reviewed as illustrative and informative of macro level, empirical research. Gray, interviewed 44 project management professionals representing 17 nationally recognized UK organizations across 7 industry sectors (2001). Among the findings, Gray states that an organizational climate characterized by open communication, participation in goal definition , and innovation engenders project success. Conversely, "project success is shown to decline as the level of personal and environmental threat perceived by project staff increases" (2001:103). Gemunden, et al. collected data from project management professionals in a sample of 104 companies to ascertain the "influence of project autonomy on project success" (2005). More specifically, autonomy was operationalized as Structural (Organizational Separation and Reporting Level), Resource (Size of Resource Base and Freedom of Using Resources), and Social (was team co-located or not). Project success was operationalized via an assessment of the iron triangle across multiple project stages, as well as separate measures representing internal success and external success. In each of these operationalizations, respondents evaluated project performance on Likert-scales in relation to their specific goals (2005:370). Results of the authors' analysis suggest that only one variable coming from the organization behavior tradition is significantly related to project success—co-location of teams (2005:371). Research by Agarwal and Rathod (2006) begins with the premise that different success criteria emerge depending on whether one adopts an internal or external focus. Specifically, they mention time, cost and scope attainment as illustrative of internal concerns, whereas a characteristic such as customer satisfaction would likely be emphasized if one adopted an external focus. Limiting their sample to three groups of internal stakeholders (Programmers/Developers, Project Managers, and Customer Account Managers), the researchers were interested in determining the extent of unanimity regarding the enumeration of criteria for success and the importance assigned to these criteria across three different internal constituencies. Analysis yielded surprising consistency across the groups with scope attainment (specifically, functionality) selected as the most critical success factor by all three internal groups and cost the least critical to success.

As noted in a comprehensive review of project success scholarship, Jugdev and Muller suggest that by the 21st century the emphasis was on an acknowledgement of the strategic import of project management, specifically a commitment by senior management to provide "the vision, strategy, and sponsorship....throughout—not just at the start" (2005:28). Additionally, several external factors were thought to have an impact upon project success. This list included forces as removed from the boardroom as politics and economy, as well as some closer to home, such as client, and subcontractors. Termed four necessary, but not sufficient, conditions for project success, Jugdev and Muller suggest:

1. Success criteria should be agreed on with the stakeholders before the start of the project and repeated at review points throughout the project.
2. A collaborative working relationship should be maintained between the project owner (or sponsor) and project manager, with both viewing the project as a partnership.
3. The project manager should be empowered with flexibility to deal with unforeseen circumstances , and with the owner giving guidance.
4. The owner should take an interest in the performance of the project (2005:28).

It is clear from the above that communication and collaboration between the project owner and the project manager are integral to success in the current project management environment. This suggests there is a need for hands-on knowledge and participation by all stakeholders throughout the project. Thus, one outcome of the acknowledgement of project management's strategic import has been to shorten overall project duration and adapt an iterative, evolutionary methodology.

Project Duration. Job security/longevity aside, today's economy is all about quick turnaround. The PM or team member perceived as attempting to prolong or extend a task without merit is deemed the proverbial albatross around the neck—the organization can't jettison him/her too quickly. The emphasis on expediency, on staged intermediate deliverables, is a hallmark within current project management best practices. As examples, consider the titles of two chapters in Larson and Gray's forthcoming *Project management: the managerial process* (2011): "Reducing Project Duration" and "Agile Project Management." Add to these the myriad articles (e.g., Gale 2010, Scott 2009, Swager 2010) and blogs (e.g., TechRepublic 2010, Arras 2010) that tout the merits of 'shorter is better.'

Clearly, both academics and practitioners accept the ubiquity of small (short) is beautiful in project management circles.

While each organization may present unique constraints as well as opportunities, the standard justifications given for a shorter project might include:

- decreased product to market time
- truncated timeframe for subsequent tasks due to earlier unforeseen delays
- incentive contracts
- imposed deadlines
- high overhead costs
- the need to reassign human and equipment resources (Larson and Gray, 2011).

Not surprisingly, traditional PM methodologies are a less than optimal template to employ when pursuing projects of short duration. Whereas the various waterfall approaches are predicated on an assumption that requirements are generally static, agile methodologies were created to be able to respond in dynamic environments. Fortunately, there are many 'agile' methodologies available that are specifically designed to facilitate successful completion of the short project. The general agile process relies on incremental, iterative development cycles. In essence, each iteration is a project. Furthermore, the agile iteration is significantly shorter than previous iterative methods. The agile environment is, by definition, a highly collaborative environment where all constituencies check-in at various points in each development cycle. Thus, the likelihood for timely input, course corrections, and information exchange is enhanced.

Despite the many potential advantages to adopting a shorter project duration, it's important to note that inherent risks remain in the project environment. The primary advantage when considering risk is that shorter timeframes engender frequent, close scrutiny of tasks. This reality results in quicker awareness of risks or threats and frequently affords the PM team a better vantage point for negotiating a successful solution. Other caveats regarding the use of agile management methods affect progress status, team size, and expertise. More specifically, the integrative and iterative nature of agile methods make it difficult to give a precise response to an executive's query on, "Where are we?" The more traditional methodologies allowed for a response such as, "The design phase is completed." or "The testing phase is completed." Status updates within the agile methods milieu take a little more explanation. Regarding team size, it should mirror the project duration, i.e., smaller (to medium) is better. Finally, conventional wisdom is that agile development requires individuals with higher than average skill and motivation (Sanjay 2005).

Stevenson and Starkweather Study (2010)

In a 2-year study by Stevenson and Starkweather (2010), IT project success rates were measured across companies throughout the United States. The specific focus of the study was two-fold – 1) to identify those project management characteristics or competencies that IT executives found to be indicative of successful project managers and 2) to identify which measures of project success were found to contribute most to overall project success.

The study was constructed in two phases, the first of which sought to identify those project manager characteristics that recruiters deemed critical to satisfy their corporate client needs. The second phase sought to identify corporate executive's preference of these recruiter-selected core characteristics, as well as identify those measures of project success most important to success rates in their organizations.

Phase 1

The primary goal of the first phase of this study was to identify a stable set of hiring criteria that front-line recruiters looked for when trying to satisfy corporate recruiting requirements. In an attempt to establish survey content validity and consistency, personal recruiter contacts were first interviewed by phone. As preliminary responses indicated a strong degree of rigor and coherence, 375 IT recruiters were then sampled from Oya's Recruiting List and various online recruiting listing agencies nationwide, equally distributed across all geographic regions, as identified by the U.S. Census Bureau. Each recruiter was asked, through a series of open-ended questions, to indicate what hiring criteria their corporate counterparts required and valued most when hiring a PM applicant. Out of the 375 recruiters sampled, 32 responded, identifying 15 hiring criteria that were most valued by their corporate counterparts.

Phase 2

The focus of the second phase of this study was to ascertain the agreement to which corporate executives valued the hiring criteria identified by the independent recruiters in our sample. A 32-item questionnaire was mailed to 3,258 IT managers and executives that were selected from a Dunn and Bradstreet dataset, and screened for mid sized firms with over 750 employees. Of the 3,258 questionnaires mailed, 84 were returned. As this mailing coincided with the November, 2009 economic downturn, it was not surprising to experience such a low response rate. Despite the low number of returns, however, those 84 firms that responded were highly representative of the sampling population. 80 of these questionnaires were deemed useable.

The questionnaire itself was divided into 3 major sections, the first dealing with demographics, where questions were asked regarding age, years with the company, years in the IT profession, workforce composition, average project revenues, budget allocations, and PMP Certification, among others. The second section asked executives to rank the 15 hiring criteria that recruiters identified in Phase 1, on a 7-point Likert scale, and the third section, which is the focus of this article, asked IT managers and executives to identify, on a 10-point Likert scale, the degree to which respondents experienced project success as measured by the following project success factors:

- Client/User Satisfaction
- Cost/Within Budget
- On Schedule
- Quality/Met Technical Specs
- Quality/ Met Client-Defined Business Requirements

While a variety of IT success factors have been identified over the years, these five factors remain at the core of measuring IT project success.

Analysis

In preliminary analysis, sample demographics indicated a high level of consistency with population demographics, in that 81% of the respondents were male, as compared to 73% for the population, and 23.8% of the respondents held the title of CIO, as compared to 23% of the population. It did appear, however, that fewer IT managers were represented in this sample (38%), as compared to 56% for the population. Other sample data indicated that 43% of the respondents had been employed by their current company for 5-14 years, while 47.5% of the respondents had been active in the IT industry for 25 years or more. The majority of the respondents were 51 years of age or older (58%).

Table 1 indicates the industries that were represented in this sample. As indicated, 35% of the respondents were employed in the Health Care industry, with 21.3% in Manufacturing and 12.5% employed in Public Administration.

Table 1. Industry Representation in IT Sample.

Industry	n	%
Health Services	28	35.0
Manufacturing	17	21.2
Public Administration	10	12.5
Misc. Other	24	30.0

A major objective of this study was to determine the level of IT project success that respondents experienced, as measured by the success factors of Cost, On Schedule, Quality1 – Meeting Tech Specs, Quality2 – Meeting Client-Defined Business Requirements, and Client/User Satisfaction. Table 2 indicates these results.

Table 2. Percent of Project Success Across IT Success Factors.

% of Successful Projects	Cost/Within Budget	On Schedule	Quality1-Met Tech Specs	Quality2 – Met Client-Defined Business Requirements	Client/User Satisfaction
10-19%	1.2	3.8	1.2	1.2	0.0
29-29%	1.2	5.0	0.0	0.0	3.8
30-39%	6.2	1.4	2.5	2.5	2.5
40-49%	3.8	1.4	3.8	2.5	0.0
50-59%	8.8	13.8	5.0	2.5	3.8
60-69%	2.5	8.8	3.8	8.8	6.2
70-79%	23.8	16.2	16.2	17.5	17.5
80-89%	20.0	25.0	28.8	26.2	32.5
>=90%	25.0	17.5	31.2	31.2	27.5

Contrary to current literature proclamations of high IT project failure rates, the majority of the respondents in this study indicated a relatively high level of experienced project success, as measured by the core success factors of Cost, On Schedule, Quality 1 – Met Tech Specs, Quality2 – Met Client-Defined Business Requirements and Client/User Satisfaction. Specifically, 71.2% of all respondents indicated that they experienced a 70% success rate or better, across these success factors. Of particular note, is the fact that nearly one third of the respondents indicated a 90% or greater project success rate, when measured by the two Quality success factors - meeting technical specifications and client-defined business requirements, at 31.2 % respectively. In an attempt to further understand and delineate these somewhat unexpected findings in our current economic downturn, the effect of project duration on project success rates was investigated. Given that 71.2% of respondents indicated a project success rate of 70% or higher, the original "% of Project Success" scale was aggregated into two categories: "70-80%" and ">=90%" for further analysis. To identify average project duration in this study, respondents were presented with four categories to select from: "< 6 months", "6 months to a year" "1 to 3 years" and "> 3 years". Table 3 presents the initial frequencies.

Table 3. Average Duration of Projects.

Project Duration	n	Percent
< 6 months	22	27.5
6 months – 1 yr.	42	52.5
1 – 3 yrs.	14	17.5
> 3 yrs.	2	2.5

As is clear from this distribution, 97.5% of the respondents indicated that their organizations focused on projects with durations of 3 years or less, with only 2 out of 80 respondents stating that their companies focused on long term projects of greater than 3 years. . Given this fact, these four categories were condensed to three: "< 6 months", "6 months – 1 yr", and "1 – 3 yrs", for further analysis.

The following crosstab analyses shown in Tables 4 – 8 provide some insights to the relationship between project success rates and project duration.

Table 4. Project Duration and Cost/Within Budget Success Factor.

Project Duration	70-80% Project Success Rate (n)	<= 90% Project Success Rate(n)
< 6 months	9	10
6 months – 1 yr.	18	22
1 – 3 yrs.	11	3

It is clear from these data that those projects that are more short term in nature (under 1 year), experience higher levels of project success, as measured by the Cost success factor. The implication here is that those projects under one year in duration are perhaps easier to manage or to adjust to budget or cost changes as they appear. According to this data, projects over one year experience significantly less success than those shorter term projects. The Chi Square statistic indicated significance at the .09 level.

Table 5. Project Duration and On Schedule Success Factor.

Project Duration	70-80% Project Success Rate (n)	<= 90% Project Success Rate (n)
< 6 months	9	10
6 months – 1 yr.	18	22
1 – 3 yrs.	13	2

Again, it is clear from these data that shorter projects are associated with a higher incidence of project success for the "On Schedule" success factor. Significant at the .02 level, the disparity is clear, between success rates for those projects for over one year in duration. As "On Schedule" measures project scope, it is no surprise that short term projects would be easier to manage and forestall any significant scope creep that is so prevalent in long term projects.

Table 6. Project Duration and Quality1 – Meeting Technical Specs.

Project Duration	70-80% Project Success Rate (n)	<= 90% Project Success Rate (n)
< 6 months	8	12
6 months – 1 yr.	9	30
1 – 3 yrs.	9	6

Of particular note in this presentation is the significantly increased success rate for those mid range projects with durations from 6 months to one year, as measured by "Quality1 – Meeting Technical Requirements". This suggests that perhaps there is some minimum timeline to establish and test technical requirements that cannot be achieved in very short term projects. This data was significant at the .03 level.

Table 7. Project Duration and Quality2 – Meeting Client-Defined Business Requirements.

Project Duration	70-80% Project Success Rate (n)	<= 90% Project Success Rate (n)
< 6 months	6	14
6 months – 1 yr.	12	27
1 – 3 yrs.	10	5

Again, the data in Table 7 above show, at the .04 significance level, that respondents stated that projects with durations of 6 months to 1 year experience more project success than longer term projects, based on the "Quality2 – Meeting Client-Defined Business Requirements" success factor.

Table 8. Project Duration and Client/User Satisfaction.

Project Duration	70-80% Project Success Rate (n)	<= 90% Project Success Rate (n)
< 6 months	6	14
6 months – 1 yr.	14	26
1 – 3 yrs.	7	8

Of the five success criteria that were analyzed in the presence of project duration, "Client/User Satisfaction" is the only criteria that was unaffected by the duration variable (significant at the .59 level). While it is apparent that shorter term projects were still preferred, it appears that project length was not significantly critical to client or user satisfaction.

When reviewing the results of these 5 tables, it is clear that in each case, no matter which success factor was present, respondents overwhelmingly stated that their companies preferred shorter term projects, no longer than one year in duration. The most significant relationships found between the success factors and length of project was at the .02, .03 and .04 levels, for "On Schedule", "Quality1 – Met Technical Requirements" and "Quality2 – Met Client-Defined Business Requirements, respectively.

To ascertain whether this preference for shorter term projects differed by industry, a crosstab analysis was performed and the results are presented in Table 9 below.

Table 9. Project Duration by Industry (n).

Industry	Project Duration: < 6 months	Project Duration: 6 months – 1 yr.	Project Duration: 1 – 3 yrs
Health Care	6	18	4
Manufacturing	9	8	0
Public Admin	0	4	6
Misc Other	7	12	5
Total	22	42	15

These data clearly seem to support the previous data in the overall tendency toward a preference for shorter term projects by those respondents in this study. Only those firms in the Public Administration sector appeared to engage in longer term projects, of one to three years in duration. Given the nature of this sector, federal funding cycles and personal experience, this is not surprising. Conversely, firms in the manufacturing sector seemed to prefer the shortest of projects, under six months in duration. As manufacturing has been hit hard in this economic downturn, it seems highly practical to shorten project lifecycles, minimize scope creep and increase accountability with shorter project durations.

CONCLUSION

Measuring project success has been a critical component of project management for decades. Whether in economic downturns or upswings, it is the most significant benchmark by which the project management industry judges itself -- it's value in terms of personal productivity and contribution to the overall success of a corporation. A myriad of project success measurements or factors have emerged throughout the years, ranging from the basic Iron Triangle of cost, scope and meeting technical specifications, to more sophisticated criteria measuring those factors that are most associated with success, dependent on the particular phase of the project analyzed. Regardless of the measures used, the overall objective remains the same: to increase project success.

As Larson and Gray (2011) note, the IT industry itself has been specifically plagued with low project success rates, 32% in 2009, even as that is an improvement over recent years. It is clear, from this evidence, that the search for those criteria that contribute most to project success will continue.

The Stevenson and Starkweather (2010) study sought to identify success rates of IT projects in a variety of companies across the United States based on five success criteria: Cost, On Schedule, Met Technical Requirements, Met Client-Defined Business Requirements and Client/User Satisfaction. Initial results showed that 71.2% of respondents indicated that their companies experience a 70% project success rate or better across all five success factors and a 90% or better success rate for those projects measured by "Met Technical Requirements" and "Met Client-Defined Business Requirements". This result is clearly counter to the 2009 CHAOS Summary Report project success statistic of 32%. Even more surprising, is that the respondents of this study reported such high success rates in the midst of one of this country's most significant economic downturns since the Great Depression. One would expect failure rates to increase significantly during this time, as project funding suffers, resource commitments waver and companies become less tolerant of risk.

In search of answers to this unexpected finding, other criteria were analyzed in this study, to shed light on the unusually high success rates. In recent years, one trend in project management has been to reduce project length to shorter, more measurable and accountable projects, in an effort to increase project success. The respondents of this study support that trend with 97.5% of the respondents indicating that their organizations focused on projects with durations of 3 years or less, with 52.5% of respondents stating that the most common project duration in their organizations was 6 months to 1 year . When the "Project Duration" variable in this study was then analyzed in terms of its impact on project success, the results were clear – a significant relationship emerged between project success and short term projects of less than one year, as measured by three success factors: "On Schedule", "Quality1 – Met Technical Requirements" and "Quality2 – Met Client-Defined Business Requirements. The implications of this result suggest that the shorter the project, the easier it is to keep on schedule, meet client specs as defined in smaller, more manageable chunks, and meet technical requirements. The one factor that was unaffected by project duration was "Client/User Satisfaction", which suggests that respondents believed that their companies would deliver a quality product that would satisfy their customers regardless of the length of the project.

While the data from this study clearly make a case for the implementation of short term projects, given the higher than average project success rates reported, it also serves to affirm a litany of previous studies that promote shorter term agile project methodologies, where the focus is on a series of short iterative project development cycles that produce a series of deliverables that increase accountability, control scope creep and reduce risk, and, hence, increase the chance of project success.

Whether challenged by economic downturns, or enjoying the excesses of economic upswings, the project management discipline will continue to search for answers on how to increase project success rates. Whether through investigating the effects of different success criteria in various combinations, or determining the impact that project manager characteristics have on particular types of projects, or analyzing the effect that project length has on success rates – the goal remains the same: increase project success and, hence, corporate success.

REFERENCES

[1] Agarwal, N. & U. Rathod. (2006). "Defining 'success' for software projects: *An exploratory revelation*." IJPM 24 , 358-370.

[2] Arras People. "*How to Manage a Camel – The Project Management and Recruitment Blog*." http://projectcentric.co.uk

[3] Belassi, W. & Tukel. O. I. (1996). "A new framework for determining critical success/failure factors in projects." *IJPM*, *14*, 141-151.

[4] Belout, A. & Gauvreau, C. (2004). "Factors influencing project success: the impact of human resource management." *IJPM*, *22*, 1-11.

[5] Belout, A. (1998). "Effects of human resource management on project effectiveness and success: toward a new conceptual framework." *IJPM*, *16*, 21-26.

[6] Belzer, K. (2001). "*Project management*: *Still more art than science*." A paper. 1-6. Retrieved from http://www.pmforum.org/library/papers/2001/ArtthanScience.pdf

[7] Cooke-Davies, T. (2002). "The 'real' success factors on projects." *IJPM*, *20*, 185-190.

[8] Fortune, J. & White, D. (2006). "Framing of project critical success factors by a systems model." *IJPM*, 24, 53-65.

[9] Gale, S. F. (2010). "*The bigger picture*. PM Network Trend Report." PM Network. May.

[10] Gemunden, H. G., Salomo, S. & Krieger. A. (2005). "The influence of project autonomy on project success." *IJPM*, *23*, 366-373.

[11] Gray, R. J. (2001). "Organisational climate and project success." *IJPM*, *19*, 103-109.

[12] Jugdev, K. & Muller, R. (2005). "A retrospective look at our evolving understanding of project success." *Project Management Journal*, *36*, 19-31.

[13] Larson, E. W. & Gray, C. F. (2011). *Project management: the managerial process*. 5th Ed., NY: McGraw-Hill/Irwin.

[14] Lee-Kelley, L. K. Leong, & Loong, (2003). "Turner's five functions of project-based management and situational leadership in IT services projects. *IJPM*, *21*, 583-591.

[15] Morris, P. W. G. & Hough, G. (1987). *The anatomy of major projects: A study of the reality of project management*. Chichester, UK: Wiley.

[16] Pinto, J. K. & Prescott, J. E. (1988). "Variations in critical success factors over the stages in the project life cycle." *Journal of Management*, 1988, *14*, 5-18.

[17] Sanjay, A. V. "*Overview of agile management and development methods*." Retrieved 3/15/2010: www.projectperfect.com.au

[18] Scott, L. A. "How to maximize short term project management contracts." Retrieved 3/1/2010: http://projectcentric.co.uk/how_to_manage_a_camel/projectmanagement

[19] Slevin, D. P. & Pinto, J. K. (1986). "The project implementation profile: New tool for project managers." *Project Management Journal*, *18*, 57-71.

[20] Stevenson, D. & Starkweather, J. (2010). "PM critical competency index: IT execs prefer soft skills." *IJPM*, *28*, forthcoming.

[21] Swager, E. (2010). "*No small task*: *Project management isn't just for big corporations and their flashy megaprojects*." PM Network. May 26-27.

[22] Turner, J. R. & Muller, R. (2005). "The project manager's leadership style as a success factor on projects: A literature review. *Project Management Journal*, *37*, 49-61.

[23] Turner, J. R. (1993). *The Handbook of Project-based Management*. NY: McGraw-Hill.

[24] Wateridge, J. (1995). "IT projects: A basis for success." *IJPM*, *13*, 169-172.

[25] Wateridge, J. (1998). "How can IS/IT projects be measured for success?" *IJPM*, *16*, 59-63.

In: Project Management
Editor: Robert J. Collins, pp. 137-152
ISBN: 978-1-61761-460-6
© 2011 Nova Science Publishers, Inc.

Chapter 5

MEASURING STRATEGIC ICT ADOPTION FOR BUILDING PROJECT MANAGEMENT

Vanita Ahuja[1*], Jay Yang[2] and Ravi Shankar[3]
[1]Project Management Consultant, New Delhi, India, 204, Sector-A, Pocket – C, Vasant Kunj, New Delhi, India, 110070
[2]Professor, Faculty of Built Environment and Engineering, Queensland University of Technology, Brisbane, Australia
[3]Professor, Dept. of Management Studies, Indian Institute of Technology Delhi, New Delhi, India

ABSTRACT

Building project management requires real time information systems and in present scenario required information systems can be achieved by effective use of Information Communication Technologies [ICT] at the industry level. This chapter reports a benchmarking framework developed to rate the construction organizations for their ICT adoption for building project management, administration of its first phase comprising rating of organizations and through Data Envelopment Analysis measurement of their efficiency in implementing strategic adoption of ICT for building project management. Data analysis leads to the development of a model for defining a 'Best Practice Organization' for ICT adoption for building project management.

Keywords: ICT, building project management, benchmarking, data envelopment analysis

INTRODUCTION

Building project management information systems are measured by the effectiveness of all project team agencies to communicate with and feedback to the rest of the project team

* Corresponding author: Email: vanita_ahuja@yahoo.com, +91 9811472372.

throughout the project life-cycle. In present scenario when project team members are geographically separated, such information systems can be achieved by the project teams through ICT adoption. People, who are a part of different project team organizations, manage projects and the project team organizations are a part of the construction industry. Also, at any given time, each construction organization is involved in multiple projects or is a part of multiple supply chains. Thus, effective adoption of ICT for building project management requires improvement of the system in the whole industry.

Measurement is one of the first steps in any improvement process [Lee, Thomas and Tucker, 2005]. So, to strategically increase effective adoption of ICT in the construction industry, a system of evaluation of the ICT based Information Systems [IS] is required to be developed. But, researchers have serious doubts about the efficacy of using traditional capital investment appraisal techniques for the appraisal of ICT adoption and a multi-layer evaluation process is suggested [Milis and Mercken, 2004]. This chapter utilizes benchmarking and Data Envelopment Analysis [DEA] technique for measuring strategic adoption of ICT by the construction industry for building project management.

Slow adoption of ICT in the construction industry is due to a number of historical, industrial and market forces that perpetuate the industry's culture, thus affecting the extent of ICT adoption in day-to-day business processes [Baldwin, Thorpe and Carter, 1999] and the issues for slow adoption can be categorized as technical, managerial, cultural and socio/political due to differing perceptions of project team members. The requirement is to match technological innovation with the perceived needs and preparedness for change on the part of the industry [Weippert and Kajewski, 2004].

The objective of the research study discussed in this chapter is to provide construction organizations with a generic benchmarking framework to assess their extent of ICT adoption for building project management processes and to measure their efficiency in implementing their strategies for ICT adoption. The developed framework is also applicable at the industry level for rating the construction organizations for ICT adoption and performance measurement in this context.

In construction industry, majority of the organizations can be categorized as Small and Medium enterprises [SMEs] [Dainty, Briscoe and Millett, 2001; Hegazy and Ersahin, 2001; Love, Irani and Edwards, 2004; Ribeiro and Lopes, 2002] and constitute important component of the project supply chains. Thus, the research discussed in this chapter is focused on measurement of ICT adoption for building project management by SMEs.

The chapter discusses the adopted research methodology, introduction of Data Envelopment Analysis [DEA] technique and the developed Benchmarking Framework. It further leads to the detailed discussion on Benchmarking Framework administration in the construction industry including performance measurement of organizations for strategic adoption of ICT for building project management conducted through DEA.

RESEARCH METHODOLOGY

The study focused on ICT adoption by SMEs in the construction industry and with respect to SMEs it is important to understand the processes, their indicators and measures in the local context and this research studied issues with respect to the Indian construction industry. Based on the literature review, for the research study, an SME is defined as an organization with its number of staff upto 250.

The research utilized a sequential mixed methods approach focused on collecting and analyzing both quantitative and qualitative data in a sequential manner. Factors affecting ICT adoption for building project management are the research variables and were identified through extensive literature survey. A questionnaire survey [quantitative analysis] was conducted in the Indian Construction Industry to examine the current practices of ICT adoption for building project management in the Indian construction industry, to test the hypotheses formulated in the research and to identify the issues that required further study [Ahuja et al., 2009].

Questionnaire survey data analysis led to the development of a benchmarking framework for rating construction organizations for ICT adoption for building project management. The developed framework is discussed in detail in a supporting paper by the authors [Ahuja et al., 2010a]. The structure of the framework is discussed briefly in the subsequent sections.

Benchmarking framework administration and finalization included Semi-structured interview survey data collection and analysis including Data Envelopment Analysis [quantitative and qualitative method]; and Case Studies analysis conducted by SAP [Situation-Actor-Processes] –LAP [Learning-Action-Performance] analysis [qualitative method] leading to synthesis of the results of all the stages of research [Ahuja et al., 2010b]. Such sequential mixed methods approach helped in establishing ICT adoption status and trends at industry level, followed up with study of research variables at the level of organization and projects to probe, explore and validate the results in more depth.

DATA ENVELOPMENT ANALYSIS TECHNIQUE [DEA]

DEA is a data-oriented [Li et al., 2005], non-parametric methodology based upon Input-Output system [Chiang, Cheng and Tang, 2006] and utilizes the application of linear programming. It is used for measuring the performance efficiency of organizational units, which are termed as Decision-Making Units [DMUs] and aims to measure how efficiently a DMU uses the resources available to generate a set of outputs [Charnes, Cooper and Rhodes, 1978]. DMUs can include manufacturing units, departments of big organizations, a set of organizations or even practicing individuals and can also be systems such as scenarios, options, etc. [Chiang, Cheng and Tang, 2006]. Most of these DMUs are those where the measurement of performance efficiency is difficult [Ramanathan, 2003]. DEA has been successfully employed for assessing the relative performance of a set of DMUs that use a variety of identical inputs to produce a variety of identical outputs.

In DEA, the performance of DMUs is assessed using the concept of efficiency or productivity, which is the ratio of the total outputs to the total inputs. Efficiency can range from 0-1. For such a comparison to occur, **a set of criteria must be established, which have to be classified as inputs and outputs** [Cooper, Park and Pastor, 1999]. The efficiencies estimated using DEA are relative i.e relative to the best performing DMU[s]. The best performing DMU is assigned an efficiency score of unity or 100% and the performance of other DMUs varies between 0-100% relative to this best performance. Functional specifications are avoided in expressing production relationships between inputs and outputs

[Li et al., 2005]. If all the DMUs operate in a similar environment, it is realistic to measure performance of the studied DMUs with that of the best DMU [Ramanathan, 2003].

The analysis can be conducted mathematically as well as graphically. The DEA analysis checks whether the DMU under consideration could improve its performance by decreasing its input and increasing its output. A DMU which cannot improve its performance is efficient or non-dominated. The analysis does not reflect that the performance of the best performing DMU[s] cannot be improved. It may or may not be possible. These are the best DMU[s] with regard to the data used for analysis [Ramanathan, 2003]. The performance of all the other DMUs is assessed in relation to this best achieved performance. Thus, relative efficiencies are calculated based on the data available and not as absolute efficiencies.

DEA has been applied to various areas of efficiency evaluation [Chen, 2003; Zhu, 2002] such as: health care [hospitals, doctors], education [schools, universities], banks, manufacturing, **benchmarking**, management evaluation, fast food restaurants, retail stores [DEA Homepage, 1996], defense bases [army, navy, air force], tax offices, prisons, non-profit making organizations, etc. [DEA Notes].

It has been discussed that exploring the role of the construction sector in terms of the consumptions and inputs may help formulate strategies to maximize construction productivity [Chiang, Tang and Leung, 2001; Ganesan, Hall and Chaing, 1996]. With respect to the construction research: Lacouture, Medaglia and Skibniewski [2007] have discussed a DEA based tool for optimizing purchasing decisions in B2B construction marketplaces; Chiang, Cheng and Tang [2006] have examined repercussions of consumptions and inputs placed on the construction sector by the use of Input–Output tables and DEA; Cheng and Li [2004] have applied DEA to evaluate a set of locations for construction projects; Chiang, Cheng and Tang [2006] and Li et al. [2005] have applied DEA in a longitudinal study of the measurement of productivity of Chinese construction industry; and Anderson et al. [1998] have applied DEA to measure efficiency of franchising in the residential real estate brokerage market.

In the research study reported in this chapter, DEA has been conducted using 'Frontier Analyst' software developed by University of Warwick and Banxia Software Ltd. UK. It helped in measurement of the efficiency of organizations in implementing their strategies for the adoption of ICT.

Developed Benchmarking Framework

The developed Benchmarking framework includes eight measurement indicators [MIs]. Each indicator is measured by one or more performance measures derived from the questionnaire, as the questionnaire survey data analysis provided the validity, relevance and significance of these performance measures. The measures have their own metrics, data sources and minimum and maximum limits relevant to the industry standards and established after the questionnaire data analysis. The maximum limits of the measures reflect the 'Best Practice' in the Indian Construction industry. Eight MIs forming the Benchmarking framework are categorized as under:

Strategic Indicators

Strategic use of ICT indicator [MI1] measuring present strategic use and long-term strategic goals of the organization with respect to ICT adoption in the organization and measured by 7 performance measures.

Strategic project communication indicator [MI2] measuring strategic planning for use of ICT and communication methodologies for the projects and measured by 4 performance measures.

Measuring benefits of use of ICT indicator [MI3] also a strategic indicator and measuring ICT adoption benefits evaluation initiatives within the organization. Tangible as well as intangible measures are evaluated by 7 performance measures structured in a lead on format.

Use of ICT for General Administration Works Indicators

ICT infrastructure indicator [MI4] measuring ICT infrastructure maturity at an organization's head office and project sites and measured by 15 performance measures.

ICT for general administration indicator [MI5] measuring extent of ICT adoption for general administration within office and with external agencies and measured by 12 performance measures.

Use of ICT for Building Project Management Processes Indicators

ICT for time management [MI6], ICT for cost management [MI7] and ICT for project administration and resource management [MI8] indicators measuring extent of ICT adoption for specific project management processes of time management, cost management and project administration and resource management at different stages of the projects. These indicators are measured by 13, 6 and 11 performance measures respectively.

Benchmarking Process

Causal relationships established between performance indicators after Structural Equation Modeling analysis defined the relative importance of the groups of indicators and led to the establishment of weights for groups of indicator variables and the formula for calculating the rating of organizations at three levels of High, Medium and Low.

The suggested Benchmarking process includes four phases of Benchmarking and BenchMeasurement, BenchLearning, BenchAction and BenchMonitoring.

Benchmarking and BenchMeasurement phase comprises two components:

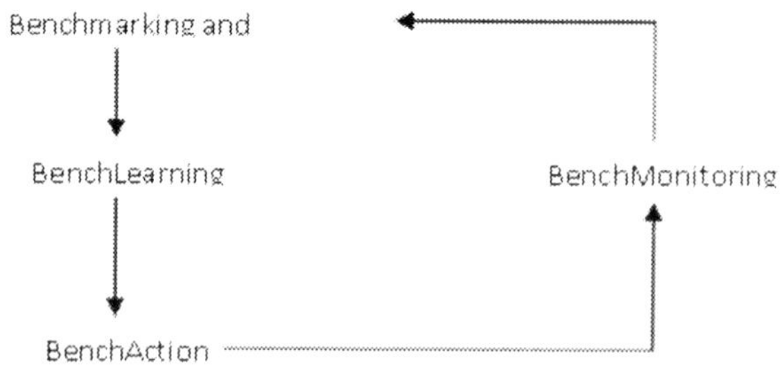

Figure 1. Benchmarking Process.

- Benchmarking for rating the organizations into three levels of low, medium and high and identifying trends and gaps in practices in the industry.
- BenchMeasurement to measure the efficiency of organizations in implementing their strategies for ICT adoption for building project management and conducted through 'Data Envelopment Analysis' [DEA] technique.

BenchLearning would include qualitative study of results of BenchMeasurement incorporating study of gaps in practices and trends identified at the Benchmarking stage. It would be conducted through case study analysis for each organization under study. SAP [situation-actor-processes] – LAP [learning-action-performance] framework for research enquiry is suggested for case study analysis. BenchLearning would suggest actions to overcome the trends, gaps in practice and other identified issues. These actions would form a component of the BenchAction stage. Accordingly 'BenchMonitoring' stage includes periodic Benchmarking and BenchMeasurement exercise conducted in the organizations followed by BenchLearning and BenchAction. Figure 1 schematically shows the developed Benchmarking process.

Benchmarking and BenchMeasurement Administration

Benchmarked Organizations

One organization from each group of the surveyed organizations i.e Builders, Project Management Consultancy Organizations and Architectural Organizations was selected for benchmarking framework administration and finalization. Organizations with higher ICT adoption were selected and approached. A semi-structured interview was conducted for benchmarking or measurement of ICT adoption by these organizations for building project management processes and measurement of the efficiency of the organizations for implementing their strategies for ICT adoption. Selecting organizations from the previous respondents helped in providing continuity to the research. Introduction of the three organizations is given below. But, their names are not disclosed for the purpose of confidentiality.

Builders [BO]

The studied Builders organization is based in New Delhi, India with a branch office in another metropolitan city of India. It was setup in 1971 as a contracting organization executing soil testing and piling works. In 1978, the organization started building construction and in 1984 the real estate division of the organization was started. Organization's expertise is in construction and development of residential projects. Recently it has also started construction of commercial buildings. It is headed by a chairman, two managing directors and its staff strength including the administrative staff is upto 240. The staff strength has recently increased due to the boom in the construction activity in the country. An in-house project management group manages projects. But, architectural services and most of the construction work are outsourced. It is an ISO certified organization and regular audits are conducted with respect to this certification. The value of each project executed by the organization ranges between INR 100 crores to INR 300 crores [approx. US$ 25 million to US$ 75 million] and turnover of the organization is about INR 8 crores [approx. US$ 2 million].

Project Management Consultancy Organization [PMCO]

The studied Building Project Management Consultancy organization is based in New Delhi, India. It was setup in 1995. The organization has managed a vast range of projects: from institutional buildings, commercial building to townships. It is headed by a managing director and has around 75 technical staff including the staff at project sites. A trained cadre of administrative staff supports the administrative work. At the time of data collection, the organization was planning to expand and it was envisaged that by 2008 the technical staff strength would be doubled. Specialized works are outsourced to consultants. But, for maintaining the quality and timely completion of work, maximum work is done inhouse. It has been awarded ISO certification for 'construction project management' and regular audits are conducted with respect to this certification. The value of each project executed by the organization ranges between INR 50 crores to INR 100 crores [approx. US$ 12.5 million to US$ 25 million] and turnover of the organization is between INR 2 crores to INR 4 crores [approx. US$ 0.5 million to US$ 1 million].

Architectural Organization [AO]

The studied Architectural organization is based in New Delhi, India with a branch office in another metropolitan city of India. It was set up in 1987. The organization specializes in designing and managing institutional buildings, cultural centers and commercial interiors. It also executes commercial interiors as a turnkey agency. The staff in each branch office includes 2 principals, a project architect, 2 draughtsmen, a site engineer and the administrative staff. A site engineer is also posted at each project site. Most of the specialized work is outsourced to consultants. The organization collaborates with a regular team of consultants, but sometimes new consultants are also included in the project team at clients' reference. The value of each project executed by the organization ranges between INR 4 crores to INR 50 crores [approx. US$ 1 million to US$ 12.5 million] and turnover of the organization is upto INR 2 crores [approx. US$ 0.5 million].

Benchmarking

With reference to the developed Benchmarking framework, all the three organizations are in the middle level rating with PMCO having the highest ranking and AO the lowest. Comparison of performance measurement values of the three organizations for all the MIs as discussed below helped in the identification of gaps in practices.

MI1 - Strategic use of ICT

All the three organizations except AO had a strategy for use of ICT within the organization and all the three organizations had a disaster recovery plan in case of breakdown of IT infrastructure. With respect to strategic planning for adopting higher technology: all the three organizations either plan to adopt intranet within next 0-5 years or already have it installed; BO and PMCO plan to utilize project web sites for project management in next 0-5 years, but AO has no plan of adopting this technology; all the three organizations feel that within next 5-10 years it would be viable and imperative to adopt videoconferencing. Only BO and PMCO provide training to their employees for updated IT infrastructure and use of ICT and all the three organizations either have an in-house IT department or take services of IT consultants for planning, implementing and maintaining IT systems.

MI2 - Strategic project communication

All the three organizations strategically plan for project communications in terms of report formats, periodicity of reports and periodicity of meetings to be conducted during the project execution. But, only PMCO implements and regulates required and uniform ICT adoption by project agencies through project scope.

With respect to the MI ‘Strategic project communication’ PMCO reflects best practice for the industry.

MI3 - Measuring benefits of use of ICT

All the three organizations measure benefits of use of ICT. But, it is subjective or qualitative measurement and not quantitative measurement. All the three organizations assess benefits with respect to project success. Only PMCO assesses benefits with respect to effective team management, AO assesses benefits of effective use of technology and all the three organizations assess benefits with respect to increased organizational efficiency. Thus, project success and increased organizational efficiency are considered as important areas by all the three organizations.

MI4 - ICT infrastructure

In all the three organizations more than 90% of office staff has access to computers. In BO and PMCO 45%-90% of site staff has access to computers. As indicated earlier also in MI1, none of the organizations utilize project web sites for project management. AO does not have a centralized database and only BO has intranet facility in the organization. All the organizations have Internet connection at project sites, LAN connection in office, use of MS Office for general administration works at office and at sites and adobe acrobat reader installed in office computers. Only BO has adobe acrobat reader installed in computers at project sites. BO and PMCO keep backup of electronic data in storage disks as well as external/internal hard disk, but AO keeps it only in storage disks. In all the three organizations, portable communication technology being utilized is only mobile phone.

Issues of project web sites and intranet facility have been included in MI1 as well as MI4 because both the indicators need reference to these issues for complete definition. Thus, such a framework would allow the participants to evaluate their organizations for individual indicators also.

MI5 - ICT for general administration

In all the three organizations majority of the information flow within the office and between office and project sites for general administration is through e-mail and hard copies. With respect to communication between the head office and clients, BO primarily communicates through hard copies, PMCO through e-mails and AO primarily uses a combination of the two methods. With respect to communication between head office and consultants, PMCO again primarily communicates through e-mails, and BO and AO primarily use a combination of the two methods.

In all the three organizations, communication between head office and contractors/material suppliers and other external agencies flows as a combination of e-mails and hard copies. In BO and AO, information from the project sites to other agencies primarily flows through hard copies, but in PMCO it is through a combination of the above discussed methods. In BO, meetings between head office and site staff, between head office and clients and joint meetings between all the agencies are primarily conducted as teleconferences. But in PMCO and AO these are primarily conducted as personal meetings. In all the three organizations meetings between head office and clients and consultants are primarily conducted as personal meetings. AO accesses majority of external information as hard copies, though other two organizations access it through e-sources.

MI6 - ICT for time management

In BO, time schedules of all the project stages and between all the agencies are primarily communicated as e-mails and hard copies. In PMCO trend is the same only for communicating time schedules between head office and clients or consultants. With respect to the communication between head office and project sites or contractors/material suppliers it is primarily through e-mails. In AO also trend is the same as in BO except for some time schedule reports that are communicated primarily as hard copies. Variance analysis reports are primarily communicated as hard copies and e-mails.

MI7 - ICT for cost management

In BO, cost management reports at all the project stages and between all the agencies are primarily communicated as e-mails and hard copies. In PMCO also trend is primarily the same except for the detailed cash flow report to contractors/material suppliers and cost variance reports to clients or consultants. In AO more communication flows through hard copies only.

MI8 - ICT for project administration and resource management

In all the organizations majority of the bids for the project work are received as hard copies, tender meetings and negotiations are primarily conducted as personal meetings and interviews for hiring project staff and majority of design review meetings are conducted as personal meetings. In PMCO and AO design changes are primarily communicated as e-mails, but in BO these are communicated both as e-mails and hard copies. In PMCO, information regarding materials is primarily accessed through e-sources, but in BO and AO as hard copies. In all the organizations, meetings with the material suppliers are primarily conducted as personal meetings and materials management records at sites are primarily prepared in MS Excel or through customized software. For manpower resource management records, trend is the same for BO and PMCO, but in AO these are primarily prepared in MS Word even though MS Excel has more features for analysis of data. In all the three organizations, project documents are primarily stored as hard copies and electronic copies at offices. At project sites, trend remains the same for BO and PMCO, but in AO these are primarily stored as hard copies.

Overall comparison

Comparison of the three organizations with respect to total MI values [Figure 2] shows that for strategic planning indicators [MI1, MI2, MI3], PMCO has the highest value and AO has the lowest. PMCO reflects best practice for 'Strategic project communication' [MI2]. BO is a relatively larger organization as compared to other two organizations but benefit assessment values of BO [MI3] are less as compared to the other two organizations and AO lags in 'Strategic planning for use of ICT' [MI1].

Rating values of three organizations for Strategic indicators [MI1+ MI2+ MI3] could range from [3-24]. Their calculated values are as given below:

BO: 19, PMCO: 21, AO: 16.

Thus, the strategic indicators are leading indicators for PMCO and BO. But, they are lagging indicators for AO.

With respect to indicators measuring use of ICT for general administration works [MI4, MI5], AO is lagging for both the MIs, BO has better IT infrastructure as compared to other two organizations, but PMCO's use of ICT for general administration works is highest. In indicators measuring use of ICT for project management processes, PMCO has the highest values and BO has values a little higher than those of AO.

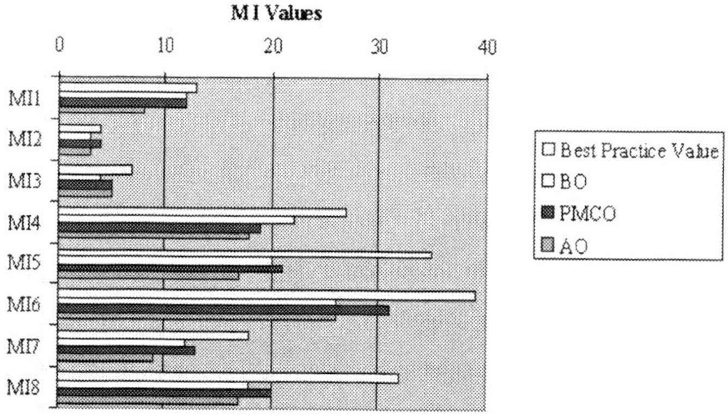

Figure 2. Comparison of measurement indicator values for three organizations.

Rating values of three organizations for two groups of indicators are as given below:

[MI4+MI5]		[MI6+MI7+MI8]	
Range: 18-62		Range: 30-69	
BO:	42	BO:	56
PMCO:	40	PMCO:	64
AO:	35	AO:	52

The analysis shows that the organizations' strategic planning for use of ICT is high, but gap between their use of ICT and the best practice is more. With respect to the best practice, indicators MI4 to MI5 are lagging indicators for all the three organizations and MI6-MI8 are leading indicators for PMCO.

Above analysis identified trends indicating the reasons for less values of use of ICT and gaps in practices for the individual organizations. The reasons for these gaps in practices and trends required qualitative study that constitutes 'BenchLearning' conducted through case study analysis.

BenchMeasurement

Benchmarking showed that inspite of strategically planning for ICT adoption, the organizations were lagging in use of ICT for building project management processes as compared to the best practice in the industry. Thus, the objective of BenchMeasurement was to:

Measure performance of the three benchmarked organizations for efficiently implementing their strategies for use of ICT for building project management.

BenchMeasurement was conducted through 'Data Envelopment Analysis' [DEA] technique. The decision making units [DMUs] were the three benchmarked organizations. Study of causal relationships between the factors affecting ICT adoption helped in identifying first two groups of indicators as inputs and third group as the output as indicated in Table 1. The values and weights of inputs and outputs are derived from the benchmarking framework [Table 1].

Table 1. Inputs and outputs for DEA analysis.

Indicators	Measurement Indicators	Weights
Inputs		
Strategic Indicators	MI1+MI2+MI3	3
Use of ICT for General Administration Works Indicators	MI4+MI5	2
Outputs		
Use of ICT for Building Project Management Processes Indicators	MI6+MI7+MI8	1

Table 2. Data values for three analyzed organizations.

Organization	Strategic Indicators [Input]		Use of ICT for General Admin. Works Indicators [Input]		Use of ICT for Building PM Processes Indicators [Output]	
	Value	Weighted Value	Value	Weighted Value	Value	Weighted Value
Builders [BO]	19	57	42	84	56	56
Project Management Consultancy Organization [PMCO]	21	63	40	80	64	64
Architectural Organization [AO]	16	48	35	70	52	52

The analysis was conducted in the 'Output Maximization' mode with the assumption that the requirement is to have maximum use of ICT for building project management processes with respect to the strategies formulated in the organizations. The analysis was also conducted in the 'Variable Returns Scale' mode with the assumption that changing all the inputs i.e. strategies formulated for use of ICT and use of ICT for general administration works' by the same proportion changes the output i.e. 'use of ICT for building project management processes' by a greater extent than the proportional value. Final weighted values of the inputs and outputs for each organization are as shown in Table 2.

Analysis results showed that based on the data available, PMCO and AO are the best performing DMUs or the organizations with 100% efficiency scores and BO has 89.65% efficiency score. It signifies that PMCO and AO are able to efficiently implement their strategies for use of ICT, but BO is lagging in it.

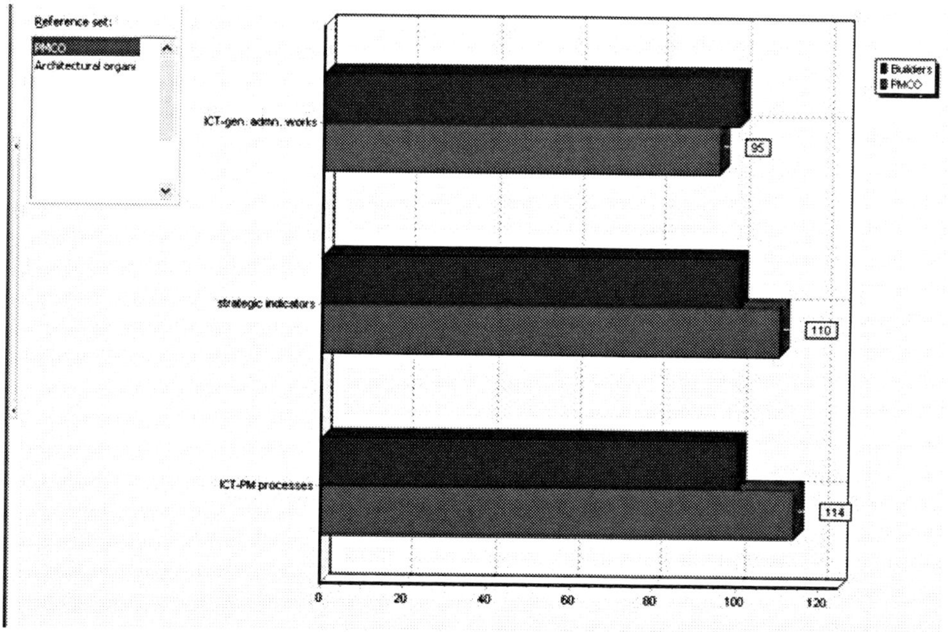

Figure 3. Reference comparison values of PMCO with respect to BO.

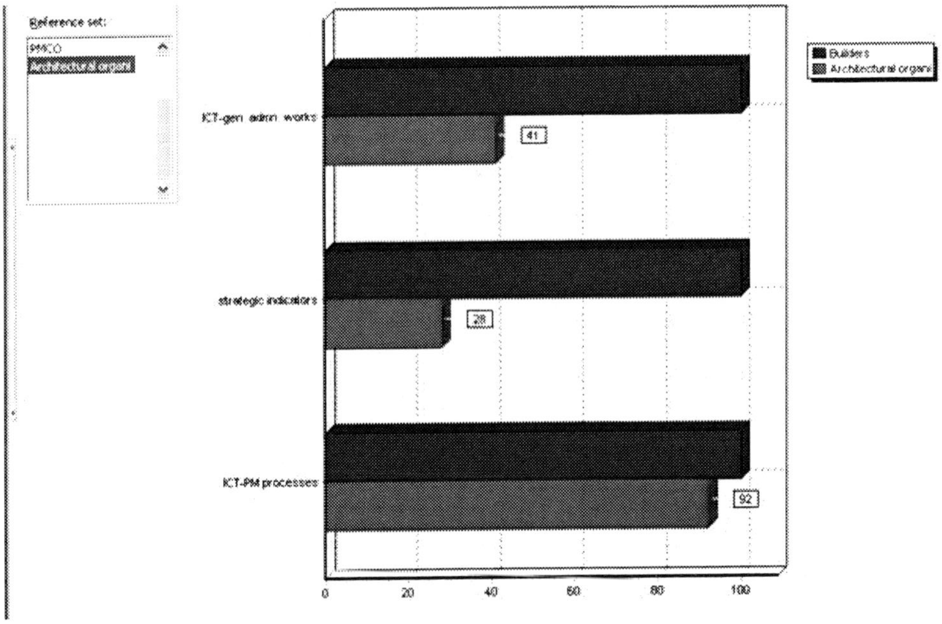

Figure 4. Reference comparison values of AO with respect to BO.

With respect to the data values, 'Reference comparison' values are calculated. These values show performance of the DMU being studied in comparison to 100% efficient DMUs or 'reference units'. The values of the DMU under study are scaled to 100% in the graph, with comparison values also scaled accordingly to make the relationship more obvious. Figure 3 and Figure 4 show comparison of data values of PMCO and AO with respect to the data values of BO, where data values of BO are scaled to 100%. It shows that the values of two indicators of PMCO are higher than those of BO. Values of input indicators of AO are very less in comparison with those of BO, but the value of output indicator is only 92% of that of BO.

For BO to be 100% efficient, with the same level of 'strategic planning', 'use of ICT for general administration works' can reduce by 11.6 points [approx. 14%] and 'use of ICT for building PM processes' should increase by 11.55 points [approx. 21%] [Table 3].

Table 3. Potential improvement required in BO.

Input/Output	Actual	Target	Potential Improvement
Strategic Indicators	57	57	0
Use of ICT for General Administration Works Indicators	84	74.26	-11.6
Use of ICT for Building Project Management Processes Indicators	56	62.47	11.55

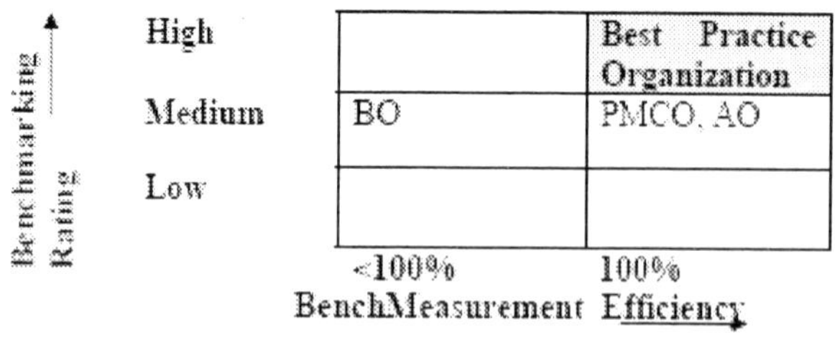

Figure 5. Relation between rating and efficiency of analyzed organizations.

Best Practice Organization Model

Above analysis shows that PMCO has the highest benchmarking ranking amongst the three organizations and is also efficient in implementing its strategies. BO has the middle level ranking but it is not efficient in implementing its strategies. AO is lowest in the ranking but it is efficient in implementing its strategies, because its strategic use of ICT is also less. Relation between rating and efficiency of analyzed organizations is shown in Figure 5.

Data analysis leads to the development of a model defining a Best Practice Organization for ICT adoption for building project management. The derived model indicates that a Best Practice Organization in the industry would have 'High' Benchmarking rating and 100% BenchMeasurement efficiency i.e it would be 100% efficient in implementing its strategies for ICT adoption for building project management.

Conclusion

The chapter discussed administration of a Benchmarking framework developed for assessing the extent of ICT adoption for building project management by construction organizations. The research study reported in the chapter focused on ICT adoption by SMEs in the construction industry and with respect to SMEs it is important to understand the processes, their indicators and measures in the local context and this research studied issues with respect to the Indian construction industry. Data analysis was conducted with respect to the Indian construction industry, but the benchmarking framework would be applicable in other countries after due considerations as the measurement indicators were identified after extensive literature review. The framework is applicable at the industry level for rating the construction organizations for ICT adoption and performance measurement and also provides construction organizations with a generic framework to assess their extent of ICT adoption for building project management processes and to measure their efficiency in implementing their strategies for ICT adoption. The framework was administered in three organizations for rating these organizations under high, medium and low level of ICT adoption for building project management and for measuring their efficiency in implementing their strategies for ICT adoption through Data Envelopment Analysis technique. Data analysis led to the development of a model for defining the 'Best Practice Organization' in the industry with respect to use of ICT for building project management.

REFERENCES

[1] Ahuja, V., Yang, J. & Shankar, R. (2009). Study of ICT Adoption for Building Project Management in the Indian Construction Industry, *Automation in Construction, Vol. 18*, No. 4, 415-423.

[2] Ahuja, V., Yang, J. & Shankar, R. (2010a). Benchmarking Framework to Measure Extent of ICT Adoption for Building Project Management. *Journal of Construction Engineering and Management* [Accepted for publication]

[3] Ahuja, V., Yang, J. & Shankar, R. (2010b). IT Enhanced Communication Protocols for Building Project Management, *Engineering, Construction and Architectural Management* [Accepted for publication]

[4] Anderson, R. I., Fok, R., Zumpano, L. V. & Elder, H. W. (1998). The efficiency of franchising in the residential real estate brokerage market. *Journal of Consumer Marketing, 15(4)*, 386-396.

[5] Baldwin, A. N., Thorpe, A. & Carter, C. (1999). The use of electronic information exchange on construction alliance projects. *Automation in Construction, 8(6)*, 651-662.

[6] Charnes, A., Cooper, W. W. & Rhodes, E. (1978). Measuring the efficiency of decision making units. *European Journal of Operations Research, 2*, 429-44.

[7] Cheng, E. W. L. & Li, H. (2004). Exploring quantitative methods for project location selection. *Building and Environment, 39*, 1467-76.

[8] Chen, Y. (2003). A non-radial Malmquist Productivity Index with an illustrative application to Chinese major industries. *International Journal of Production Economics, 83*, 27-35.

[9] Chiang, Y. H., Cheng, E. W. L. & Tang, B. S. (2006). Examining repercussions of consumptions and inputs placed on the construction sector by use of I–O tables and DEA. *Building and Environment, 41*, 1-11.

[10] Chiang, Y. H., Tang, B. S. & Leung, W. Y. (2001). Market structure of the construction industry in Hong Kong. *Construction Management and Economics, 19(7)*, 675-87.

[11] Cooper, W. W., Park, K. S. & Pastor, J. T. (1999). RAM: A range adjusted measure of inefficiency for use with additive models, and relations to other models and measures in DEA. *Journal of Productivity Analysis, 11*, 5-42.

[12] Dainty, A. R. J., Briscoe, G. H. & Millett, S. J. (2001). New perspectives on construction supply chain integration. *Supply Chain Management: An International Journal, 6(4)*, 163-173.

[13] *Data Envelopment Analysis [DEA] Homepage*, (1996). [online information] Available from: http://www.etm.pdx.edu/dea/ [accessed January 2007].

[14] *Data Envelopment Analysis [DEA] Notes*, [online information] Available from: http://people.brunel.ac.uk/~mastjjb/jeb/or/dea.html [accessed January 2007].

[15] Ganesan, S., Hall, H. & Chiang, Y. H. (1996). Construction in Hong Kong: *Issues in Labour Supply and Technology Transfer*, Aldershot: Avebury.

[16] Hegazy, T. & Ersahin, T. (2001). Simplified spreadsheet solutions I - Subcontractor information system. *Journal of Construction Engineering and Management, 127(6)*, 461-468.

[17] Lacouture, D. C., Medaglia, A. L. & Skibniewski, M. (2007). Supply chain optimization tool for purchasing decisions in B2B construction marketplaces. *Automation in Construction, 16(5)*, 569-575.

[18] Lee, S. H., Thomas, S. R. & Tucker, R. L. (2005). Web-based benchmarking system for the construction industry. *Journal of Construction Engineering and Management, 131(7)*, 790-798.

[19] Li, H., Chen, Z., Yong, L. & Kong, S. C. W. (2005). Application of integrated GPS and GIS technology for reducing construction waste and improving construction efficiency. *Automation in Construction, 14(3)*, 323-331.

[20] Love, P. E. D., Irani, Z. & Edwards, D. J. (2004). Industry-centric benchmarking of information technology benefits, costs and risks for small-to-medium sized enterprises in construction. *Automation in Construction, 13(4)*, 507-524.

[21] Milis, K. & Mercken, R. (2004). The use of the balanced scorecard for the evaluation of information and communication technology projects. *International Journal of Project Management, 22(1)*, 87-97.

[22] Ramanathan, R. (2003). An Introduction to Data Envelopment Analysis: *A Tool for Performance Measurement*, New Delhi, India: Sage Publications India Pvt. Ltd.

[23] Ribeiro, F. L. & Lopes, J. (2002). An approach to E-Business in construction. *Proceedings of ARCOM 18th Annual Conference, September 2002*, University of Northumbria, UK, 2, 475-484.

[24] Weippert, A. & Kajewski, S. (2004). AEC industry culture: A need for change. *Proceedings of CIB World Building Congress 2004: Building for the Future*, Toronto, Canada.

[25] Zhu, J. (2002). Quantitative Models for Performance Evaluation and Benchmarking: *Data Envelopment Analysis with Spreadsheets*, Boston: Kluwer Academic.

In: Project Management
Editor: Robert J. Collins, pp. 153-167
ISBN: 978-1-61761-460-6
© 2011 Nova Science Publishers, Inc.

Chapter 6

Application of Systems Engineering and Systems Thinking to Project Management

Simon P. Philbin*

Imperial College Business School, Imperial College London,
South Kensington, London, United Kingdom

Abstract

The management of technology and engineering projects within an organizational context continues to fall short on a number of levels, especially when considering that projects and programs undertaken across different industries do not always achieve the required project outputs satisfactorily. Moreover, there is also an apparent disconnect between technical activities and project management processes as well as difficulties caused by inadequate project planning. In order to address these issues, engineering systems thinking has been found to contribute to a number of favourable project management features. Consequently, this chapter will identify approaches for improving the project management process through exploring the application of systems engineering and systems thinking to the management of projects. This will be undertaken through an extensive literature review of supporting material and conceptual analysis of how systems engineering and systems thinking can be applied to project planning. Through building on this analysis and from work in the literature, a new model for project management has been developed that is based on four systems-based levers, which are: multidisciplinary and holistic; requirements-driven; project interdependencies; and systems techniques. The utility and flexibility of this innovative management framework has been explored through an initial application to a case study involving a technology project on the development of composite materials for aerospace applications. This case study revealed that there are a range of systems methodologies that can be deployed in order to improve the project planning process and ultimately contribute to project success.

* Corresponding author: Email s.philbin@imperial.ac.uk

INTRODUCTION

Organizations across a range of industries operate according to project-based activities (Hobday, 2000) and this includes companies from the aerospace and defense, pharmaceutical, IT/IS, construction and general engineering sectors (Salem and Mohanty, 2008). Managing workloads according to projects and larger programs where necessary can have a number of benefits (Clelan and Ireland, 2002). There is a clear structure provided so that the required resources can be managed to deliver project outputs, which will have been specified at the project initiation stage. Moreover, projects will be traditionally delivered according to fixed parameters that are a known deadline, a pre-determined cost basis and a stated quality or performance level. In this regard, there are internationally recognized standards and processes that have been developed, such as the project management body of knowledge (PMI, 2003) in the United States and the PRINCE2 methodology (OGC, 2005) in the United Kingdom.

Whilst these sets of processes and structures have provided rigor to the field of project management, there continues to be numerous examples and across different industries of project's failing to generate the required deliverables (Linberg, 1999; Pinto and Mantel, 1990; Pinto and Slevin, 1989), and one of the main reasons for such failures has been attributed to the lack of detail and foresight at the beginning of projects in the planning stage, the so called 'fuzzy front end' (Smith and Reinertsen, 1991). Although there is debate over what constitutes project success as well as the role of critical success factors (CSFs) for projects (Jugdev and Müller, 2005). Furthermore, in technical project management, there can also be an apparent disconnect between the technical work undertaken and general organizational management constructs, including project management. Therefore, in order to address these challenges it is proposed that systems engineering and systems thinking can be utilized as an underpinning approach to improve technical project management. Indeed in some respects, systems engineering and project management can be regarded as being complementary (Dasher, 2003) and so this application is a logical extension.

As a methodology for designing and implementing technological products and services, systems engineering has matured over a number of years as an important enabler for technology-based organizations (Stevens et al., 1998). Similarly, the underpinning subject of systems thinking (Davidz and Nightingale, 2008) is focused on an examination of problems through consideration of the components of the wider system of interest as well as from the relationships between the individual components. In this regard, it is proposed that the application of systems engineering and systems thinking to project management can be achieved through the use of four main systems-based levers, which are:

- Integrating multidisciplinary viewpoints and holistic considerations into the project context.
- Driving projects through a requirements-based approach.
- Developing an improved understanding of interdependencies between projects and project activities.
- Applying existing systems knowledge, techniques and best practice to projects.

SYSTEMS ENGINEERING AND SYSTEMS THINKING

The discipline of systems engineering has been established for a number of years (Buede, 1999) and this provides a recognized set of processes and techniques for the design and implementation of complex products and services through adoption of a holistic or systems-wide viewpoint. Systems engineering is an interdisciplinary approach that has developed a range of tools, which can be deployed to help in the management of complexity. Fundamental to this approach is a holistic assessment of factors that contribute to the performance of system performance, and as part of the integrated system design process this starts with the requirements capture stage. Decomposition of systems according to subsystem connectivity can be undertaken, followed by analysis, design, implementation, integration, acceptance and finally evaluation. The subject of systems thinking (Senge, 2000) underpins systems engineering through the use of common sets of principles that are applicable to the structure and operation of systems of different types (Skyttner, 2006). Consequently, systems engineering and systems thinking offer the potential to supplement general project management processes with a complementary toolset that can handle the technical complexity, and provide a framework to help tackle the need for enhanced problem structuring and improved project planning.

Through further consideration, engineering systems thinking (Frank, 2000) can be regarded as a set of learning theories, which are focused on applying systems viewpoints; such as a holistic perspective and a focus on the inter-related nature of system components, as well as the design and implementation of engineering initiatives. Applying engineering systems thinking to project management (Philbin, 2008a) can be analyzed through consideration of a number of supporting areas, as put forward by Frank and Waks (2001), and together with the resulting project management features is summarized in Table 1.

The benefits described highlight the merits of applying engineering systems thinking to project management and through building on this analysis and from work in the literature it is possible to discern four main systems-based levers for project management and these are depicted in Figure 1.

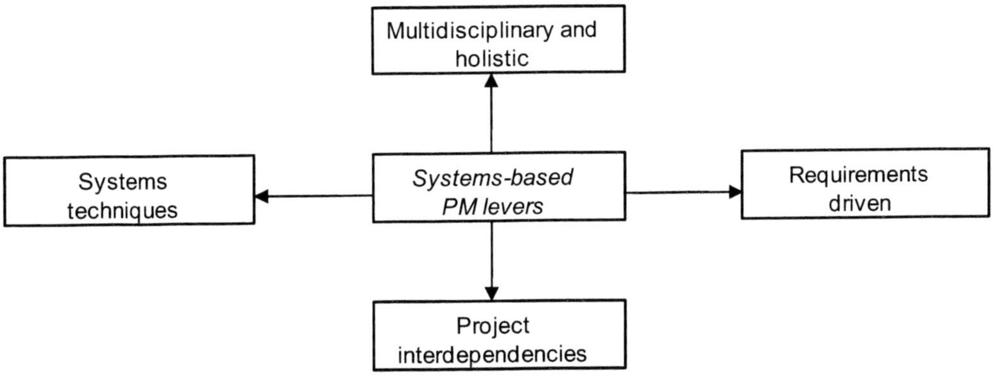

Figure 1. Systems-based project management levers.

Table 1. Application of engineering systems thinking to project management.

Engineering systems thinking	Project management features
Ability to see the 'big picture'.	Viewing projects as part of a wider program or business perspective will help to identify project dependencies.
Implementation of overall management considerations.	Aligning projects with organizational structures will enhance the cascade down of strategic management issues or changes.
Acquisition and use of interdisciplinary knowledge.	Managing across different functional areas (technical, contracts & legal, business, human resources and finance) in order to ensure project success.
Analysis of customer needs and internal capabilities.	Ensuring all project or contract requirements are adequately specified and delivered according to a systematic requirements capture process.
Use of underpinning systems knowledge.	Using recognized systems techniques and methodologies to enable project planning and implementation and the co-ordination of technical project activities.
Understanding of synergies and emergent properties.	Analyzing project activities and how they are interdependent in order to effectively control project critical pathways as well as interdependencies with activities external to the project.
Ability to challenge existing approaches.	Challenging existing project management approaches, such as iterative life cycle methodologies, in order to improve project performance through utilizing systems-based management best practice.
Creativity and creative management.	Creatively managing people in a project environment through, for example, enhancing responsibilities for project engineering staff in order to improve motivation and enthusiasm in the project.

The premise of this new conceptual framework is that adoption of the systems-based project management (PM) levers during project planning and implementation will enhance project performance through improving the integration of technical project activities with the organization and also from reducing uncertainties at the early stages of projects. In order to illustrate how these systems-based levers can be deployed in a project management context, the following discussion provides an initial application of the four levers to a case study involving project planning for a materials development project for an aerospace application.

Applying Systems-Based Levers to a Project Planning Case Study

Case Study Project Background

This project involves the assessment of different types of composite materials for use in advanced airframes. The project activities involve an assessment of light-weight, high-temperature composite materials; analysis of materials preparation, heat and pressure curing, machining techniques, and manufacturing methods for composites; and development of an economic cost-benefit model for the use of composite materials on airframes for civil airlines. The project represents the first part of a technology demonstration program for a new airframe that is required by an OEM (original equipment manufacturer) aerospace company, and the project is undertaken by a technology consultancy company under contract from the OEM.

Systems-Based Lever: Multidisciplinary and Holistic

This systems-based lever encapsulates both multidisciplinary and holistic approaches, since both of these features of systems thinking are linked, due to being focused towards distributed analysis and implementation, i.e. a wider consideration of underlying factors. Moreover, a systems viewpoint is predicated on a broad or holistic analysis of the contributing factors that can impact on the performance of the system. Applying this approach to projects would encourage a wider analysis of how the project relates to the wider organizational structure as well as any external dependencies. This would be particularly useful in regard to project risk management, since consideration needs to be taken of risks that can originate within the project as well as potential risks from external sources. Correspondingly, there are a number of risk management methodologies that are linked to systems analysis (Le Coze et al., 2006).

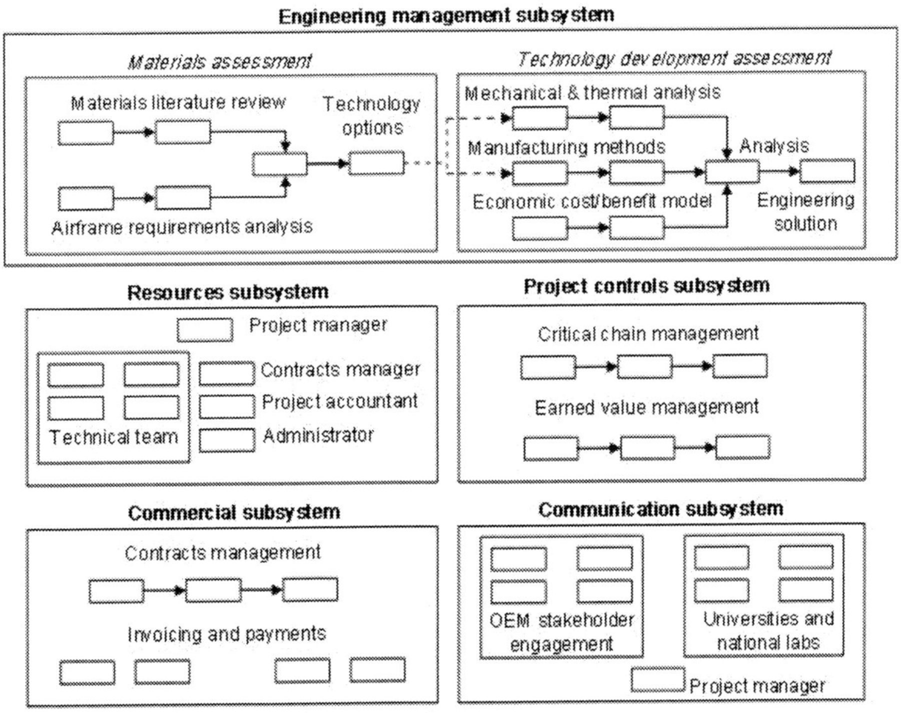

Figure 2. Project organizational architecture.

System risk analysis based on computational approaches, such as Monte Carlo simulation, is a recognized method for technical risk management (Evans and Olson, 1998) but such quantitative methodologies can also be applied to project risk management, industrial engineering management and business administration. Furthermore, work by Helton (1994) provides a useful treatment of risk and uncertainty in terms of being stochastic or subjective for the case of complex systems, such as the performance assessment of a waste isolation pilot plant. In the application of project planning, the ability to draw on robust risk management approaches that can be used to identify and manage risks on a system level will help to ensure projects include adequate resources and supporting costs to mitigate against such risks.

Effective project management requires planning, control and organization of project activities across different disciplines and therefore an inherent multidisciplinary approach will be beneficial. Systems engineering rests on an ability to integrate different disciplines so that the system can be designed and implemented effectively. Moreover, systems architecting can be used to illustrate the multidisciplinary nature of project management and Figure 2 provides a project organizational architecture generated for the case study.

The architecture includes five main subsystems of operation that would need to be formulated as part of the project planning stage. The main technical subsystem is based on engineering management but this is further broken down into materials assessment and technology development assessment. The output from the materials assessment is a set of technology options that can be further assessed in order to generate an engineering solution. The solution would include details on composite materials that can offer the requisite performance benefits over metallic airframes, such as structural rigidity and damage tolerance, as well as being based on a satisfactory cost/benefit approach. Other subsystems in project planning include the resources subsystem that describes key project staff; project controls subsystem that relates to recognized project management techniques such as EVM (earned value management); commercial subsystem that includes routine contracts management; as well as the communication subsystem that describes how the project will engage with OEM stakeholders as well as third-party research providers such as universities and national laboratories.

The project organizational architecture illustrates the range of disciplines and supporting activities that will need to be planned in the case study project and consequently the project management role would require effective management of these different areas (i.e. being multidisciplinary focused). In this regard, project managers need to have good communication skills to be able to engage with different disciplines as well as a consultative approach that is able to motivate people from different organizational backgrounds.

Systems-Based Lever: Requirements-Driven

Requirements capture is a fundamental component of systems engineering (Parnell, et al., 2008) and this initial stage is directed towards detailing the technical specifications or requirements for a particular project, contract or initiative. These requirements provide a definition of what the system will be required to do and hence there will be vital information on the required state of the system to be developed. Requirements can be defined according to user or customer viewpoints and encapsulated in formats, such as user requirements documents. The importance of adequate requirements capture activities has been reported by Dvir et al. (2003) and this study found a positive correlation between requirements management and rigorous assessment of technical specifications with the performance of defense projects.

There are a wide range of approaches to requirements capture and engineering. This includes formalistic (Navarro et al., 2006) and systemic definition processes (Agouridas et al., 2008) that can provide a highly structured methodology for building up requirements across different stakeholders and for example as part of software architecture development. There also exist 'softer' approaches that can be used to generate requirements, including workshops and group discussions (Macaulay, 1996) as well as informal information channels (Macdonald and Williams, 1993), which are likely to be particularly effective in elucidating requirements of a more tacit nature (i.e. not explicit or easily codified information). Moreover, effective requirements management (Robertson and Robertson, 1999) can rest on a number of supporting activities and processes and this can include the following:

- Technical specification formulation according to functional, performance, constraint or physical requirements.
- Requirements documentation.
- Requirements specification analysis via threshold or goal parameters.
- Multidisciplinary team working.
- Structured workshops.
- Quality assurance.
- Issuing and following work instructions.
- Generating derived requirements (i.e. requirements established from other requirements).
- Avoiding requirements creep.

Use of a requirements-driven approach in the case study would help provide valuable structure to the technical project activities. In this case a requirements database could be compiled that details key areas of project information, such as materials compositions, thermal properties, mechanical properties and economic factors. To this end, Figure 3 provides a representative view of the requirements capture process.

In the example provided, for each of the four areas, there are a number of specific requirements detailed, e.g. for materials compositions, this could be carbon-fiber reinforced plastic (RS11), metal-matrix composite (RS12) and thermoset composites (RS13). Subsequent to requirements capture and formulation of the requirements database, analysis of requirements dependencies can be undertaken and in the example shown, it can be seen that for the metal-matrix composite (RS12) (e.g. discontinuously reinforced aluminum metal matrix composite), there is dependency on having a tailorable coefficient of thermal expansion (RS22) and high stiffness (RS33). As can be seen from the example, analysis of these dependencies would provide valuable information to help in the project planning stage and this can contribute significantly to the project's eventual outcome.

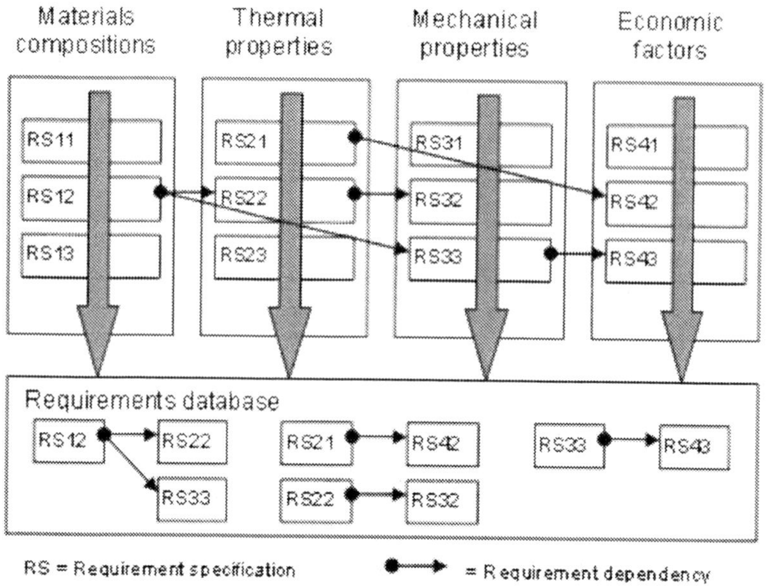

Figure 3. Requirements specification process.

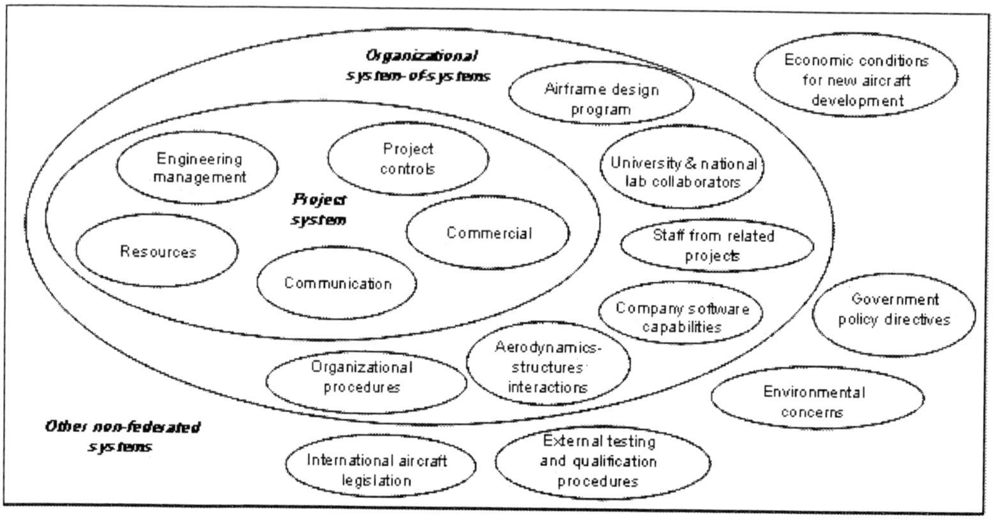

Figure 4. System-of-systems map for composite materials project planning.

Systems-Based Lever: Project Interdependencies

A key feature of systems is the interdependence of activities (i.e. subsystems) within the system, where the performance or status of a particular activity can affect the performance of other activities and which collectively contribute to the performance of the whole system. There is an obvious parallel to project management, since the performance of a project activity can have a direct impact on the project's overall performance. At the planning stage, it can be difficult to assess this interdependence of project activities. Project risk management can clearly be a useful process to employ in determining the likely impact of a particular risk or in this context if a certain project activity does not produce the required result. However, there continues to be difficulty in assessing and then managing the interdependencies between project activities Indeed research by Verma and Singh (2002) has indicated the benefits from managing interdependencies between projects in terms of resources and technology factors. Moreover, work by Liesiö et al. (2008) has applied robust portfolio modeling to project interdependencies, incomplete cost information and variable budget levels; this approach helped in the selection of robust projects and portfolios as well as identifying projects that required further attention.

A four-stage linear model has been put forward (Philbin, 2008b) that allows system complexity to be managed as part of a structured framework and the model includes scope for the planning and management of project interdependencies. The model is based on a sequential progression through the four stages, which are integrated system design; system architecture development; systems integration; and system-of systems management. The fourth stage, system-of-systems management, can be particularly useful from a planning perspective in order to assess different hierarchies and interdependencies between project activities. The system-of-systems view (Keating et al., 2003) seeks to place the system in connection to partially federated systems (which constitute the system-of-systems) as well as in relation with other non-federated systems. The system-of-systems perspective has been brought to bear on a number of different applications. DeLaurentis and Callaway (2004) have looked at next generation transport systems using this perspective in order to improve decision-making in regard to public policy. As an integrating framework, the system-of-systems view was found to offer a 'negotiation aid' that encourages consideration of diverse capabilities and distributed systems including those from policy, economic and technology sources. The system-of-systems approach has also been explored for telecommunications applications (Noam, 1994) as a tool for describing increasing complex networks and the consequences on telecommunications regulation. In order to illustrate application of this perspective, Figure 4 provides a system-of-systems map for the composite materials project.

The system-of-systems map provides a hierarchical view of the project system and this can be used as a planning tool to examine project interdependencies. The project system itself includes the five subsystems previously identified (engineering management; resources; project controls; commercial; and communication). The project system can then be viewed as part of a wider organizational system-of-systems, which includes partially related or federated systems, such as airframe design program; university and national laboratory collaborators; staff from related projects; company software capabilities; aerodynamics-structures interactions; and organizational procedures. Finally there are other non-federated systems that will need to be considered in the project planning stage, including economic conditions; government policy directives; environmental concerns; external testing and qualification standards; and international aircraft legislation.

For illustrative purposes, the following set of interdependencies can be identified for the case study project. The engineering management subsystem and specifically the mechanical testing parameters for composite materials will have a dependency on the airframe design program. Therefore, changes to the program specifications will need to inform the engineering subsystem, so that any required modifications to the testing can be undertaken.

LIVERPOOL JOHN MOORES UNIVERSITY
LEARNING SERVICES

This interaction is part of a federated system-of-systems, since both areas can influence the performance of the other and so there is two-way connectivity. However, the airframe design program will have a one-way connection to other non-federated systems, such as external testing and qualification procedures, and environmental concerns. Changes to these two systems will impact on the airframe design program, e.g. changes to the qualification procedures to take account of emerging environmental issues may require different airframe configurations to be developed. This interaction would be one-way though, as any changes to the airframe design program would not influence either the external testing and qualifications procedures or environmental concerns. Through system-of-systems planning, it is therefore possible to highlight project interdependencies that contribute to the performance of the project and consequently areas that need to be addressed in project planning.

Systems-Based Lever: Systems Techniques

Systems engineering is able to provide project management with a large range of structured techniques that have significant potential to improve the project management process. The ability to represent a system as a model can have benefits in the design and management of systems and so by extension it is postulated that application of system architecting and modeling techniques to project management can also provide benefits. This will include improving project risk management as mentioned earlier. Furthermore, there are a range of formalistic modeling techniques that be utilized in technical project management. Unified modeling language (UML) provides an established methodology for designing and implementing systems (Rumbaugh et al., 2004) and in the case study UML could be used to describe the process for correlating different technical performance parameters for composite materials. Further adaptation of UML has been undertaken to develop the related modeling approach, SysML (Holt and Perry, 2007). The SysML methodology is based on four underpinning pillars, which are structure (including definition and use); behavior (including interaction, state machine and activity/function); requirements; and parametrics. In the case study, a SySML communication diagram could be used in order to describe the different cost drivers that need to be incorporated in the economic assessment of composite materials as part of the cost/benefit analysis.

As discussed previously, projects inevitably have a number of different areas of operation that encompass different disciplines and consequently there will be activities undertaken in parallel. System dynamics is a technique that can be used to model parallel activities through the dynamics of multiple-loop systems (Sterman, 2000). This modeling technique includes the use of causal loop diagramming, which can be used to model the relationships between different system variables that are represented as nodes in the diagram. The relationship is described through being either a positive causal link (+) where the two nodes change in the same direction, or a negative causal link (-) where the two nodes change in the opposite direction.

Lyneis et al. (2001) have explored the use of system dynamics to support a project bid as a tool for assessing project risk as well as different organizational configurations, and the study pointed to the need to include system dynamics as part of ongoing learning approaches within organizations. Love et al. (2002) have used system dynamics as a tool to improve the understanding of change and rework in construction projects and the study included a causal loop model of the project management system. This approach demonstrated the potential utility of modeling as a mechanism for determining project dynamics that have the potential to undermine project progress. Building on this work, it is possible to apply system dynamics to the case study and Figure 5 provides a causal loop model for the project planning system.

Through analysis of the causal loop diagram various project planning issues can be identified, for instance, in order to maintain project progress there are a number of supporting activity loops. These include project technical variables, centered on the availability of materials, which drives the need for favourable thermal and mechanical properties, and other factors, which feed back into project progress through the quality of technical recommendations. Another loop starts with the level of requirements capture, leading to other project work parameters within the system and back to project progress through the schedule to deliver technical recommendations.

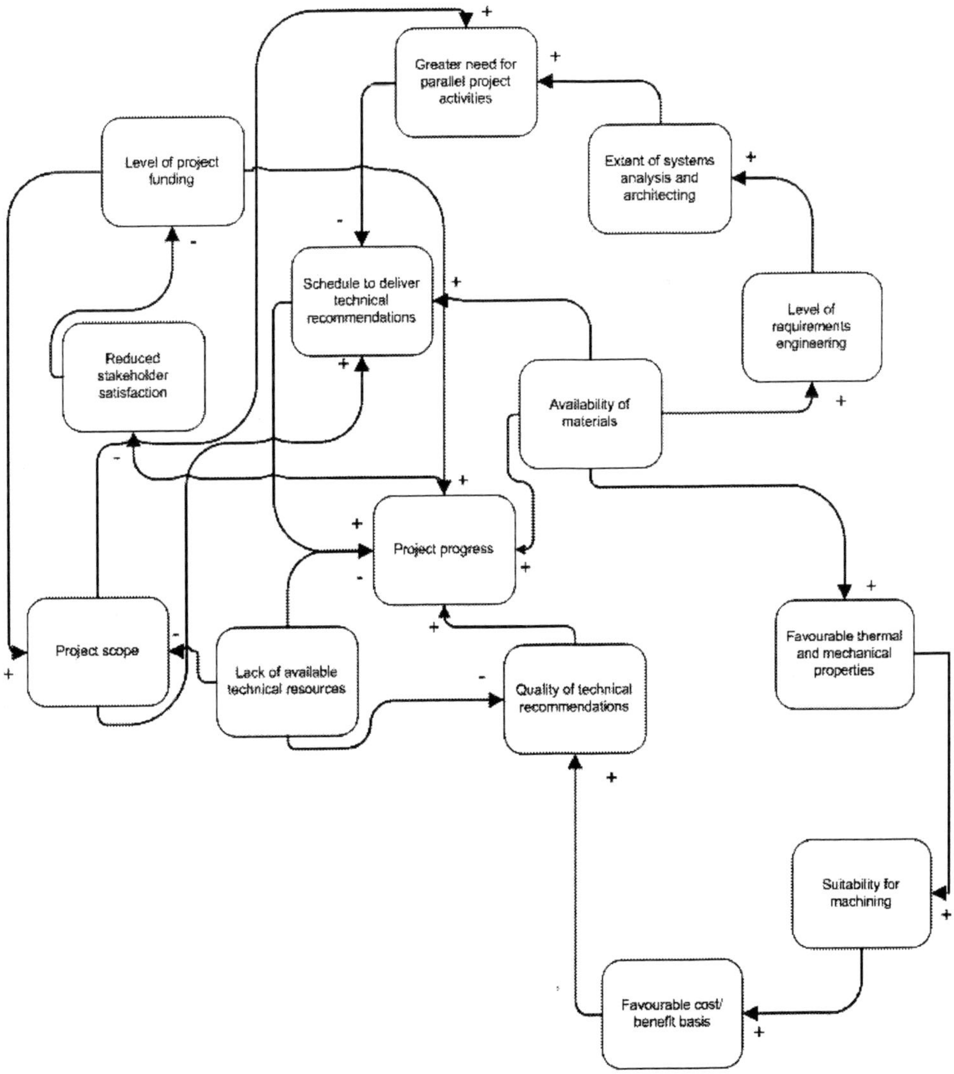

Figure 5. Causal loop model for project planning system.

Moreover, key project work features can drive multiple areas, e.g. project scope contributes to both the schedule to deliver technical recommendations, and the need for parallel activities. Through the use of the causal loop diagramming technique, it is therefore possible to identify critical project activities that have the ability to contribute to areas across the project and consequently there needs to be adequate planning for such work activities. It is also possible to assess the causal link direction in order to reveal more information on project work activities and variables as part of the project planning process, e.g. a lack of available technical resources will likely cause a decrease in the quality of the technical recommendations (hence a negative causal link), whereas an increase in the project scope will likely drive an extension to the schedule to deliver technical recommendations (hence a positive causal link). The causal loop model generated for the composites materials case study highlights a range of features of the project management system. Indeed causal loop modeling can be a highly instructive approach that can help in the analysis of systems through creating 'mental models'.

Conclusion

This chapter has set out the premise for a research agenda on the application of systems engineering and systems thinking to project management. This has been done through description of some of the main challenges in project management and how systems methodologies can be utilized to address these areas. Through application of engineering systems thinking, it has been possible to conceptualize four systems-based project management levers, which are as follows: multidisciplinary and holistic; requirements-driven; project interdependencies; and systems techniques. It is proposed that the use of these management levers and the supporting processes and activities, as part of the project management lifecycle, will improve project performance.

In order to advance the new conceptual model it has been initially applied to a case study involving planning for a project on the technology development of composite materials for aerospace applications. The case study provided the opportunity to demonstrate the utility of the model and the four systems-based levers through the use of a number of systems methodologies. These have ranged from requirements capture and systems dynamics, through to multidisciplinary architecting and system-of-systems mapping. This approach has highlighted how the application of systems engineering and systems thinking can provide a structured framework to improve the planning process for technical projects.

The system-based project management levers described in this paper have been formulated in order to help technical project management practitioners through provision of a toolset of systems methodologies to improve the project planning process. Inevitably there will be trade-offs and uncertainties in project planning (Smith-Daniels and Smith-Daniels, 2008), and the individual systems-based levers have been developed so as to enhance decision-making so that such trade-offs can be effectively managed. A cautionary note, however, on the use of structured management approaches, such as the systems-based levers described here, is that the use of formal planning techniques should not be allowed to prohibit creative thinking and problem-solving (Caughron and Mumford, 2008) to the detriment of the project and where such an outcome occurs, then the planning approach will need to be modified accordingly so as to eliminate such an effect.

It is suggested that future work is carried out through the application of the systems-based project management levers to different types of projects and at different stages in the project lifecycle. It would also be useful to undertake performance assessment of the conceptual model reported here alongside other technical project management approaches and to develop further the quantitative aspects of the model through using numerical systems-based levers.

REFERENCES

[1] Agouridas, V., McKay, A., Winand, H. & de Pennington, A. (2008). Advanced product planning: a comprehensive process for systemic definition of new product requirements, *Requirements Engineering*, *Vol. 13*, No. 1, 19-48.

[2] Buede, D. M. (1999). *The Engineering Design of Systems: Models and Methods*, John Wiley & Sons.

[3] Caughron, J. J. & Mumford, M. D. (2008). Project Planning: the Effects of Using Formal Planning techniques on Creative Problem-Solving, *Creativity and Innovation Management*, *Vol. 17*, No. 3, 204-215.

[4] Clelan, D. I. & Ireland, L. R. (2002) Project Management: *Strategic Design and Implementation,* McGraw-Hill Professional, 4th edn.

[5] Dasher, G. T. (2003). The Interface Between Systems Engineering and Program Management, *Engineering Management Journal*, *Vol. 15*, No. 3, 11 -14.

[6] Davidz, H. L. & Nightingale, D. J. (2008). Enabling Systems Thinking To Accelerate the Development of Senior Systems Engineers. *Systems Engineering*, *Vol. 11*, No. 1, 1-14.

[7] DeLaurentis, D. & Callaway, R. K. (2004). *A System-of-Systems Perspective for Public Policy Decisions, Review of Policy Research*, *Vol. 21*, Issue 6, 829-837.

[8] Dvir, D., Raz, T. & Shenhar, A. J. (2003). An empirical analysis of the relationship between project planning and project success, *International Journal of Project Management*, *Vol. 21*, Issue 2, 89-95.

[9] Evans, J. R. & Olson, D. L. (1998). *Introduction to Simulation and Risk Analysis*, Prentice-Hall Inc.

[10] Frank, M. & Waks, S. (2001). Engineering Systems Thinking: A Multifunctional Definition. *Systemic Practice and Action Research*, *Vol. 14*, No. 3, 361-379.

[11] Frank, M. (2000). Engineering Systems Thinking and Systems Thinking. *Systems Engineering*, *Vol. 3*, No. 2, 163-168.

[12] Helton, J. C. (1994). Treatment of Uncertainty in Performance Assessment for Complex Systems, *Risk Analysis*, *Vol. 14*, Issue 4, 483-511.

[13] Hobday, M. (2000). The project-based organisation: an ideal form for managing complex products and systems. *Research Policy*, *Vol. 29*, No. 7/8, 871-893.

[14] Holt, J. & Perry, S. (2007). *SysML for Systems Engineering*, Institution of Engineering and Technology.

[15] Jugdev, K. & Müller, R. (2005). A retrospective look at our evolving understanding of project success, *Project Management Journal*, *Vol. 36*, No. 4, 19-31.

[16] Keating, C., Rogers, R., Unal, R., Dryer, D., Sousa-Poza, A., Safford, R., Peterson, W. & Rabadi, G. (2003). System of Systems Engineering. *Engineering Management Journal, Vol. 15*, Issue 3, 36-45.

[17] Le Coze, J. C., Salvi, O. & Gaston, D. (2006). Complexity and Multi (Inter or Trans)-Disciplinary Sciences: Which Job for Engineers in Risk Management, *Journal of Risk Research, Vol. 9*, No. 5, 569-582.

[18] Liesiö, J., Mild, P. & Salo, A. (2008). Robust portfolio modeling with incomplete cost information and project interdependencies, *European Journal of Operational Research, Vol. 190*, Issue 3, 679-695.

[19] Linberg, K. R. (1999). Software developer perceptions about software project failure: a case study, *Journal of Systems and Software, Vol. 49*, Issue 2-3, 177-192.

[20] Love, P. E. D., Holt, G. D., Shen, L. Y., Li, H. & Irani, Z (2002). Using systems dynamics to better understand change and rework in construction project management systems. *International Journal of Project Management, Vol. 20*, 425-436.

[21] Lyneis, J. M., Cooper, K. G. & Els, S. A. (2001). Strategic management of complex projects: a case study using system dynamics, *System Dynamics Review, Vol. 17*, No. 3, 237-260.

[22] Macaulay, L. A. (1996). *Requirements Engineering*, Springer-Verlag.

[23] Macdonald, S. & Williams, C. (1993). Beyond the Boundary: An Information Perspective on the Role of the Gatekeeper in the Organization, *Journal of Product Innovation Management, Vol. 10*, No. 5, 417-428.

[24] Navarro, E., Letelier, P., Mocholi, J. A. & Ramos, I. (2006). A Metamodeling Approach for Requirements Specification, *Journal of Computer Information Systems*, Special Issue, *Vol. 47*, 67-77.

[25] Noam, E. M. (1994). Beyond liberalization: from the network of networks to the system of systems, *Telecommunications Policy, Vol. 18*, Issue 4, 286-294.

[26] Office of Government Commerce (OGC), UK (2005). *Managing Successful Projects with PRINCE2*, London: TSO.

[27] Parnell, G. S., Driscoll, P. J. & Henderson, D. L. (2008). *Decision Making in Systems Engineering and Management*, Wiley-Interscience.

[28] Philbin, S. P. (2008a). Bid management: A systems engineering approach. *Journal of High Technology Management Research, Vol. 19*, Issue 2, 114-127.

[29] Philbin, S. P. (2008b). Managing Complex Technology Projects. *Research-Technology Management, Vol. 51*, No. 2, 32-39.

[30] Pinto, J. K. & Mantel, S. J. J. (1990). The causes of project failure, *IEEE Transactions on Engineering Management, Vol. 37*, No. 4, 269-277.

[31] Pinto, J. K. & Slevin, D. P. (1989). Critical success factors in R&D projects, *Research-Technology Management, Vol. 32*, No. 1, 31-36.

[32] Project Management Institute (PMI), USA (2003). *Guide to the Project Management Body of Knowledge*, PMBoK, 3rd Edn.

[33] Robertson, S. & Robertson, J. (1999). *Mastering the Requirements Process*, Addison-Wesley.

[34] Rumbaugh, J., Jacobson, I. & Booch, G. (2004). *Unified Modeling Language Reference Manual*, Second Edition, Pearson Higher Education.

[35] Salem, O. & Mohanty, S. (2008). Project Management Practice and Information Technology Research. *Journal of Construction Engineering and Management, Vol. 134*, Issue 7, 501-508.

[36] Senge, P. M. (1990). *The fifth discipline: The art and practice of the learning organization,* Doubleday, New York.

[37] Skyttner, L. (2006). General Systems Theory: *Problems, Perspectives*, Practice, World Scientific Publishing.

[38] Smith, P. G. & Reinertsen, D. G. (1991). *Developing Products in Half the Time*, Van Nostrand Reinhold.

[39] Smith-Daniels, D. E. & Smith-Daniels, V. L. (2008). Trade-Offs, Biases, and Uncertainty in project Planning and Execution: A Problem-Based Simulation Exercise, *Decision Sciences Journal in Innovative Education*, *Vol. 6*, No. 2, 313-341.

[40] Sterman, J. D. (2000). Business Dynamics. *Systems Thinking and Modeling for a Complex World*, Irwin McGraw-Hill.

[41] Stevens, R., Brook, P., Jackson, K. & Arnold, S. (1998). *Systems Engineering*, Coping with Complexity, Pearson.

[42] Verma, D. & Singh, K. K. (2002). Toward a theory of project interdependencies in high tech R&D environments, *Journal of Operations Management*, *Vol. 20*, Issue 5, 451-468.

[43] Winter, M. (2006). Problem structuring in project management: an application of soft systems methodology. *Journal of Operational Research Society*, *Vol. 57*, Issue 7, 802-812.

In: Project Management
Editor: Robert J. Collins, pp. 169-182
ISBN: 978-1-61761-460-6
© 2011 Nova Science Publishers, Inc.

Chapter 7

INSTITUTIONAL ARRANGEMENTS IN CHINA'S CONSTRUCTION INDUSTRY

Ping Yung*

School of Architecture, Design and the Built Environment,
Nottingham Trent University, Nottingham, United Kingdom

ABSTRACT

This chapter documents the institutional arrangements in China's construction industry. It concentrates on the three major differences between China and the UK system, namely, the mandatory tender evaluation by an Independent Specialist Committee (ISC), the mandatory construction supervision system, as well as the mandatory use of bills of quantities procurement method for government funded projects. It is hoped that this will provide some insights for international construction professionals seeking to work in China. The effects of the former two arrangements on the efficiency of property developers, and the quality and safety performance of construction projects will be evaluated. The study indicates that the ISC tender evaluation system has actually reduced the efficiency of property developers in terms of capital-output ratio. However, the mandatory construction supervising system has improved both the safety during construction and the quality of finished projects. The reasons why the old Quota procurement system is still widely used is also discussed.

Keywords: Institutional arrangements, construction industry, tender evaluation, construction supervision, procurement

INTRODUCTION

The construction industry in China is arguably the largest one in the world. The total output in 2008 was RMB 6203.7 billion (National Bureau of Statistics of China 2009). The

* Corresponding author: Email: ping.yung@ntu.ac.uk

output from companies with foreign investment has grown from RMB 6.75 billion in 2000 to RMB 38.71 billion in 2008. The increase in investment from foreign firms has resulted in a higher demand for foreign project managers or construction related personnel. Foreign construction professionals working in China have to overcome language difficulties, but the differences between the institutional arrangements in the construction industries in China and other countries will also be a significant barrier.

Professionals from the majority of the countries including the UK usually find it difficult to understand the institutional arrangements in China. This paper seeks to bridge the gap by highlighting the three major differences between China and the UK systems. These are:

- The mandatory tender evaluation by an Independent Specialist Committee (ISC).
- The mandatory construction supervision system.
- The mandatory use of bills of quantities procurement method for government funded projects.

This paper will not only introduce the policy backgrounds, it will also evaluate the effects of the policies. It is hoped that this paper will provide some insights into the current structure of China's construction industry for the construction professionals or academia.

The remainder of the paper is arranged as follows. The next section will introduce the mandatory tender evaluation system and evaluate its effects on the efficiencies of property developers. The mandatory construction supervision system will then be introduced, followed by an evaluation of its effects on both construction quality and safety. The mandatory use of bills of quantities procurement method for government funded projects will then be introduced. The reason why the previous Quota system still persists will also be discussed. The last section concludes the findings.

Mandatory Tendering and Mandatory Tender Evaluation

Policy Background

The mandatory adoption of tendering for construction projects formally started in 1999, when *the Tendering Law of the People's Republic of China* (The *Tendering Law*) was enacted. The *Tendering Law* prescribes that site investigation, design, construction, construction supervision, and related important equipment and materials for virtually any kind of building that exceeds the prescribed minimum range and scale requirements shall be procured through (competitive) tendering.

This generally ruled out the option of negotiated tendering. In the UK, negotiated tendering is used when the client has a preference for a particular firm, often because it has done satisfactory work in the past (Ramus et al. 2006). Negotiated tendering may result in a higher price, but it saves the cost of tendering which could be quite significant. Hence, it is quite popular in the UK.

Mandatory tendering alone is not enough, as it could be easily manipulated in the tender evaluation process. Hence, the discretionary power of the property developers in choosing contractors was also largely restricted. This was achieved by the adoption of an Independent Specialist Committee (ISC) tender evaluation system.

There are representatives of the client in an ISC, but they can not exceed one third of the committee. The majority of the members of an ISC are randomly selected from a specialist panel two days before a tender's opening day. The specialist panel shall be formed by relevant departments from governments at the provincial level or above or by tender agencies formed by law. The specialists eligible for election to the panel shall fulfil the following requirements:

(a) They must have practiced in the relevant professional field for at least eight years and possess a "senior" professional title[1] or be at the same professional level.
(b) They must be familiar with the laws and regulations relating to tendering.
(c) They must be able to perform duties diligently, fairly, honestly, and incorruptibly.
(d) They must be healthy enough to perform the tender evaluation works.

The ISC will, based on the criteria listed in the tender documents and the procedural requirements of the Tender Administration Office, recommend three tenderers in order of priority. Normally, the first prioritized tenderer will be awarded the job.

This mandatory adoption of tendering and tender evaluation by ISCs was considered necessary to reduce the possibility of corruption in real estate / construction related enterprises, as the dominant form of governance in these enterprises was still state ownership. Yung and Lai (2009) argued that these policies were largely influenced by the Principal-Agent Theory (PA Theory) popular in China (Yung 2009b). The standard PA Theory suggests that the discretionary powers of the managers in State-Owned Enterprises (SOEs) shall be restricted to reduce their shirking behaviours / corruptions.

In contrast, the tender evaluation of a construction project in the UK or Hong Kong is normally performed by either the developer's in-house professional team, or more commonly, by an independent professional advisor, who is most likely a quantity surveying firm.

Hypothesis

As the laws have specifically addressed the possibility of corruption in real estate / construction related enterprises, we shall observe that, other things being equal, the efficiencies of real estate developers will increase as the laws are implemented.

Evaluation Method and Data

Yung (2008a) and Yung and Lai (2009) have used capital-output ratio, an essential part of the Harrod-Domar growth model, to examine whether the mandatory tender evaluation by ISCs have actually improved the efficiency of developers. They found no evidence of any improvements in efficiencies. In fact, the efficiencies measured by the capital-output ratio

---

[1] The "titles" such as "engineer," "senior engineer," and "engineer at the professor level" are awarded by the relevant human resource departments of the government.

actually decreased for both SOEs and non-SOEs (Yung and Lai 2009). This chapter will follow the method used in Yung (2008a) and Yung and Lai (2009). However, instead of comparing the efficiencies of SOEs and non-SOEs, only the overall efficiencies for the whole nation will be used. In addition, the data range will be extended to cover the period from 1990 to 2007. The possible deficiency in data will also be addressed.

The capital-output ratio measures the efficiency of converting inputs into outputs. Inputs are measured in terms of monetary investment in construction and installations, while outputs are measured by the floor space of buildings that are under construction or have been completed. The data for evaluating the hypotheses was obtained from the *China Statistical Yearbook* compiled by the National Bureau of Statistics of China. The nominal monetary investments will be discounted with the Construction and Installation Price Index (CIPI) published by the same authority. The results are presented in the next section.

Results and Discussion

Figure 1 shows the capital-output ratio in China from 1991 to 2007, discounted to 2007 constant prices. Obviously the capital-output ratio has been decreasing over the years. There are three possible reasons.

First, the efficiency of developers actually decreased over the years. If this is the only reason, the results of Yung (2008) and Yung and Lai (2009) will be confirmed.

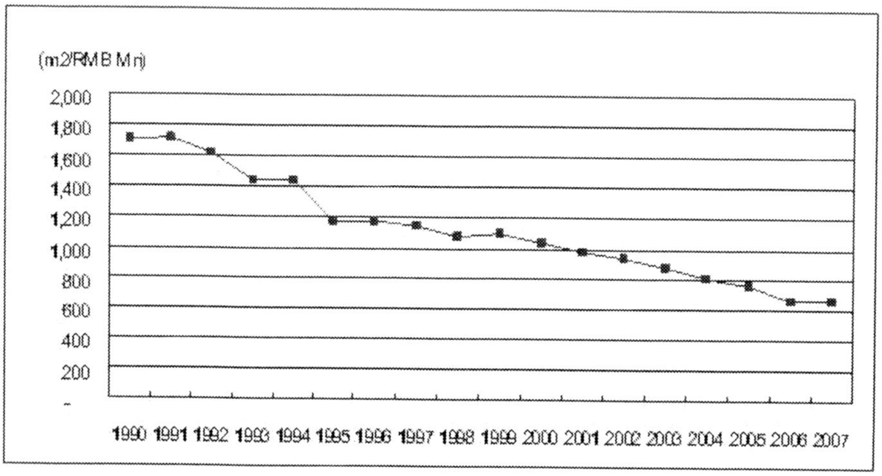

Source: China Statistical Yearbook, various years

Figure 1. Capital-Output Ratio in China (2007 constant prices).

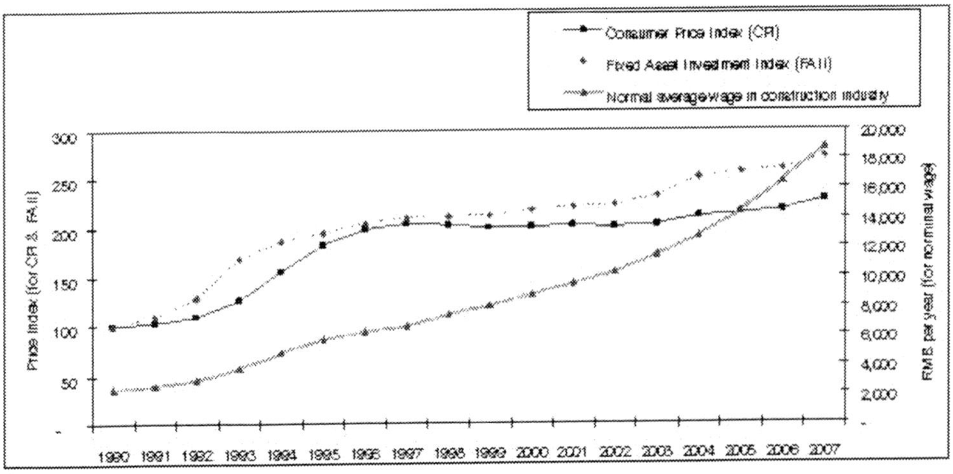

(Source: China Statistical Yearbook, various years)

Figure 2. Trends of Price Indices and Nominal Average Wages.

Second, the Construction and Installation Price Index (CIPI), which we used for discounting, have been under-estimated. Figure 2 shows the trends of Consumer Price Index (CPI), CIPI as well as the nominal average wage in construction industry over the period from 1990 to 2007. We can see that over the period of 18 years, CPI in 2007 was 2.28 times that in 1990, slightly less than the increase in CIPI (2.71 times). However, both are significantly less than the rise in wages (7.87 times). As labour normally forms 40-50% of construction costs, average construction costs in 2007 shall be about 3.15-3.94 times of those in 1990, assuming material and plant costs remain the same. However, we know that materials and plant costs have gone up in this long period. As a result, there is evidence that the Construction and Installation Price Index has been underestimated.

Although we found some evidence that the price indices might have been underestimated, we don't know the "true" level of the price indices. Since *China Statistical Yearbooks* are the official publications of the Chinese government, we have to accept this deficiency and interpret the results with care.

Third, the specification levels of buildings have been increased. The economy of China has been developing at an amazing rate of about 10% for nearly 30 years (Cheung 2008). As the economy has grown, specification levels increased. People in China 30 years ago lived in properties generally without building services. Electricity was the only type of building service a building in an urban area provided for many years. It only became available in rural areas much later. Plumbing and drainage systems and fire services were gradually provided in residential buildings during the 1980s, while air conditioning only became widely affordable during the late 1990s. Today, fast lifts, building automation systems, and advanced telecommunications are standard in many parts of China. As the specification levels increased, unit construction cost increased, hence lowering the capital output ratios.

To summarize, decreases in capital output ratio might be due to the underestimate in price indices or increases in specification levels. However, at least we can say that we found no evidence that efficiency of property developers had increased over the period, and we can conclude that the mandatory tendering and mandatory Independent Specialist Committee tender evaluation system did not improve their efficiency. Yung and Lai (2009) suggested that one way to improve the efficiency of developers is to better delineate the property rights of the enterprises, as the capital-output ratios of non-State-Owned Enterprises (SOEs) have always been much higher than those of SOEs.

MANDATORY CONSTRUCTION SUPERVISION

This section will introduce and evaluate the mandatory construction supervision system which is another important institutional arrangement in the construction industry in China. The effects of this system on both construction quality and safety will be evaluated.

Policy Background

The mandatory construction supervision system was introduced to China's construction industry in 1988. It was formally adopted in the *Construction Law of the People's Republic of China* in 1997. Under the law and its subsidiary regulations, virtually all "large or medium-sized" buildings or building blocks of "extensive" scale need construction supervision. Large or medium refers to a project commanding an investment of over RMB 30 million, while the term "extensive" means a project with a gross floor area of over 50,000 square metres.

The construction supervision works shall be conducted by licensed construction supervision firms. There are three categories of qualification licences (zizhi). The categorization of qualification licences is based on the registered capital, the qualifications of the technical staff employed and their professional job experience. Construction supervision firms shall confine their business to those projects of the scale permitted in their qualification licenses.

Only those who have passed in the construction supervisor qualification examination and obtained the Construction Supervisor Qualification Certificate are eligible to registration as construction supervisor. By the end of 2007, there were 71,133 registered construction supervisors in China (Ministry of Construction 2008).

The theoretical role of construction supervisors in China, save for a few minor distinctions, resembles that of project managers in the West (Liu et al 2004). The design institutes in China seldom perform any contract administrative roles in the post-contract stage. The construction supervisors will perform many of these contract administration tasks. In contrast, in the UK system, the architect will normally be the contract administrator in the traditional procured projects.

However, despite the numerous services that could be provided by construction supervision firms and the complexity of system, it has been reported that construction supervisors were often limited to the quality control of works in the construction stage, and that the system has brought about improvements to the Chinese construction industry (Chan et al. 1999, Liu et al. 2004).

In contrast, the JCT Standard Building Contract in the UK stipulates that contractors are always responsible for the quality of construction works stipulated in the contract bills, while the contract administrator only needs to express opinion on the quality of works which are stated to be "to the satisfaction of the contract administrator".

The construction supervisor acted as the "Engineer" as defined in the International Federation of Consulting Engineers (FIDIC) contract in some projects. One may think that the "Engineer" in a FIDIC contract will take up most of the contract administration tasks. However, the clients in China generally have a large project management team. One major problematic area in the roles of construction supervisor lies in the division of authorities between the client's project managers and the construction supervisors. It seems that there is no commonly agreed rule on the division of authorities. As a result, documents are often required to be signed by four parties, namely, the client, the contractor, the design institute and the construction supervisor.

Hypothesis

It has been reported that construction supervisors were often limited to the quality control of works in the construction stage, and that the system has brought about improvements to the Chinese construction industry (Chan et al. 1999, Liu et al. 2004). As the mandatory construction supervision has been implemented only gradually due to lack of qualified personnel, we shall expect *gradual improvements in construction quality over the years* after the introduction of the new system.

Yung and Lai (2008) found that the construction qualities, measured by the "Good Quality Rates", of both projects by State-Owned Enterprises (SOEs) and non-SOEs at national level gradually improved over the years. Yung and Yip (2010) took a further step to show that Good Quality Rates of both projects by SOEs and non-SOEs at province level gradually improved. This study will examine the trends of the overall Good Quality Rates at national level, without distinguishing SOEs and non-SOEs, similar to Yung (2008a).

As to construction safety, Yung (2009a) has documented and evaluated how institutional arrangements in construction industry had affected construction safety at a macro level. Essentially, there are three institutional reasons. First, construction workers consist of mainly "farmer workers", a concept unique in China. Farmer workers work for salaries but were registered in the Census Register as "farmers". They cannot enjoy the social benefits like their urban counterparts do. Historical reasons have made their social status very low. They have very low bargaining powers against either property developers or contractors. They cannot negotiate a good and safe working environment. Second, the contractual arrangements in construction industry merely consider time, cost and quality of the project. Safety has never been seriously addressed. The most a contract will do is to stipulate that contractors must comply with the relevant laws and regulations on safety. Hence, laws are the only protection construction workers may have. Third, the extensive subcontracting in the industry will cause more safety problems.

Hence, we can see that the more the law protects the workers, the better the safety performance will be. The laws and regulations enacted during 1990s tend to protect the workers more. For instance, contractors are made responsible for site safety[2], and they shall compensate workers who suffer from accidents. For a detailed discussion, see Yung (2009a).

Hence, we shall observe that as the laws protecting the workers are gradually implemented, *the safety performance will increase gradually.*

---

[2] Clause 45 of the Construction Law of the People's Republic of China.

Yung (2009a) evaluated the safety performance at province level and found that safety performance increased gradually. This study will evaluate the trends of safety performance at national level. In addition, the fatality cases and serious injury cases will be treated separately.

Evaluation Method and Data for Construction Quality

For the purpose of this study, quality is defined as the total floor areas of "Good Quality Projects" as a percentage of total floor area of completed projects in a particular year (referred to as "Good Quality Rates"). Good quality projects here refer to those projects accredited as "good quality" by the relevant government quality supervision department according to the quality standard prevailing at the time of inspection. The quality standards prevailing during our study period were those prescribed by the *Standards for Assessment of Quality of Construction and Installation Projects* (GBJ300-88), in which three categories of quality, namely, good, pass and fail were defined.

All the data will be collected from various issues of *China Statistical Yearbook*. The longest data set one can get is from 1991 to 2001. A different quality measure, namely, the percentage of projects qualified (as "pass") at the first check, was reported for the year 2002. This measure is not compatible with those of early years. Hence, it was not included in this study. Moreover, no measure of construction quality of whatsoever, has been published for the years afterward.

We shall observe the trends of the Good Quality Rate over the years. If there was a general increase in the trend, the hypothesis will be confirmed.

Evaluation Method and Data for Construction Safety

The mandatory reporting of "serious accidents" started in 1989 when the *Provisions on the Procedures of Reporting and Investigating Serious Construction Accidents*[3] came into effect. "Serious accidents" are classified into four categories as shown in Table 1. For the purpose of this study, there will be three measures of safety performance, namely the number of accidents (of Class 4 and above), fatalities and serious injuries per 10,000 workers in a particular year (referred to as Accident Rate, Fatality Rate, and Injury Rate respectively).

We shall observe the trends of Accident Rate, Fatality Rate and Injury Rate over the years. If there were general decreases in the trend, the hypothesis will be confirmed. All the data was collected from various issues of *China Building Industry Year-book*. Only six years of data (1994, 1996-2000) were available. As it covered the years immediately after the adoption of the mandatory construction supervision system, the period is considered of sufficient duration to evaluate the hypothesis.

[3] These were enacted on 30 September 1989 by Order No. 3 of the Ministry of Construction of China, effective from 1 December 1989.

Table 1. Classification of Serious Accidents in China.

	Accidents resulting in one of the following conditions		
Class	Fatalities	Injuries	Economic Loss
1	Not less than 30		Not less than RMB 3 million
2	10 - 29		RMB 1 – 3 million
3	3 - 9	Not less than 20	RMB 0.3 – 1 million
4	No more than 2	3 - 19	RMB 0.1 – 0.3 million

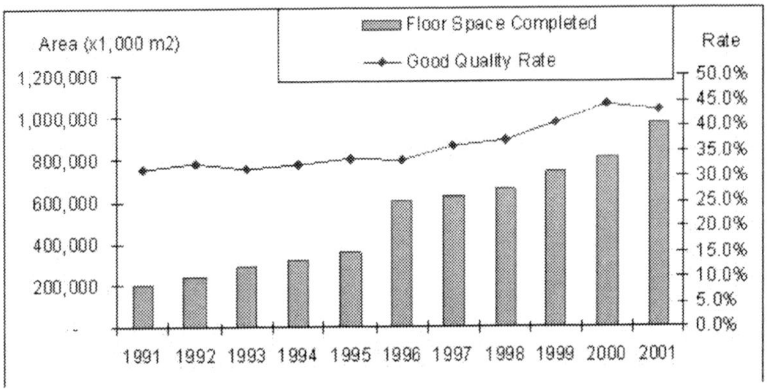

(Source: China Statistical Yearbook, various years)

Figure 3. Total Floor Space Completed and Rate of Good Quality Projects.

Results and Discussion for Construction Quality

Figure 3 shows the results of total areas of floor space completed in various years and their associated good quality rates. We can see that the total areas of floor space completed in each year went up quite rapidly during the period, reflecting the rapid economic development in China during the period. Despite the sharp increase in the total areas of buildings completed, the Good Quality Rate still went up generally during the period. This indicated that the general quality levels of construction projects increased.

Of course, one may argue that construction quality is affected by many factors, for instance, Yung and Lai (2008) and Yung and Yip (2010) found that availability of resources, and nature of construction firms (whether being SOEs or not) would affect Good Quality Rates as a measure of construction quality. However, by merely observing the increasing trends in the Good Quality Rates, we could safely conclude from our results that our hypothesis has not been refuted.

Results and Discussion for Construction Safety

Figure 4 shows the Accident Rate, Fatality Rate and Injury Rate per 10,000 workers in China over the period from 1994 to 2000. We can see that every rate shows a decreasing trend.

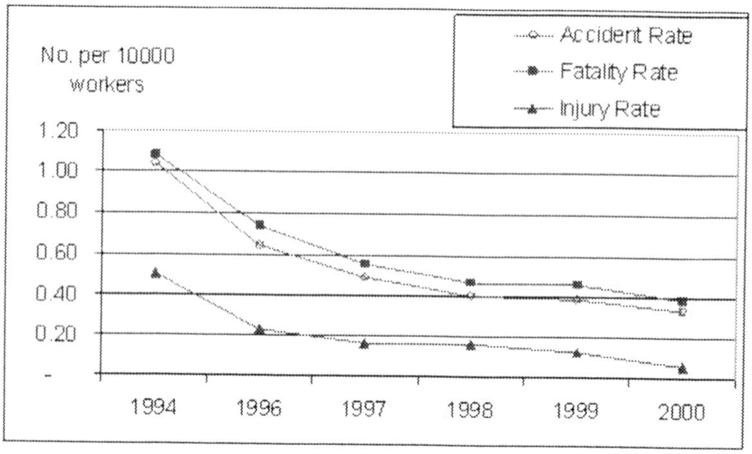

(Source: China Building Industry Year-book, various years)

Figure 4. Accident Rate, Fatality Rate and Injury Rate.

Again, there are many factors that may affect construction safety. For instance, most studies concluded that support from higher management (Cheng, et al 2004, Hinze and Rabound 1998, Jannadi 1996, Jaselskis, et al. 1996, Sawacha, et al. 1999, Tam et al. 2004) and safety training (Cheng, et al. 2004, Hinze and Gambatese 2003, Jannadi 1996, Jaselskis, et al. 1996, Lee and Halpin 2003, Tam and Fung 1998, Tam et al. 2004) are two of the most important factors affecting construction safety. In addition, Yung (2009a) approached the matter from a macro perspective of institutional arrangement, and found that the subcontracting rate is also a significant factor.

However, by merely observing the decreasing trends in all the three rates, we could safely conclude that our hypothesis has not been refuted. Indeed, the safety performance had been improving continuously in the study period.

MANDATORY USE OF BQ PROCUREMENT METHOD

Policy Background

The traditional procurement method, or the "Quota" system, had been practiced for decades before 2003. The Quota system was quite similar to a pre-priced standard schedule of rates re-measurement procurement method in the UK quantity surveying system.

There are, of course, some major differences. First, the Quota system itself incorporates a method of measurement. In contrast, the British system has a separate Standard Method of Measurement. Second, there are different versions of Quota systems complied for buildings, landscaping, civil engineering works, etc. Each province will publish its own version of Quota. Third, some parameters, e.g. the percentage add-on for site overhead, etc., are prescribed according to the "social average". Last but not least, in the UK pre-priced standard schedule of rates re-measurement procurement method, the tenderers are not allowed to change individual rates. Instead, they compete on a percentage addition or deduction. Similarly, the Quota system is a pre-priced standard schedule of rate. However, the rates are not regularly updated. This was not a problem twenty years ago as the economy was still centrally planned and all prices were controlled. However, this could not satisfy the demand of rapidly changing markets nowadays. Hence, the parties to a contract will normally refer to some official price document published, usually monthly, by a certain authority. An example will illustrate this. Suppose an item "concrete", measured in cubic metres, consists of certain quantities of materials (cement, sand, aggregate, water, etc), certain quantities of labour and plant use. The prices of materials, labour and plant will be adjusted, but not the quantities.

In 2003, a procurement method reform took place in China when the *China National Standard GB50500-2003* (Ministry of Construction 2003) came into effect. This is an attempt by the Chinese government to replace the previous Quota system with a procurement system based on bills of quantities (BQ). The majority of the standard is actually the methods of measurement for all the trades. All the projects mainly funded by public funds are required to use this BQ procurement system, while private projects are urged to use this system.

The Chinese government was very keen to promote this system. It has been seven years since the adoption of the BQ system, supposedly there should have been enough time to abandon the use of the old Quota system. However, the old Quota system seems to be persisting in many parts of the country. For instance, the Liaoning Province published an updated version of Quota system in 2008. There must be some reasons for the persistence of the Quota system. These are discussed in the next section.

Discussion

There are several reasons why the old Quota system persists. These are mainly based on the observations of the author as a quantity surveyor working on China projects for nearly 5 years. First, the old Quota system was built upon the ideology that cost determines price. All the rates and prices were built up with all the resources required, reflecting the productivity level in the society. The new BQ system was built upon the ideology that market forces determine prices. This fundamental shift in ideologies has proved difficult.

The Terminal 3 project of Beijing Capital International Airport was one of the earliest large projects that used this BQ system. The shift from the old Quota system to the new BQ system was one of the reasons why a very complicated governance structure of consultant teams was formed (Yung 2008b). When the author was preparing pre-tender estimates for this project, the client frequently asked questions such as "what labour rate have you allowed in your costing?" This to some extent reflected the ideology that cost determines price. A quantity surveyor in the UK or Hong Kong will care more about the all-in supply and installation rates instead of the labour contents within the rates.

Second, the education system in China can hardly cope with the new system. There is no course in China equivalent to the UK quantity surveying courses. There are indeed courses on construction management or construction cost management. However, the old Quota system is still taught with much emphasis. The students graduating from this education system are likely to be familiar with the Quota system, perhaps even more than the new BQ system.

Third, unlike the case in the UK where the majority of the buildings are low rise small-scaled ones, the buildings in China cities tend to be high rise large-scaled ones. There are generally hundreds of variations in each project. Quota system offers a convenient and widely accepted mechanism to solve the problems of "star rates".

The experience in Hong Kong will demonstrate its importance. Star rates are the rates for the work items, created by variations, hence not covered in the bills of quantities. The parties need to agree on the rates of these items. Where there are a lot of star rates in a project, it is often a lengthy process for the quantity surveyor, on behalf of the client, to agree on all the rates with the contractor. That is why sometimes it takes years to settle the final account after the practical completion. It is not infrequent that the matter shall be settled by commercial ways, where the client and the contractor agree on a lump sum to settle the final account, because the quantity surveyor cannot agree on everything with the contractor within a reasonable time.

Given the difficulties in agreeing the prices of items new to the bills of quantities, the availability of a universally agreed method of pricing is valuable. Having been practised in China for decades, the Quota system serves this function perfectly. This is probably one major reason why Quota system persists. The SPON's price books or the like in the UK serve similar functions, although they are complied by private quantity surveying firms.

CONCLUSION

This chapter documents the institutional arrangements in China's construction industry. It concentrates on the three major differences between the Chinese and the UK systems, namely, the mandatory tender evaluation by an Independent Specialist Committee (ISC), the mandatory construction supervision system, as well as the mandatory use of bills of quantities procurement method for government projects.

The mandatory tender evaluation by an Independent Specialist Committee (ISC) was meant to reduce the discretionary power of developers in selecting contractors. The efficiency of developers, measured by capital-output ratio, showed no signs of improvement from 1990 to 2007. This means the ISC tender evaluation system did not achieve its intention.

The mandatory construction supervision system was meant to improve the quality and safety performance of the construction projects. The construction quality was measured by the Good Quality Rate which is the total floor areas of projects accredited as "good quality" as a percentage of the total floor areas completed in a certain year. The Good Quality Rate from 1991 to 2001 did generally increase. As the study period covers both the times before and after the implementation of the mandatory construction supervising system, we can conclude that the system did improve construction quality. The construction safety was measured by the accident rate, fatality rate and injury rate per 10,000 workers in a particular year. All the rates from 1994 to 2000 decreased, showing that construction safety did improve during the period.

The effects of the mandatory bills of quantities procurement system were not covered in the study, as the effects on the construction industry were still unknown. However, the persistence of the old Quota system in many parts of China is worth of attention. The author believes there are three reasons, namely the difficulty in changing ideologies, the continuous emphasis on the Quota system in the education system, and the practical purpose of providing a universally agreed method of pricing items not included in the bills of quantities. Further studies could be directed towards this topic.

It is hoped that this chapter will provide some insights for academia or international construction professionals seeking to work in China.

REFERENCES

[1] Chan, W. K. L., Wong, F. K. W. & Scott, D. (1999). Managing construction projects in China - the transitional period in the millennium. *International Journal of Project Management, 17(4)*, 257-263.

[2] Cheng, E. W. L., Li, H., Fang, D. P. & Xie, F. (2004). Construction safety management: an exploratory study from China. *Construction Innovation, 4(4)*, 229-241.

[3] Cheung S. N. S. (2008). The economic system of China. Hong Kong: Arcadia Press.

[4] *China Building Industry Year-book,* (1995-2002). China: China Building Industry Publication.

[5] Hinze, J. & Gambatese, J. (2003). Factors that influence safety performance of specialty contractors. *Journal of Construction Engineering and Management, 129(2)*, 159-164.

[6] Hinze, J. & Rabound, P. (1988). Safety on large building construction projects. Journal of *Construction Engineering and Management, 114(2)*, 286-293.

[7] Jannadi, M. O. (1996). Factors affecting the safety of the construction industry. *Building Research and Information, 24(2)*, 108-111.

[8] Jaselskis, E. J., Anderson, S. D. & Russell, J. S. (1996) Strategies for achieving excellence in construction safety performance. *Journal of Construction Engineering and Management, 122(1)*, 61-70.

[9] Lee, S. & Halpin, D. W. (2003) Predictive tool for estimating accident risk. *Journal of Construction Engineering and Management, 129(4)*, 431-436.

[10] Liu, G., Shen, Q., Li, H. & Shen, L. (2004) Factors constraining the development of professional project management in China's construction industry. *International Journal of Project Management, 22*, 203-211.

[11] Ministry of Construction. (2003). China National Standard GB50500-2003, *Code of Valuation with Bill Quantity of Construction Works*. Beijing: China Planning Publication. [In Chinese]

[12] National Bureau of Statistics of China. (1996-2009). *China Statistical Yearbook*. Beijing: China Statistics Press.

[13] Ramus, J., Birchall, S. & Griffiths, P. (2006). *Contract Practice for Surveyors*. 4th ed. Oxford: Elsevier.

[14] Sawacha, E., Naoum, S. & Fong, D. (1999). Factors affecting safety performance on construction sites. *International Journal of Project Management, 17(5)*, 309-315.

[15] Tam, C. M. & Fung, I. W. H. (1998). Effectiveness of safety management strategies on safety performance in Hong Kong. *Construction Management and Economics, 16(1)*, 49-55.

[16] Tam, C. M., Zeng, S. X. & Deng, Z. M. (2004). Identifying elements of poor construction safety management in China. *Safety Science, 42*, 569-586.

[17] Yung, P. & Lai, L. W. C. (2008). Supervising for quality: an empirical examination of institutional arrangements in China's construction industry. *Construction Management and Economics, 26(7)*, 723-737.

[18] Yung, P. & Lai, L. W. C. (2009). Quality assurance in construction by independent experts: a case study of the efficiency performance of state-owned enterprises in China. Environment and Planning B: *Planning and Design, 36(4)*, 682-697.

[19] Yung, P. & Yip, B. (2010). Construction quality in China during transition: A review of literature and empirical examination. *International Journal of Project Management, 28(1)*, 79-91.

[20] Yung, P. (2008a). The Effects of Institutional Reforms on China's Construction Industry. Projects and Profits – Icfai University Press VIII(5), 57-61. Reprinted in Asis Kumar Pain ed. (2009). *Construction Industry: Changing Paradigm.* India: The Icfai University Press, 216-223.

[21] Yung, P. (2008b). Multi-level contractual links among project teams: A case study. *Construction Information Quarterly, 10(4)*, 171-175.

[22] Yung, P. (2009a). Institutional arrangements and construction safety in China: an empirical examination. *Construction Management and Economics, 27(5)*, 439-50.

[23] Yung, P. (2009b). Principal agent theory and private property rights in China's economic reform. China: *an International Journal, 7(1)*, 57-80.

In: Project Management
Editor: Robert J. Collins, pp. 183-192

ISBN: 978-1-61761-460-6
© 2011 Nova Science Publishers, Inc.

Chapter 8

THE TRADITIONAL AND VIRTUAL MODELS AS INSTRUMENTS OF VALUE DELIVERY IN CONSTRUCTION PROJECTS

O.K.B. Barima
University of Hong Kong

ABSTRACT

Physical face-to-face interaction is often used in traditional construction product delivery. However, in recent times a progressively important concept (the virtual model) has emerged in construction project delivery. Via the virtual model, construction actors maintain less physical presence and rely on information and communication technology (ICT) tools to operate irrespective of time and space constraints to deliver common value delivery goals. This paper explores the perceived utility in the use of the 2 models (traditional and virtual) in value delivery in construction projects.

The study uses qualitative methods to examine the topic. Twenty-nine semi-structured interviews were done. Cross-verified data were analyzed and consolidated into themes. The results were then examined by 8 experts to illuminate the findings.

The following four segmented views emerged. First, the virtual model is seen as better than the traditional concept in value delivery in projects. Second, the 2 concepts are perceived to be complementary in value delivery in projects. Third, value delivery via the 2 media are seen to be the same. Fourth, the traditional concept is perceived to provide better value than the virtual concept in construction project delivery. The complementary use of the strengths of both concepts in a synergistic manner is, however, recommended to attain improved value delivery in construction projects.

Keywords: Virtual projects; traditional construction projects; value delivery

INTRODUCTION

Construction project delivery has traditionally relied greatly on traditional methods such as high face-to-face interaction, the use of traditional media (e.g. postal mail delivery) and two dimensional (2D) drawings for task delivery. These methods have been used over the years to deliver construction products and services worth several billions of dollars across the world.

However, recent technological developments in the information and communication technology (ICT) sector has enabled the introduction of innovative tools such as the so-called virtual model in task delivery in construction projects. Through the use of this model construction actors can, for example, rely on ICT tools to access task delivery information irrespective of their geographic location in project delivery. The virtual model has the potential to give relative benefits such as time and cost savings in construction task delivery (Barima, 2003a, b; Laudon and Laudon, 2005; Oustuizen et al., 1998).

Though the virtual model has been suggested as one of the innovative tools which can improve on traditional construction task delivery (Barima, 2003a,b; Barima, 2009; CIRC, 2001), there are however potential threats in the use of the model in project delivery. For example, the intrinsic nature of construction products make the use of traditional methods such as high physical face-to-face interaction in task delivery important. Maintaining less physical presence (as used in the virtual model) can affect the quality of task supervision at the construction project sites. What then are the perceived utility in the use of the traditional and virtual models in task delivery in construction projects?

This study investigates the perceived utility in the use of the virtual and traditional models as instruments of value delivery in construction projects. The study explores the perceptions of construction professionals on this topic and adds the following to the literature. First, it increases understanding on the topic. Second, it provides empirical evidence on the perceived utility of the 2 models in construction project delivery. Third, it gives insight which can support the making of better informed decisions on the subject.

The virtual model is defined as the reliance by construction actors on ICT tools to collaborate irrespective of time and space constraints to deliver common project goals, whilst maintaining less physical presence(Barima, 2003a,b; Barima, 2009; Oustuizen et al., 1998). The traditional model is defined as the major use of traditional methods such as physical face-to-face interaction, 2D drawings, and other traditional media (e.g. postal mails) in construction project delivery (Barima, 2003a, b; Oustuizen et al.,1998). The traditional methods are deemed in this study to exclude the use of ICT tools. Since value can mean different things to different people, value in this study is defined as the attainment of the project end delivery attributes via the use of efficient processes to achieve effective results delivery (Barima, 2009).

The rest of the paper is structured as follows. The next section provides the background and context of the study. Then the research methods used in this study are given. The findings, discussion and limitations of the study precede the conclusions of the paper.

BACKGROUND

The construction industry is a key sector in many economies. The industry accounts for the supply of products which support the delivery of goods and services in other sectors of the economy (CIRC, 2001; Tulacz, 2005). Several billions of dollars are therefore spent across the world in the procurement of construction products each year (Tulacz, 2005).

As an important industry, concerns have been raised in many places in the world about the construction industry in recent times (CIRC, 2001). These relate to issues such as the poor delivery of works, the slowness of the industry to adopt/adapt innovative tools and technologies, increasing costs in works delivery, and persistent disputes (CIRC, 2001).

To deal with some of the identified problems of the industry, scholars have made a number of recommendations. One of the key recommendations concerns the adoption of innovative tools and technology by actors in the industry to support the efficient and effective delivery of goods and services (Barima, 2003a, b; CIRC, 2001; Oustuizen et al., 1998). It is often argued that the infusion of innovative tools into the traditional modes of works delivery (in construction projects) can provide immense benefits in terms of parameters such as costs, time, functional and quality improvements (Barima, 2003a, b; Barima,2009; CIRC, 2001; Oustuizen et al., 1998).

Traditionally, construction works delivery in many places often entail the dominant use of physical face-face interaction, relatively lower application of sophisticated technology (depending on type of work), reliance on traditional communication tools (e.g. postal delivery systems), and significant reliance on physical presence in the delivery of tasks (Barima, 2003a,b; CIRC, 2001).

However, recent revolutionary strides in the Information and Communication Technology (ICT) sector has brought to the fore an innovative tool in the delivery of construction works. The so-called virtual model has emerged in construction project delivery.

The virtual model is progressively becoming important in construction project delivery (Barima, 2003a,b; Barima, 2009). Construction actors are increasingly relying on ICT tools such as the internet, project webs, intranets, extranets, emails and other ICT based tools to operate irrespective of location and time constraints to deliver common project delivery goals (Barima, 2003a,b;Oustuizen et al., 1998). Via the virtual model, actors also maintain less physical presence and collaborate to provide task deliverables (Barima, 2003a,b ; Oustuizen et al., 1998).

The use of the virtual model in construction project delivery has benefits and risks. Therefore there has been a number of studies on the utility and challenges of the use of this model (virtual) in project delivery in the construction industry. For example, Andresen, Christensen, and Howard (2003) observed that increases in the use of project webs in projects (especially large ones) were linked to expectations of increased efficiency and benefits. They used 4 case studies to investigate the use of project webs focusing on areas such as management, costs and benefits, and functionalities (Andresen, Christensen and Howard, 2003). The study found that the application of the tools did not give monetary benefits, but rather intangible benefits (Andresen, Christensen and Howard, 2003). Also, the study reported that one of the challenges was that users often lost patience with the use of the tools and completed their tasks via traditional methods (Andresen, Christensen and Howard, 2003).

Rivard et al. (2004) used case studies to examine the use of IT (Information Technology) in the Canadian construction industry. Architects, engineers, general contractors, and owners were interviewed. Electronic distribution of documents was identified to be more efficient and cheaper. Improvement in task delivery via the use of IT were also noted in the study. These include, for example, the ability of architects to handle design complexities better via the use of 3D tools to reduce errors, better exchange of information among project partners, improved productivity, better requirements planning and Bill of Quantities (BQ) preparation (Rivard et al, 2004). The study concluded that the wide use of IT could provide significant benefits (Rivard et al, 2004) in the industry. They noted however that the short span of projects coupled with unfavorable monetary conditions made the introduction of new technology difficult (Rivard et al., 2004). Also, lagging companies reduced the potential benefits of IT (Rivard et al., 2004).

Other noted potential benefits in the use of the virtual model include time and cost savings, flexibility and improved convenience in tasks delivery, potential access to massive information, information certainty, better access to information and financial control, improved product design and product delivery via the use of digital tools (Barima, 2003 a, b; Barima,2009; Samuelson, 2002).

In spite of the potential benefits of the virtual model, additional challenges in the use of the virtual model include the following. Loss of rich face-to-face interaction; potential poorer supervision of construction tasks; potential communication problems due to the lack of physical presence, the cost of systems and their attendant upgrading costs (Barima, 2003 a, b; Samuelson, 2002). Other issues also relate to problems associated with differences in the actors' culture, use of language, time zone issues, etc (Barima, 2003 a, b). Also a longitudinal study by Dorgan and Dowdy (2004) found that technology can give no better value unless it is linked with better management policy.

Certain studies have also given other triangulated perspective to the subject. For example, Barima (2003a,b) examined in detail the traditional and virtual concepts in project delivery. He argued that the virtual and traditional concepts are better seen to be in a form of a continuum. He explained that there can be various hybrids of combinations of the two concepts (with extreme versions of each concept on the extreme ends of the continuum). Also, he observed that though the virtual concept could give potential savings in time and cost it was important to deal with its potential challenges in order to increase these benefits.

Other works have also examined tactical applications of tools which can be used to enhance the use of the virtual model. For example, Waly and Thabet (2003) has shown the importance of the use of the virtual model to simulate alternate execution strategies before their actual implementation (Waly and Thabet, 2003). The use of such methods can enhance decision making, and assist in choosing better execution strategies in construction project delivery.

Though the efforts of scholars in examining aspects of the subject are commendable, further studies on the topic can enhance better understanding of the topic to help users make better informed decisions. This paper investigates the perceived utility in the use of the virtual and traditional models as instruments of value delivery in construction projects. This adds empirical evidence to the emerging body of knowledge on the topic (in this nascent field) to enhance understanding.

RESEARCH METHODS

The objective of this study was to examine the perceived utility in the use of the traditional and virtual models in value delivery in construction projects. To achieve this objective qualitative methods were used. The reason for this choice was as follows. This approach was deemed important in providing a deeper and richer inquiry of the subject. The qualitative methods included the use of observation, semi-structured interviews and desk studies.

The qualitative studies entailed the use of 32 professionals. The respondents were selected via theoretical/purposive sampling, and theoretical saturation guided the further selection of respondents. The respondents worked for companies with varied backgrounds. These companies included large, medium and small companies. Also, the companies operated locally (in Hong Kong) and internationally. The respondents occupied senior to middle level positions in their respective companies. They also comprised key professionals in the construction industry in Hong Kong. They included architects, engineers (structures, mechanical and electrical engineering services, planning), quantity surveyors, management information systems, risk and systems management analysts, estimators, and construction and project managers.

A qualitative research protocol was prepared to guide the studies. This protocol clearly defined the aims and objectives of the study, the study's background, the definition of the key constructs of the study, and the study's questions (among others).

Only respondents with adequate knowledge of the topic were selected for the study. Copies of documents containing the research aims/objectives, questions and definition of terms (among others) were sent to the respondents for their prior study before each interview. The respondents were also given the opportunity to clarify issues with the principal researcher before each interview. Also all the interviews were arranged at the convenience of the respondents.

The interviews were conducted in the offices of the respondents. The interviews lasted for an average of 1.15 hours. About 15 minutes was spent before and after each interview to build rapport. The responses were both recorded [audio] and transcribed. Both sources were used in tandem to capture an accurate record of the answers. To enhance quality assurance, the answers were cross verified by the respondents before they were used in the analysis.

Microsoft word was the primary software which was used to support data analysis. Data reduction via record and summary of repeating ideas was the first step in data analyses (Patton, 1980; Yin, 1994). This latter activity supported the consolidation of the ideas into themes. The findings from these activities were then incorporated into a draft report. Prior to the release of the draft report, presentations on the research findings were given at seminars to obtain feedback on the study. The draft report was also given to 8 experts on the topic to put the results into context. The next section provides the findings of the study.

FINDINGS/DISCUSSION

The respondents were asked to state in their own words the perceived differences in the utility in the use of the traditional and virtual models in value delivery in construction projects. Four themes were consolidated from the study. These were as follows.

1. The first school of thought holds that the virtual model is better than the traditional concept in value delivery.
2. The second school of thought sees value delivery via the 2 media to be the same.
3. The third school of thought perceives the 2 concepts as complementary in value delivery.
4. The fourth school of thought holds that the traditional concept provides better value than the virtual concept in construction project delivery.

The distribution of the respondents' views (in terms of percentages) was as follows.

Fifty two percent of the respondents supported the first theme. The second school of thought was held by 28 % of the respondents. The 3rd school of thought: 16 %. Four percent of the respondents supported the fourth theme.

Table 1 provides a summary of the key themes and corresponding comments which were distilled from the analyses of the study.

Typical Responses

The following are typical responses from some of the respondents on the perceived utility in the use of the virtual and traditional models in value delivery in construction projects.

Table 1. A summary of key themes and distilled comments.

Key theme	Distilled embedded comments
1.	Value from the 2 concepts are different. The virtual concept provides better value, and can give the following benefits. Visibility and certainty over traditional concepts; potential costs and time savings; savings in paperwork, storage space; potentially provides better environmental friendliness; opportunity to work over the 24 hours daily cycle; potential to perform tasks irrespective of location; easier access to overseas consultants and knowledge base; instant delivery/access to information; potential to be better in tune with the needs of clients.
2.	The 2 concepts give the same value. The end value through the use of the 2 concepts is the same. The key difference between the 2 concepts is via the means used in value delivery.
3.	Value from the 2 concepts differ, but it is better to see them as complementary.
4.	The traditional concept is superior since it provides better opportunity to evolve team/social events with stakeholders.

Theme 1: The virtual model is better than the traditional concept in value delivery

The consolidated responses under theme 1 support the view that the virtual model is better than the traditional concept in value delivery. The following are examples of typical responses under theme 1.

The contracts manager of a large construction client firm articulated the following view. The use of the virtual concept is better than the traditional concept in value delivery. The virtual model provides better opportunity for time and costs savings in value delivery.

Also, according to the director of a leading construction company, 'the use of the virtual model in the company has given better value by improving visibility and certainty in the company's activities. All authorized staff can access the same authorized information irrespective of where they are (in real time) and accordingly help in decision making or taking appropriate actions. Compared to the previous system (i.e. reliance on traditional methods) this would have been very difficult or impossible'.

To the Chief engineer of a medium sized subcontracting company, the virtual model is environmentally friendly, and it also helps to conserve storage apace. Via the use of the model there is lesser use of paperwork and physical hardcopies in routine task delivery.

Theme 2: Value delivery via the 2 media to be the same

Respondents who expressed views under this theme perceived the value delivered via the 2 concepts to be the same. A typical view was expressed by the contracts manager of a large construction company.

The 2 concepts are means towards an end. The end value via the use of the 2 concepts will be the same.

Theme 3: The 2 concepts are complementary in value delivery

The respondents who expressed views under this theme perceived the 2 concepts to be complementary. A civil engineer and a director of an engineering consulting firm articulated this typical view:

I believe that the 2 concepts (virtual and traditional) can be used in a complementary manner. None of the 2 concepts can wholly provide absolute value. Hence, a complementary use of the 2 concepts is better.

Theme 4: The traditional concept provides better value than the virtual concept in construction project delivery

Under this theme, the traditional concept was seen to be better than the virtual concept in value delivery. The construction site manager of a large construction client company articulated this deviant view.

Construction is production-oriented, and unless one gets this right even 1000 computers cannot help you. It is extremely important to maintain physical presence at construction project sites to get things done rightly. Hence, the traditional concept is far better than the virtual model, since one cannot replace rich face-to-face interaction by less physical presence and reliance on computers to get things done.

Discussion

The findings of this study are consistent (in part) with past studies. For example, previous studies have articulated the importance of the virtual model in the value delivery processes of construction projects, and articulated these benefits in the use of the concept. Cost and time savings (Barima, 2003a, b; Oustuizen et al., 1998) ; potential to perform tasks irrespective of location; instant delivery/access to information ; better exchange of information among project partners, improved productivity, and better product design and improved process design (Barima, 2003a,b ; Oustuizen et al., 1998; Rivard et al., 2004; Samuelson, 2002; Waly and Thabet, 2003).

Also studies sponsored by governments have recommended the introduction of ICT tools in the value delivery processes of construction projects to help improve on productivity and better service delivery (CIRC, 2001). These findings and recommendations (in a way) support the first theme in this study.

However, the construction industry (in many international locations) has been slow in adopting ICT in value delivery (Rivard et al., 2004). This perhaps suggests a high resistance to change and an affinity for the status quo (i.e. use of traditional methods). There may be many reasons for this: e.g. initial costs of systems and the costs associated with upgrading ICT systems (CIRC, 2001; Samuelson, 2002). Another reason can be the strong conviction of some practitioners in the industry for their preference for the traditional methods in task delivery (Barima,2003a,b; CIRC, 2001). This latter position can also be deduced from the findings of the 4th theme of this study. Indeed, as noted by one of the respondents in the study, construction is a production-oriented business. And the intrinsic nature of the products of the industry make certain attributes of the traditional concept very attractive. For example, rich face-to-face interaction is useful for physical supervision at the site where a slight error can even lead to huge losses.

There are also certain degrees of merit in the other 2 opinions articulated in the 2 additional themes. Thus, the view that the 2 concepts are means and hence the end delivered value via them is the same (i.e. theme 2). Also, the view expressed by some of the respondents that the 2 concepts have to be used in a complementary manner (i.e. theme 3). The merits in these positions are as follows. In relation to theme 2, it can be argued that if the focus in the construction delivery process is its end (or target) value, then the 2 concepts (virtual and traditional) can be seen as instruments of value delivery. Hence, irrespective of whatever means which is used the end delivered value is the same. However, the weakness in this position is that sometimes the use of 2 different means can give 2 different answers or ends. For example, in terms of construction products the end product may be say a house, yet, the quality, time and cost of the delivered house can be affected by the type of model used in its delivery.

Also in relation to theme 3, one can use the synergistic fusion of the strengths of each model for a better value delivery (from a bigger picture), instead of a focus and an extreme reliance on only one of the models. Indeed, as noted by Barima (2003 a, b), the 2 concepts are in a continuum and potential hybrids in the use of the 2 concepts can be useful to strengthen value delivery.

In summary, a better recommended opinion is the use of the 2 concepts in value delivery, where the strengths of the 2 can be used to support the weaknesses of the other. This position was accepted by the experts who reviewed the findings of this study. Previous studies by Barima (2003 a,b) has also articulated this view.

LIMITATIONS

Qualitative studies have been criticized to lack certain important virtues. These include issues such as methods which may be used in the selection of respondents (e.g. use of purposive sampling), reliability and dependability, potential deficiency in generalizing from such studies due to the lack of the use of scientific methods (such as random sampling) in the selection of respondents. It is worthy to note that the focus of this study was on analytic generalization and not statistical generalization. Also, the use of purposive/theoretical sampling in this study ensured the selection of theoretically helpful cases, and hence constrained unnecessary variation (as recommended by Einsenhardt, 1989; Yin, 1994). The use of a research protocol in the study also reinforced reliability in the study. All the methods used in the study were recorded, and hence this can support replication by other scholars in other research contexts (locally and internationally).

Also, to enhance the findings of the study, attention was given to quality assurance issues in the research. These included for instance the following. The use of respondents with adequate knowledge of the subject (for focus); the use of a research protocol to structure the investigation. The cross-verification of recorded data by the respondents to enhance credibility, the use of respondents with varied triangulated backgrounds (to capture a better breadth and depth of opinions across the industry on the subject). These activities helped to boost the credibility of the study.

CONCLUDING REMARKS

Four themes emerged from the investigation of the utility of the traditional and virtual models in value delivery in construction projects. The dominant view relates to the conception that the virtual concept provides better value than the traditional concept in construction projects. Some of these include time and cost savings, reduction in storage space, improved certainty and visibility in the use of information for task delivery.

The deviant theme concerned the perception that the traditional concept is better than the virtual model in value delivery. Reasons include the following. Construction is seen as production-oriented, and hence the rich use of physical face-to-face interaction is important for task delivery, and this cannot be replaced by less physical presence and reliance on computers (as done via the virtual model).

The other 2 themes support the following positions. The 2 concepts are complementary and have to be used to support each other. Also, the perception that the 2 models are better seen as means for the delivery of end targets, hence the end value via the use of the 2 models are the same. The latter view is weak, since the use of 2 different means (virtual and traditional) can provide different construction end products. The former view provides a potentially useful view in the use of the 2 concepts.

Both concepts (virtual and traditional) have strengths and weaknesses, and the synergistic use of the concepts is therefore recommended to support value in construction projects. Further studies are needed on this topic to accumulate evidence on the subject.

References

[1] Andresen J. L., Christensen, K. & Howard, R. W. (2003). *Project management*, ITcon *8*, 29-41.

[2] Barima, O. K. B. (2003a). The management of risks within the virtual construction project Environment. *Proceedings of CIB TG 23 International Conference on Professionalism in Construction(CD ROM)*, Hong Kong.

[3] Barima, O. K. B. (2003b). An exploratory study of the usage of virtual project management in South Africa. *Proceedings of CIB TG 23 International Conference on Professionalism in Construction(CD ROM)*, Hong Kong.

[4] Barima, O. K. B. (2009). Crucial tactical variables for value delivery in virtual projects. *Automation in Construction, 18(7)*, 865-1010.

[5] CIRC, (2001). Construct for excellence: Report of the construction industry review committee. *Hong Kong Administrative Government*, Hong Kong.

[6] Dorgan, S. J. & Dowdy, J. J. (2004). When IT lifts productivity: companies should beef up their management practices before focusing on technology. *The McKinsey Quarterly*, *4*. Retrieved June 5, 2004, from http: www. mckinsey quarterly.com/article_page.aspx?ar=1477&L2=13&L3=11&srid=63&gp=1

[7] Eisenhardt, K. M. (1989). Building Theories from case study research. *Academy of Management Review*, *14(14)*, 532-550.

[8] Laudon, K. C. & Laudon, J. P. (2005). Essentials of management information systems: Managing the digital firm (6th ed.). *Pearson Education International*, New Jersey.

[9] Ousthuizen, P., Koster, M. & Rey, P. D. L. (1998). Goodbye MBA: a paradigm shift towards Project management. *International Thomson publishing*, Johannesburg.

[10] Paton, M. Q. (1980). *Qualitative evaluation methods*. Sage publications Inc, Beverly Hills.

[11] Rivard, H., Froese, T., Waugh, L. M., El-Diraby, T., Mora, R., Torres, H., Gill, S. M. & O'Reilly, T. (2004). *Case studies on the use of information technology*, ITcon *9*, 19-34.

[12] Samuelson, O. (2002). *IT-Barometer 2000 - The Use of IT in the Nordic Construction Industry*, ITcon 7, 1-26.

[13] Tulacz, G. J. (2005). *World Construction Spending Nears $4 Trillion for 2004. Engineering News-Record,* (1/3-10/2005). Retrieved May 2, 2005 from http://www.enr.com/news/bizlabor/archives/050103-1.asp.

[14] Waly, A. F. & Thabet, W. Y. (2003). A virtual construction environment for pre-construction planning. *Automation in Construction, 12(2)*, 139-153.

[15] Yin, R. K. (1994). *Case study research: design and methods* (2nd edition). Sage publications Inc, Beverly Hills, California.

In: Project Management
Editor: Robert J. Collins, pp. 193-204

ISBN: 978-1-61761-460-6
© 2011 Nova Science Publishers, Inc.

Chapter 9

CONCURRENT ENGINEERING/SUPPLY MANAGEMENT PRINCIPLES IMPLEMENTATION BY SUBCONTRACTORS IN THE CONSTRUCTION INDUSTRY

Ander Errasti[1], Chike F. Oduoza[2] and Javier Santos[3]

[1]Industrial Organization, MGEP, University of Mondragon, Spain
[2]School of Engineering and Built Environment, University of Wolverhampton, WV1 1SB, UK
[3]Tecnun University of Navarra, Spain

ABSTRACT

This research aims to investigate the adoption of good practices in the construction industry based on practices applied in other sectors that could help to gain competitive advantage. Typical practices such as Concurrent

Engineering and Supply Chain Management are already established and have been applied by other researchers, however their deployment in the field of construction has not been widely explored.

The research methodology adopted is based on Action Research, in which researchers are involved in the change process. This method has been chosen because it is realistic and practical oriented.

Research carried out in the last three years has focused on the implementation of these practices with a view to improve performance of a case firm in the construction industry sector .The outcome is a total cost reduction achieved through production and assembly productivity increases as well as significant improvement in on-time deliveries to customers. The conclusion is that the benefits of the implementation of these principles in the construction sector are completely demonstrated.

1. Introduction

1.1. Paper Structure and Origins of the Research

The format for this paper describes the origin of the research, presents research questions supported with relevant literature review on Supply Chain Management and Concurrent Engineering. It then presents the research methodology and finally research outcomes followed by conclusions and future research questions.

This paper also presents the company, which has taken part in the action research, and the characteristics of the reengineering project carried out. Various authors have already identified the applications / uses of good practices in the Construction Sector. [1, 2] "Concurrent Engineering (CE) and Supply Chain Management (SCM) principles have been successfully implemented in the manufacturing industry and there is a possibility that they can be used to integrate the various disciplines of construction at the project level" Nevertheless the industry could be a critical factor to be taken into account in the relationship between customers and suppliers. [3]. Value management has been recognised as one of the most effective methodologies for achieving "best value for money" for clients since its introduction in the construction industry in the early 1960s. Shen and Liu [4] have identified the degrees of critical success factors for value management studies in construction.

2. Research Questions and Objectives

The literature has revealed that contractors and subcontractors work as a project based system. The trend in subcontractors project management is toward an integrated organisation [5], [6] and toward the implementation of Concurrent Engineering and Supply Chain Management Principles, [1], [2], [3], taking into account the position of the facility in the supply chains [7].

Construction Process Reengineering (CPR) can be successfully applied in the construction sector [8]. This approach considers applying techniques such as value analysis workshops in each project and partnering. A value analysis should be applied to the "product value stream" or system [9] [10], nevertheless subcontractors in the construction sector have difficulties to collaborate with customers and purchasing managers are skeptical about the benefits afforded through integration with suppliers [11]. Thus partnering issues become difficult to implement.

Consequently there appears to be a gap on how value analysis workshop techniques could be implemented by subcontractors in the construction sector taking into account that:

- subcontractors sometimes implement a project more than once providing an opportunity for improvement in the delivery process as well as for a family of new projects.
- managers of firms need to support project teams [5] to improve project delivery process.
- concurrent engineering principles need to be implemented as value analysis workshop technique.

This research aims to develop a methodology based on the CPR approach by applying Action Research (AR) in the construction industry sector. AR promoted by Rowley [12] suggests a case study approach to answer the "how and why" questions, and Westbrook [13] defines AR as a variation of case research. In addition, Vignalli [14] and Coughlan [15] state that AR is an appropriate method to extend theories. This paper therefore explores the manner in which value analysis techniques, supply chain management and concurrent engineering practices could be implemented in the construction industry, in order to minimise cost, enhance process and product quality and achieve on time delivery to the customer.

3. Review on Action Research, Supply Chain Management and Concurrent Engineering Practices

3.1. Action Research

There are various research methods available in operations management and researchers therefore, are able to choose the research strategy / methodology depending on the research questions to be answered [12]. Case Studies can be used for different types of research purposes such as exploration, theory building, theory testing and theory extension/refinement. AR can be seen as a variation of case research, in which the action researcher is not an independent observer [13]. Two dominate paradigms are striving for dominance in social sciences, the positivism and phenomenology. AR is a phenomenological method and could be used to generate or to extend new theories [14, 15].AR is a generic term, which covers many forms of action-oriented research and can be contrasted to positivist science. The aim of positivist science is the creation of universal knowledge, while AR focuses on knowledge in action [15]. AR needs the researchers to be involved in the cycle of planning, acting, observing and reflecting on their work more deliberately and systematically [16] and should be based on research questions as well as have conclusions as an output.

3.2. Supply Chain Management in the Construction Sector for Value Chain Improvement

The need to balance efficiency, quality assurance with compressed delivery times has compelled firms to link various functions, such as engineering, purchasing, operations and logistics. That highlights the need to manage firm resources as a series of interrelated flows and processes, [17] hoping to fulfil customer satisfaction as well as minimise the total cost of the chain. These principles have been named as Supply Chain Management, as it is concerned with the flow of materials and information from suppliers to customers. In construction industry supply chains, based on the client's brief, design consultants design and produce with the cost and bill of quantities. Thereafter, the project is passed on to the contractor who takes responsibility for the construction of the facility. The contractor subcontracts to subcontractors (Figure 1).

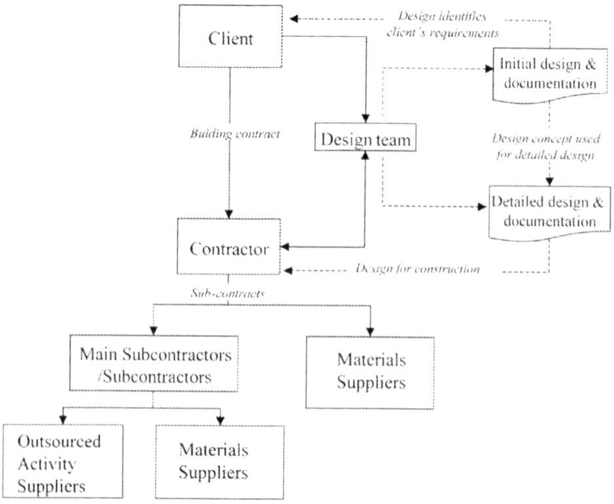

Figure 1. Agents involved in Design and Construction Projects and their relationships adapted from [18].

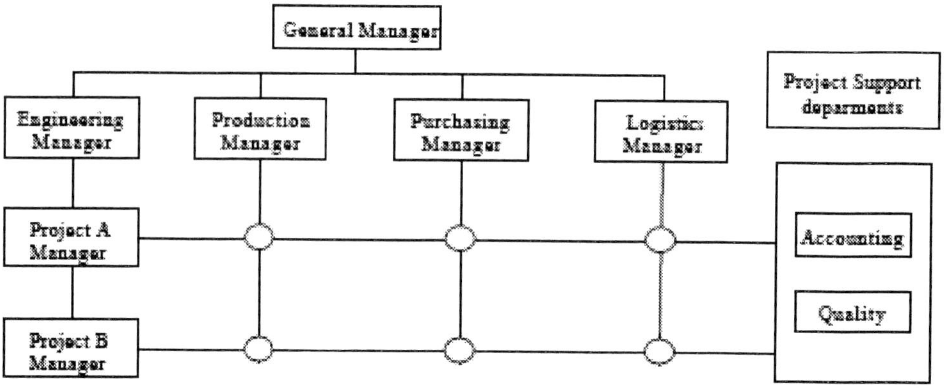

Figure 2. The matrix structure of a Project based organisation adapted from [5].

These subcontractors are subject to tremendous pressures in terms of Quality, Service and Cost [19]. In the construction industry the environment in which construction projects are delivered is not very friendly in the associated "form of contract". Each member of the project team would have to accept responsibility for failure to deliver, with the consequences for incurring penalty [6]. Thus, a supply chain management strategy is important for individual manufacturers explaining why subcontractors must develop a manufacturing strategy which is appropriate to the business environment and which takes account of the position of the manufacturing facility in the value chain [5].

Contractors and subcontractors work as a project based system. The trend in subcontractors' project management is toward an integrated organisation [18]. It is also a fact that organisational development is geared toward the management of projects. The company exists to support its project (Figure 2), while project teams are provided organisational support by the relevant line managers.

Multidisciplinary project teams [3] are compelled to apply Concurrent Engineering Principles in order to achieve reduced delivery times, improve quality and reduced cost by the integration of design and manufacturing activities [1], while simultaneously considering product and process structure [2] as well as integrating design and manufacturing functions [9]. They are therefore obliged to create value if they want to survive in a global competitive environment. Value in this context is defined as "the amount buyers are willing to pay, for what a firm is able to provide them" [22].

Some authors argue that value analysis may not only be restricted to value added by the company itself, but must also consider the extended enterprise including suppliers, distributors, customers and other stakeholders. Consequently the value chain concept must be extended beyond the value system of the company concerned [10]. Even if many enterprises are sacrificing cost effectiveness and customer satisfaction because they are unable to work effectively across the firms. not all trading relationships are collaborative [11]. For instance, Purchasing Managers are far more sceptical about the benefits afforded through such close integration, because they recognise the dependency on a small number of suppliers.

Different authors [8] conclude that all these paradigms can be renamed under a new concept called "Construction Process Reengineering (CPR). CPR therefore, is a holistic approach aimed to develop an improved project delivery process in construction. In this approach value analysis workshops are encouraged especially during the early design stage of each project and partnering with suppliers is also promoted.

4. Case Research Methodology: Role of the Researchers

The role of the researchers was to conduct the Value Analysis Workshops. The researchers have taken part in the reengineering process using a model called KATAIA [19]. This model is based on firstly giving priority to what and why analyse, secondly defining how to analyse and thirdly defining how to improve and measure the improvement issue (Figure 3). For this purpose different management and analysis tools such as BCG matrix and Value Chain have been used.

To apply this model to the company involved in the research, researchers have taken into account the recommendations from Boddy [20] for project planning, structure and implementation.

- Project planning: Setting clear goals, ensuring agreement with goals and having senior management commitment.
- Project structure: Creating structure to manage the change, ensuring adequate resources, having a respected champion, and appointing a capable project management team.
- Project implementation: Creating a project team with the right membership, preparing a detailed yet flexible project plan, consulting widely with those affected and setting up adequate controls

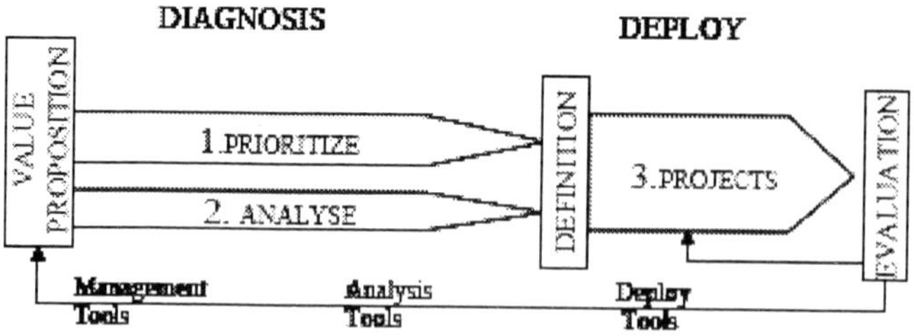

Figure 3. KATAIA Diagnoses and Deployment Model.

5. Case Study

5.1. Company Presentation

Company A is a Steel Construction company engaged in Integral Project Management, and performs basic design (and calculation) and production engineering, supply, manufacture, surface treatment and erection of all kinds of steel structures, from the simplest to the most elaborate, which stand out because of their size / complexity, for the following construction sectors: Industrial, Buildings, Public Works and Equipment Goods. To achieve this objective, Company A has a qualified and experienced staff, modern and up-to-date design, production and erection facilities, and financial resources.

5.2. Value Analysis Technique Implementation

5.2.1. Diagnosis stage

a. Prioritize: What and Why analyse

In order to prioritize the "family" of projects to undertake, Company A managers aided by the researchers fulfilled a BCG matrix. This management tool helped to determine the evolution of market growth and market share of each "family" of projects in order to prioritize the projects according to the need of the reengineering process.

The organisation's "families" of project situation and potential are represented in the BCG portfolio. Building sector family of projects was perceived to be changing from cash cows to dogs and Public Works projects were moving from Stars to Cash Cows. However, Equipment Goods market on the other hand had a growth tendency and seemed to migrate from Question Marks to Stars, if changes were successfully implemented in the project delivery process.

Equipment Goods "family" of projects thus were distinguished because of the potential and the possibility to increase their market share and market growth rate (Figure 4).

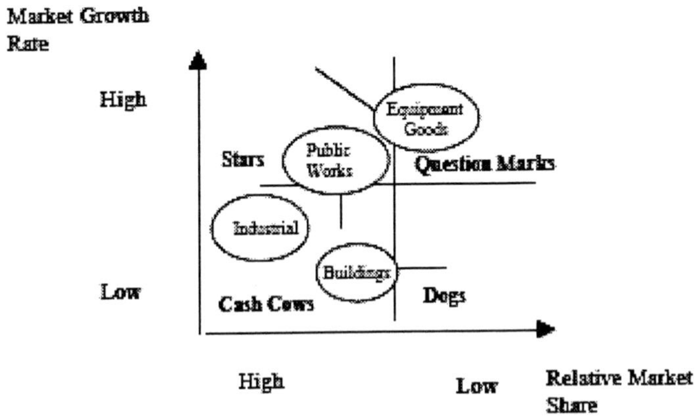

Figure 4. Market position of Company A family of projects represented in BCG Matrix.

There are known change drivers that force firms to start with a Reengineering process [21]. These change drivers are in Haque´s [6] opinion, improving product quality, reducing lead-time to market, reducing product cost and improving human resource utilisation. The most important reasons, in company A managers opinion, to start with the reengineering process of Equipment Goods projects were to reduce product cost and reduce lead-time to market in order to increase market share and market growth (Figure 4). These factors tend to maintain and promote product quality and human resource utilisation.

b. Analyse: Analysis Methodology

Since the diagnosis stage was focused on Equipment Goods projects, the researchers conducted the following analysis (Figure 5).

A. Define the Scope of the project

The research team members were identified taking into account that managers should support the improvement process [5]. Thus the Engineering, Production, Purchasing, and Logistics Managers took part in the study (Figure 2) as well as the project managers involved in the Equipment Goods "family" of projects including the researchers.

To monitor "how big the problem was" the team members collected the following data;

- Deviation of Cost in Public Works projects for the last ten years; 42 projects were carried out, where the mean deviation to cost was 3%. This deviation was found to be due to:
  (a) Low efficiency in production and assembly, as a result of the lack of coordination of engineering, logistics and production managers at the project planning phase
  (b) Low efficiency in production and assembly, from the lack of communication at the project delivery process definition upstream of the project life cycle.
- The number of lost proposals / tenders in Equipment Goods for incorrect pricing for the last ten years was identified:
  (a) 22 projects were lost for not meeting the customer target cost.
  (b) The estimate of needed improvement to reach the target cost was 4%.

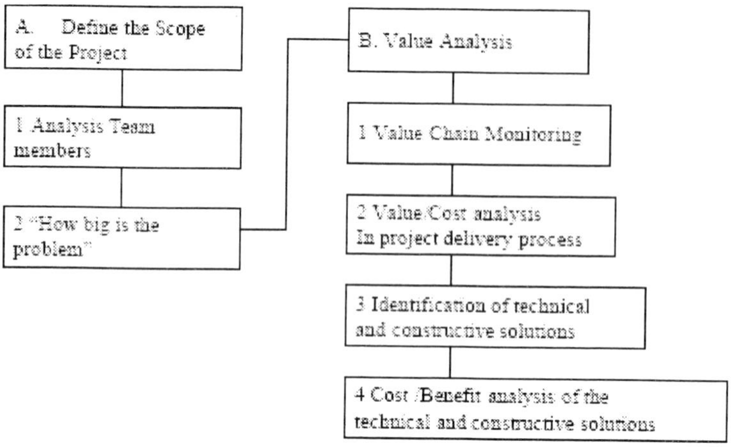

Figure 5. Steps in the analysis stage.

Based on the problem identification the following goal was formulated:

> "Reduce 5% of the integral cost of the project and by 10% of the project delivery time in Equipment Goods projects in order to gain in competitiveness and increased market share"

B. Value Analysis

The research team applied the Value Chain [10] approach to study the primary activities in Equip ment Goods projects. This approach consists of identifying the activities that create and build value (Figure 6)

The mean cost distribution of the primary activities was identified in order to do a value/cost analysis.

The Value Analysis workshop was discussed at four separate meetings in which the following issues were identified:

- Design team must watch out for project delivery process efficiency, functionality, manufacturability and ease of assembly of the product. Thus design for manufacturability and ease of assembly should involve purchasing, production and logistics departments at the design stage. This team has the necessary experience, knowledge and information about how downstream issues can be affected by design decisions.
- The design task sequence should be managed to achieve an increase in productivity in the production and assembly stages. Thus, design tasks must be reorganized and reprioritised in order to enhance productivity at the production and assembly stages. If design tasks are re-sequenced adequately this should enhance production activity with a resultant gain in overall productivity The benefits expected from such changes in the project delivery process were total production cost reduction of 12% and assembly cost reduction of 10%.

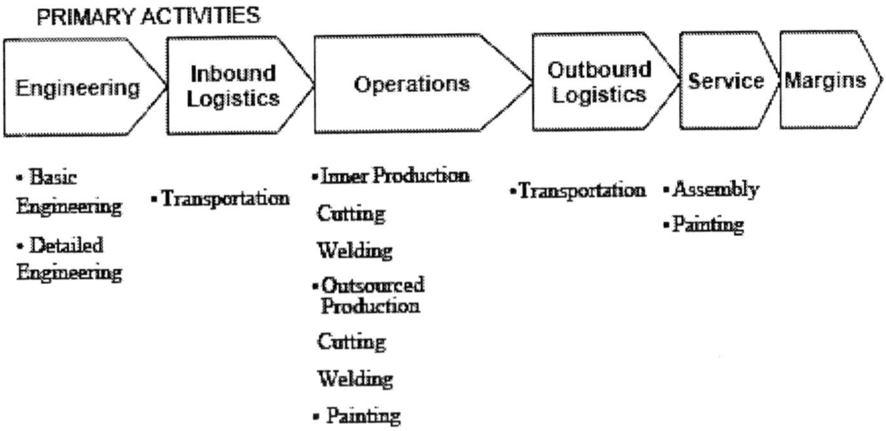

Figure 6. Primary activities of the project execution value chain.

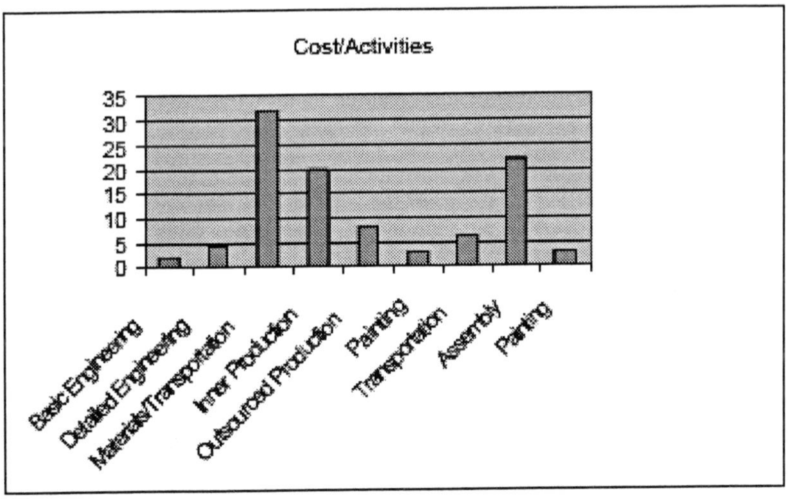

Figure 7. Cost distribution of the primary activities of the Equipment Goods projects.

5.2.2. Deployment stage

a. Projects: operational strategy deployment through projects

After the potential changes in the project delivery process were identified and the new improved process opportunities were mapped, managers decided on how to implement the changes in the organisation in terms of communication and implementation. The researchers educated all the members involved in Equipment Goods projects about this new way of managing projects.

Company A decided to implement the new ideas in a project that could be considered repetitive.

Company A works as the main subcontractor for the design, production and assembly of steel structures.

These structures are called portainer or gantry cranes, which are very large cranes used to load and unload container ships, and are only seen at container ports. They have a special lifting device called spreader for loading and discharging of containers and the whole crane runs on two railways so that it can traverse along the harbourside. These cranes are also referred to as quay cranes or dockside cranes . Lorries and container lifters, also known as straddle-carriers, can manoeuvre underneath the base of the portainer crane, and collect the 'boxes'.

The characteristics and outcomes from the reengineered process are:

- At project onset, Purchasing, Production and Logistic departments look into project process design aiming to obtain integral cost and project lead-time reduction.
- The operational strategy changes and the inner production department concentrates on procuring the final big parts while the suppliers in the subassembly concentrate on handling medium / little parts in order to increase productivity.
- The Project Delivery Process now works as a Pull System and to make it feasible , the Engineering Department, completely changed the project delivery process. It now must first of all supply the detailed Engineering of the medium / little parts and then followed by the big parts. (Figure 8)

In the next Cranes projects there was a total cost reduction of 3.5 % through production and assembly productivity increases due to:

- internal and outsourced production specialization
- minimal efficiency losses in production as a result of improvement in the coordination between production sequence and materials supply sequence The total delivery time was reduced from five to four months.

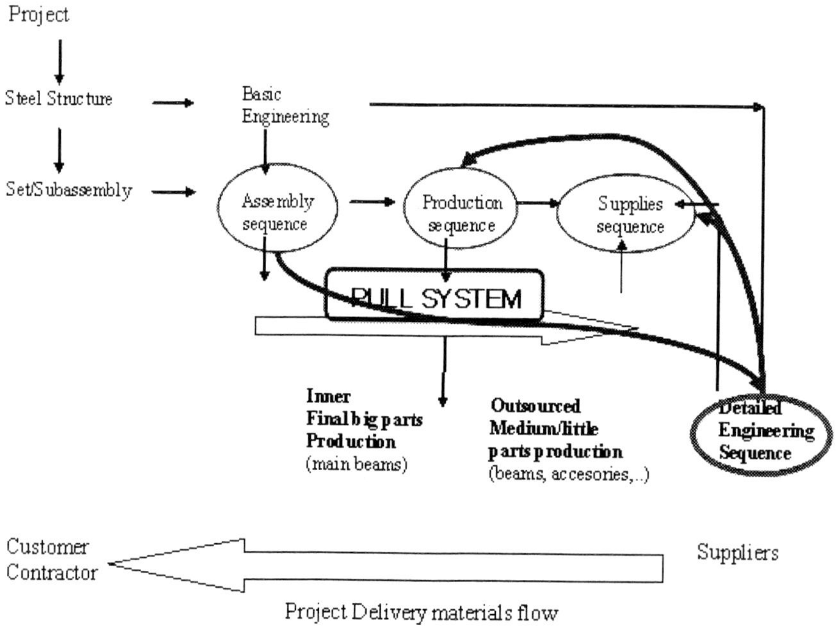

Figure 8. Project process design logic and flow of materials from suppliers to customer.

6. Conclusions

Value management is a structured, organised team approach to identifying the functions of a project, product or service with recognised techniques and providing the necessary functions to meet the required performance at the lowest overall cost. The combination of supply chain management and concurrent engineering principles applied in a value analysis workshop in a construction industry sector as demonstrated in this research can be beneficial and highly productive. The outcome is that concurrent engineering teams become more effective in the project delivery process as they expose operational constraints / conflicts encountered, as well as share design data, redefine and optimise critical tasks and also coordinate and integrate these tasks adequately (8). The overall benefit is a reduction in cost of operations, time to market, and improved product quality.

References

[1] Ngowi, A. B. "Construction procurement based on concurrent engineering principles". *2000 Logistics Information Management, Vol 13*, No 6, 361-368.

[2] Chimay, J. Anumba, Catherine Baugh and Malik M.A.Khalfan "Organisational structures to support concurrent engineering in construction". 2002. *Industrial Management and Data Systems, Vol 102*, No 5, 260-270.

[3] Lopez, Bittitci and Errasti "Business Processes: the critical link in collaborative enterprises", Euroma 2004 Qiping Shen and Guiwen Liu, "Critical success factors in value management studies in construction", *Journal of Construction Engineering and Management*, 2003, 485-491.

[4] Schermerhorn, J. "*Management for productivity*". 1993. Wiley, New York, NY, *271-90*, 311-15, 670-1.

[5] Badr Haque "Problems in concurrent new product development: an in-depth comparative study of three companies".2003. *Integrated Manufacturing Systems, Vol 14*, No 3, 191-207.

[6] Browne, J; Sackett, PJ; Wortmann, JC. " Future Manufacturing Systems-towards the extended enterprise". 1995 *Computers in Industry, Vol 25*, 235-254.

[7] Albert, PC; Chan, Linda, CN. Fan and Ann T.W. Yu "Construction process reengineering: a case study". 1999. *Logistics Information Management, Vol 12*, No 6 467-475.

[8] Kolltveit, BJ. "The importance of the early phase: the case of construction and building project". *International Journal of Projects Management*, 2004, *22*, 545-551.

[9] Porter, ME. "*Competitive Advantage*" The Free Press 1985.

[10] Robert, E. Spekman, John W.Kamauff jr and Niklas Myhr. "An empirical investigation into supply chain management a perspective on partnerships" 1998.International *Journal of Physical Distribution and Logistics Management, Vol 28*, No 8 630-650.

[11] Jennifer Rowley " Using Case Studies in Research" 2002. *Management Research News, Vol 25* No 1.

[12] Roy Westbrook " Action Research: a new paradigm for research in production and operations management". 1995. *International Journal of Operations and Production Management, Vol 15*, No 12, 6-20.

[13] Vignalli, "The marketing management process and heuristic devices: an action research investigation".2003. *Marketing Intelligence and Planning, Vol 21*, No 4, 205-219.

[14] Paul Coughlan and David Coghlan "Action Research: Action research for operations management".2002. *International Journal of Operations and Production Management, Vol 22*, No 2. 220-240.

[15] Ortrun Zuber-Skerrit " A model for designing action learning and action research programs".2002. *The learning Organization, Vol 9*, No 4 171-179.

[16] Stanley, E. Fawcett & Stanley A. Fawcett – "The firm as a value-added system; integrating logistics, operations and purchasing" 1995 *International Journal of Physical Distribution & Logistics Management, Vol 25*, No 5 24-42.

[17] Thomas, S. "Contractors risk in Design, Novate and Construct contracts". *International Journal of Project Management*, 2002, *20*, 119-126.

[18] Errasti, A; Oyarbide, A; Santos, J. "Case Research to gain competitive advantage through construction process reeingineering". Faim2005.*15thInternational Conference on Flexible Automation & Intelligent Manufacturing.*

[19] Boddy, D; Macbeth, D. Prescriptions for managing change: a survey of their effects in projects to implement collaborative working between organisations. *International Journal of Project Management*, 2000, *18*, 297-306.

[20] Hammer, M; Champy, J. *Reengineering the Corporation.* London: Nicholas Brealey, 1993.

[21] Porter, ME. "Competitive Strategy: *techniques for analyzing industries and competitors*" The Free Press, 1980.

INDEX

A

B

C

Q

R

S

T

U

V

W